The Yoga Sūtras of Patañjali

Translation and Commentary by
Sri Swami Satchidananda

Integral Yoga® Publications
Buckingham, Virginia

Originally published under the title
Integral Yoga: The Yoga Sūtras of Patañjali

First Printing: 1978
Sixteenth Printing: 2011
Revised Edition: 2012
Fourth Printing: 2015

Library of Congress Cataloging-in-Publication Data
Satchidananda, Swami
[Integral Yoga]
The Yoga Sūtras of Patañjali/translation and commentary by
Swami Satchidananda
p. cm
Includes bibliographical references, index.

ISBN-13: 978-1-938477-07-2

1. Patañjali, Yoga Sūtra. 2. Yoga, Rāja. 3. Yoga
I. Patañjali, Yoga Sūtra. 1990. II. Title
B132. Y6P2787 1990
181',452-dc2O

90-5213
CIP

Printed in the United States of America

Integral Yoga® Publications
Satchidananda Ashram–Yogaville, Buckingham, Virginia 23921
www.yogaville.org

Cover photo by Amrita Sandra McLanahan, M.D.

Printed on Recycled Paper

The publication of this work
is humbly offered to my
beloved and revered
Yoga Master, Sri Gurudev,
Swami Sivanandaji Maharaj

and

to all who seek understanding
and mastery over their minds
through the glorious
science of Yoga

Books by Sri Swami Satchidananda

Beyond Words
Enlightening Tales
The Golden Present
The Healthy Vegetarian
Heaven on Earth
Integral Yoga Hatha
Kailash Journal
The Living Gita
To Know Your Self
Yoga Sūtras of Patañjali
Bound To Be Free: The Liberating Power of Prison Yoga

Integral Yoga Pocket Collection featuring the art of Peter Max

Meditation
The Key to Peace
Overcoming Obstacles
Adversity and Awakening
Satchidananda Sūtras
Gems of Wisdom
Pathways to Peace
How to Find Happiness
The Be-Attitudes
Everything Will Come to You
Thou Art That
How to Know Yourself
Free Yourself
The Guru Within
Golden Moments

Books about Sri Swami Satchidananda

Sri Swami Satchidananda: Apostle of Peace
Sri Swami Satchidananda: Portrait of a Modern Sage
Boundless Giving: The Life and Service of Sri Swami Satchidananda
The Master's Touch

Films about Sri Swami Satchidananda (DVD)

Living Yoga: The Life and teachings of Swami Satchidananda
Many Paths, One Truth: The Interfaith Message of Swami Satchidananda
The Essence of Yoga: The Path of Integral Yoga with Swami Satchidananda
In the Footsteps of a Master: The 1970 World Peace Tour with Swami Satchidananda

For a complete listing of books, CDs and DVDs: www.iydbooks.com

Contents

Preface

Beloved Students,

It gives me great joy to witness the publication of this book. For many years these *Yoga Sūtras* have been like a *Bible* to me. They have helped me in many situations on my own path of Yoga and have given me invaluable guidance at many points. I appreciate the clarity, simplicity and thoroughness with which Patañjali Maharishi has presented the entire Yoga. He has beautifully presented it as a rigorous and complete science with all its ramifications, from the most elementary to the most highly advanced points. I feel it is a living scripture to illumine our spiritual path.

The *Yoga Sūtras* are very concentrated and terse. Study them slowly and carefully and meditate on them. You can even learn some of the most important and useful ones by heart. This is not just a book to be quickly read and then tossed away like a popular novel. Nor is it a scholarly work to fill your mind with a lot of philosophy and theories. It is a practical handbook. Every time you pick it up you can absorb more for your growth. Let us slowly try to understand more and what little we understand, let us try to practice. Practice is the most important factor in Yoga.

Let us know that all these ideas and practices are there to help us forget our personal selfishness and broaden our minds more and more. As my Master Swami Sivanandaji used to say, "Just be good and do good." It's very simple. Be good and do good and the entire wisdom will be yours.

Every day let us check our progress and see that we grow a little better. Every day should elevate us a little, broaden our attitudes, reduce our selfishness and make us better masters over our own body, senses and mind. This is the kind of Yoga that will really help us. And let that highest goal toward which Patañjali's *Sūtras* point be our goal: that one day we should all attain the highest *samādhi*, the totally liberated state. This liberation is not for the remote future or for when we die; it is to be lived in the very midst of the world.

May all the holy sages and the founder of Yoga, Patañjali Maharishi, and all the saints bless us to achieve this goal with pure minds and deep meditation. May the sacred science of Yoga inspire us to become such masters, to find peace and joy within ourselves and to share the same with all humanity.

OM Śāntiḥ, Śāntiḥ, Śāntiḥ. May God bless you.

Ever yours in Yoga,

Swami Satchidananda

Yogaville
March 1978

Acknowledgments

I gratefully acknowledge the following generous souls for their assistance in the various aspects of this book:

T. M. P. Mahadevan, Ph.D., Professor of Philosophy, University of Madras, for his scholarly assistance in checking over the translations from Sanskrit to English;

Paul jj Alix for his painstaking efforts in updating and retyping the Devanagari script and the Roman transliterations of the Sanskrit in the manuscript, for checking and expanding the definitions of the Sanskrit words used in the *sūtras* so they are consistent throughout the text and for making the Roman spellings of the Sanskrit consistent throughout the text;

Vidya Vonne, Sita Bordow, Sudharshan Anderson, Anagan Stearns, Prahaladan Mandelkorn, Rev. Paraman Barsel and Rev. Prakash Shakti for help in editing the manuscript;

Swami Sharadananda for indexing and helping with many other aspects of this volume;

Prema Conan for the original book design and layout; Peter Petronio for redesigning the cover; Anand Shiva Hervé for the new book layout and for implementing the eletronic version of the *Devanāgarī* and the Indic Roman fonts.

Abhaya Thiele, Leela Heard, Rev. Lakshmi Barsel, Ph.D., Kristofer Marsh and Hanuman for proofreading;

Rev. Prem Anjali, Ph.D. for her timeless dedication in editing the text, upgrading the fonts, layout, and Devanagari, proofreading the corrections, and overseeing the entire production of the latest edition of this manuscript.

To the generous "Wisdom Offering" donors who provided financial assistance in printing this book, and to all others who directly or indirectly aided in this work, I offer my sincere thanks. May they all enjoy the peace and joy of Yoga.

Introduction

When the word Yoga is mentioned, most people immediately think of some physical practices for stretching and stress reduction. This is one aspect of the Yogic science, but actually only a very small part and relatively recent in development. The physical Yoga, or Haṭha Yoga, was primarily designed to facilitate the real practice of Yoga—namely, the understanding and complete mastery over the mind. So the actual meaning of Yoga is the science of the mind.

We all want to know more about our minds: how they work and how we can work with them. This field is closer to us than anything else in life. It may be interesting and useful to know how to fix a car or cook a meal or how atoms are split. But something that holds a more immediate and vital interest for thoughtful people is their own mind. What is the mind? Does it determine our behavior and experience or do we create and sustain its activity? What is consciousness? Can we turn within ourselves to study and understand, perhaps even control the mind? This is the subject matter of the ancient science of Rāja Yoga.

Traditionally, the word Yoga by itself refers to Rāja Yoga, the mental science. With the current burgeoning of interest in expanding consciousness and in mental science in general, it is natural that we turn to Rāja Yoga. There are of course many Western approaches to the study and control of mind, each advancing various different concepts and techniques. But compared to these, the ancient Yogic science is a great grandsire. For thousands of years the Yogis have probed the mysteries of the mind and consciousness, and we may well discover that some of their findings are applicable to our own search as well.

The primary text of Rāja Yoga is called the *Yoga Sūtras of Patañjali* (sometimes also called *Patañjala Yoga Sūtras* or *Yoga Darśana*). *Sūtra* literally means "thread," each *sūtra* being the barest thread of meaning upon which a teacher might expand by adding his or her own "beads" of experience for the sake of the students.

There are almost 200 *sūtras*, traditionally divided into four sections. The first is the Portion on Contemplation (*Samādhi Pāda*) which gives the theory of Yoga and a description of the most advanced stages of the practice of *samādhi*, or contemplation. This probably was given first as an inspiration to the student to begin the practices. The second is the Portion on Practice (*Sādhana Pāda*). There is philosophy in this section also, but of a more practical nature. And the first five basic steps out of the traditional eight limbs of Rāja Yoga are expounded, along with their benefits, obstacles to their accomplishment and ways to overcome the obstacles. The third section is called the Portion on Accomplishments (*Vibhuti Pāda*) and discusses the final three inner steps of Rāja Yoga plus all the powers and accomplishments which could come to the faithful practitioner. The final section is called the Portion on Absoluteness (*Kaivalya Pāda*) and discusses Yoga from a more cosmic, philosophical viewpoint.

It is not known exactly when Sri Patañjali lived, or even if he was a single person rather than several persons using the same title. Estimates of the date of the *Sūtras* range from 5,000 B.C. to 300 A.D. In any case, he did not in any sense "invent" Rāja Yoga, but rather systematized it and compiled the already existing ideas and practices. Since that time he has been considered the "Father of Yoga" and his *Sūtras* are the basis for all of the various types of meditation and Yoga which flourish today in their myriad forms.

****

Sri Swami Satchidananda (Sri Gurudev) is one of the most widely known and well-rounded contemporary exponents of Yoga. He terms his entire approach to Yoga "Integral Yoga," or the Yoga of Synthesis, as it takes into consideration all the aspects of an individual: physical, emotional, mental, intellectual and social. But he often states that Integral Yoga is not in any way different from Rāja Yoga.

Rāja Yoga itself is an integral approach. It does not simply advocate meditation but takes into consideration the entire life of a person. Its philosophy is scientific. It welcomes and, in fact, demands experimental verification by the student. Its ultimate aim is to bring about a thorough metamorphosis of the individual who practices it sincerely. Its goal is nothing less than the total transformation of a seemingly limited physical, mental and emotional person into a fully illumined, thoroughly harmonized and perfected being—from an individual with likes and dislikes, pains and pleasures, successes and failures, to a sage of permanent peace, joy and selfless dedication to the entire creation.

We see the fruition of this science in Sri Swami Satchidananda. He was born and brought up in a small village in South India. He later studied agriculture, science and technology and worked in various technical and commercial fields. Not satisfied with any of these things, he made the pursuit of Yoga his full-time occupation, practicing first with the help of books and later at the feet of many of India's great sages and saints, such as Sri Swami Chidbhavananda of the Ramakrishna Order, Sri Ramana Maharshi and Sri Aurobindo. In 1949, he came to the *āśram* of Sri Swami Sivananda in Rishikesh. In Master Sivanandaji, he found his Guru or spiritual teacher. He took monastic initiation from Master Sivananda and lived, worked and taught at Sivananda Ashram for several years until he was asked by Master Sivanandaji to bring the teachings of Yoga to Sri Lanka. From there Sri Gurudev was invited to other countries in the Far East and then in 1966 to the West.

Since then he has been recognized and appreciated as a universal teacher, guiding thousands of individuals and serving on the advisory boards of many Yoga, peace and interfaith organizations. Considered a pioneer in the interfaith movement, Sri Gurudev took every opportunity to bring together people of various traditions to see the oneness in all spiritual endeavors. He never called himself an exclusive member of any one faith, group or country but rather dedicated himself to the principle that "Truth is One, Paths are Many." From that inclusive vision, he went wherever he was invited, bringing together people of all backgrounds and beliefs. He felt that Yoga should stand for, and exemplify, the message of respect for all the different paths and that all sincere seekers should realize their common spirit and the universality of their goal.

In addition to Sri Gurudev's work spreading the teachings of Yoga and his life-long devotion to interfaith understanding, he also dreamed of creating a permanent place where all people could come together and worship under one roof, in a shrine that glorified both the great religious traditions of the world and at the same time, the one Truth—or Light—behind all the names and forms. In July 1986, the Light Of Truth Universal Shrine (LOTUS) was completed—inspired and designed by Sri Gurudev. It is located in the United States at Satchidananda Ashram-Yogaville in Virginia.

Over the years, Sri Swami Satchidananda received many honors for his public service, including the Albert Schweitzer Humanitarian Award, the Juliet Hollister Interfaith Award, and the U Thant Peace Award. But, for those who knew him, it was not only in his public work but in all aspects of his life that he demonstrated his attunement with nature and his transcendence of petty limitations.

He is a beautiful instrument to guide us in the study of Rāja Yoga. As he often said, if there is something useful for you in his words, take it and make use of it. If there is anything that is not useful, leave it. May your study of the great science of Rāja Yoga bring you a life of greater health and peace, joy and understanding!

****

Sri Patañjali was the epitome of acceptance of all methods and of broad-mindedness of approach. He did not limit his instructions to one particular technique, to members of any particular religion or philosophy, or in any other way. He gave general principles and used specifics only as examples. For instance, in delineating objects for meditation, rather than saying, "Jesus is the only way," or "Kṛṣṇa [Krishna] is the highest Godhead; meditate on Kṛṣṇa," or "Only meditation on a sound vibration, or *mantra*, will bring the Yogic results," he simply gave various possibilities to choose from and then concluded, "Or by meditating on anything one chooses which is elevating."

It is probably this broad-mindedness that endeared Sri Patañjali's *Yoga Sūtras* to Sri Swami Satchidananda. His ideals and methods are—like Patañjali's—universal, interfaith and all-encompassing. He denies no one, converts no one, yet recommends techniques of understanding that can expand anyone's present experience of his or her philosophy, religion and—most importantly—daily life. Although ancient, Sri Patañjali and Rāja Yoga are eminently contemporary. Experimental and scientific, they invite independent questioning and sincere study, analysis and application.

This book is unique among books on the *Yoga Sūtras* in that it is based on Sri Swami Satchidananda's informal expositions of the *Sūtras* at lectures and Yoga retreats. It was not written for publication or for any scholarly or intellectual purpose, rather it is the recorded conversation of a Yoga Master to his students in true *sūtra* exposition tradition. It is a dynamic teaching based on the needs of the modern student, expounded by one who lives those teachings. Even the translations are new, coming from the direct experience of Sri Gurudev.

In bringing out this book, it is our hope to enable seekers after truth and Yoga practitioners in particular to have the great inspiration and practical guidance of Patañjali through the illuminating vision of the modern master Sri Swami Satchidananda.

Sri Gurudev recommended that readers make note of those *sūtras* that seem particularly meaningful to their individual lives and memorize them. The words will often come back to mind throughout one's daily activities and serve as an aid in maintaining peace of mind under all circumstances. Each time you pick up the book, you might find another one or two *sūtras* that you would like to add to your memory bank.

May the grace of all the realized Yogis of every tradition be upon us that we may succeed in realizing the peace and joy which is the divine Truth within us.

OM Śāntiḥ, Śāntiḥ, Śāntiḥ (OM Peace Peace Peace),
Reverend Vidya Vonne
Satchidananda Ashram-Yogaville

Guide To Sanskrit Pronunciation

To facilitate correct pronunciation we have used the International System of transliteration for the *Sūtras*, as well as for the words in the glossary. When used within the text of the commentary, Sanskrit words have been given a more phonetic spelling for ease in reading.

The Sanskrit letters are arranged in sequence according to their origin when spoken: throat, palate, roof of mouth, teeth and lips.
Given below are the letters of the Sanskrit Devanagari script, the letters and diacritical marks used to represent their sounds in this book and some examples of those sounds in English.

Vowels:

अ	*a*	as in *up*, soda
आ	*ā*	as in father
इ	*i*	as in fill, pin
ई	*ī*	as in feed
उ	*u*	as in full, bush
ऊ	*ū*	as in fool, rule
ऋ	*ṛ*	as in Christmas (but not pronouncing the "i")
ॠ	*ṝ*	as *ṛ*, (but held twice as long)
ऌ	*ḷ*	as in slur (but not pronouncing the "l")

Please note: the letters *ṛ*, *ṝ* and *ḷ* are vowels, and are not to be confused with the consonants *r* and *l*.

ए	*e*	as in they, pray (always long)
ऐ	*ai*	as in aisle
ओ	*o*	as in go
औ	*au*	as in how
अं	*ṁ*	as in hum

ः *ḥ* is a final sound pronounced with a stronger puff of air and the suggestion of the vowel preceding it. For example, *aḥ* sounds like aha; *iḥ* like ihi.

Consonants:

क	*k*	as in seek
ख	*kh*	as in back-hand
ग	*g*	as in good
घ	*gh*	as in dig-hard
ङ	*ṅ*	as in sing, monkey
च	*c*	as in pitch
छ	*ch*	as in Church-hill
ज	*j*	as in joy
झ	*jh*	as in hedge-hog
ञ	*ñ*	as in canyon
ट	*ṭ*	as in tub
ठ	*ṭh*	as in hit-hard
ड	*ḍ*	as in deer
ढ	*ḍh*	as in red-hot
ण	*ṇ*	as in not
त	*t*	as in pat (with the tongue touching the back of the teeth)
थ	*th*	as in hit-hard (with the tongue touching the back of the teeth)
द	*d*	as in dense (with the tongue touching the back of the teeth)
ध	*dh*	as in red-hot (with the tongue touching the back of the teeth)
न	*n*	as in nut
प	*p*	as in pin
फ	*ph*	as in up-hill
ब	*b*	as in bird
भ	*bh*	as in abhor

म	*m*	as in mud
य	*y*	as in yes
र	*r*	as in ladder (when said quickly)
ल	*l*	as in light
व	*v*	as in voice
स	*s*	as in sun
श	ś	as in shun (with the top of the tongue against the palate)
ष	ṣ	as in sure (with the tongue pulled back and the tip touching the ridge of the back of teeth)
ह	*h*	as in honey

The syllable *jña* commonly occurs in Sanskrit. It sounds more or less like *gnya.*

The vowels and consonants are pronounced the same whenever they appear in a word. Each syllable of a word is stressed equally, with the long vowels held twice as long as the short. Because each short and long vowel is a different letter in Sanskrit, it is important to pronounce them correctly. Mispronunciation changes the Sanskrit spelling, making another word with another meaning. For example, *rājā* (long "a") means king, while *raja* (short "a") means dust.

Book One

Samādhi Pāda

Portion on Contemplation

This begins our study of Rāja Yoga, or Aṣṭāṅga (eight-limbed) Yoga as it is sometimes called. The *Yoga Sūtras* as expounded by the sage Patañjali Maharishi comprise the first and foremost scripture of Yoga. It was Patañjali who carefully coordinated Yogic thought and explained it to his students. As he expounded these thoughts, his students jotted them down in a sort of shorthand using just a few words which came to be called the *sūtras*. The literal meaning of the word "*sūtra*" is "thread;" and these *sūtras* are just combinations of words threaded together—usually not even well-formed sentences with subjects, predicates and so on. Within the space of these two hundred short *sūtras*, the entire science of Yoga is clearly delineated: its aim, the necessary practices, the obstacles you may meet along the path, their removal, and precise descriptions of the results that will be obtained from such practices.

अथ योगानुशासनम् ॥१॥

1. Atha Yogānuśāsanam.

Atha = now; **Yoga** = Yoga;
anuśāsanam = exposition or instruction.

Now the exposition of Yoga is being made.

Anuśāsanam means exposition or instruction because it is not mere philosophy that Patañjali is about to expound but rather direct instruction on how to practice Yoga. Mere philosophy will not satisfy us. We cannot reach the goal by mere words alone. Without practice, nothing can be achieved.

योगश्चित्तवृत्तिनिरोधः ॥२॥

2. Yogaś citta vṛtti nirodhaḥ.

Yogaḥ (Yogaś) = Yoga (is); **citta** = of the mind-stuff, mind field;
vṛtti = modifications; **nirodhaḥ** = restraint.

The restraint of the modifications of the mind-stuff is Yoga.

In this *sūtra,* Patañjali gives the goal of Yoga. For a keen student, this one *sūtra* would be enough because the rest of them only explain this one. If the restraint of the mental modifications is achieved, one has reached the goal of Yoga. The entire science of Yoga is based on this. Patañjali has given the definition of Yoga and at the same time the practice. "If you can control the rising of the mind into ripples, you will experience Yoga."

Now we will discuss the meaning of each word of the *sūtra.* Normally, the word Yoga is translated as "union," but for a union there should be two things to unite. In this case, what is to unite with what? So here we take Yoga to mean the Yogic experience. The extraordinary experience gained by controlling the modifications of the mind is itself called Yoga.

Citta is the sum total of mind. To have a full picture of what Patañjali means by "mind," you should know that within the *citta* are different levels. The basic mind is called *ahaṁkāra,* or the ego, the "I" feeling. This gives rise to the intellect or discriminative faculty which is called *buddhi.* Another stage is called *manas,* the desiring part of the mind, which gets attracted to outside things through the senses.

For example, say you are quietly sitting enjoying the solitude when a nice smell comes from the kitchen. The moment the *manas* records, "I'm getting a fine smell from somewhere," the *buddhi* discriminates, "What is that smell? I think it's cheese. How nice. What kind? Swiss? Yes, it's Swiss cheese." Then, once the *buddhi* decides, "Yes, it's a nice piece of Swiss cheese like you enjoyed in Switzerland last year," the *ahaṁkāra* says, "Oh, is it so? Then I should have some now." These three things happen one at a time, but so quickly that we seldom distinguish between them.

These modifications give rise to the effort to get the cheese. The want was created and, unless you fulfill it by peeping into the kitchen and eating the cheese, your mind won't go back to its original peaceful condition. The want is created, then the effort to fulfill the want, and once you fulfill it, you are back to your original peaceful position. So, normally you are in the peaceful state. That is the natural condition of the mind. But these *citta vṛttis,* or the modifications of the mind-stuff, disturb that peace.

All the differences in the outside world are the outcome of your mental modifications. For example, imagine you have not seen your father since your birth and he returns when you are ten years old. He knocks at your door. Opening it, you see a strange face. You run to your mama saying, "Mama, there's a stranger at the door." Your mama comes and sees her long-lost husband. With all joy she receives him and introduces him as your father. You say, "Oh, my Daddy!" A few minutes before, he was a stranger; now he has become your daddy. Did he change into your daddy? No, he is the same person. You created the idea of "stranger," then changed it to "Daddy." That's all.

The entire outside world is based on your thoughts and mental attitude. The entire world is your own projection. Your values may change within a fraction of a second. Today you may not even want to see the one who was your sweet honey yesterday. If we remember that, we won't put so much stress on outward things.

That is why Yoga does not bother much about changing the outside world. There is a Sanskrit saying, *"Mana eva manuṣyanam karaṇam bandha mokṣayoḥ."* "As the mind, so the person; bondage or liberation are in your own mind." If you feel bound, you are bound. If you feel liberated, you are liberated. Things outside neither bind nor liberate you; only your attitude toward them does that.

That is why whenever I speak to prison inmates I say, "You all feel you are imprisoned and anxiously wait to get outside these walls. But look at the guards. Are they not like you? They are also within the same walls. Even though they are let out at night, every morning you see them back here. They love to come; you would love to get out. The enclosure is the same. To them it is not a prison; to you it is. Why? Is there any change in the walls? No, you feel it is a prison; they feel that it is a place to work and earn. It is the mental attitude. If, instead of imprisonment, you think of this as a place for your reformation where an opportunity has been given you to change your attitude in life, to reform and purify yourself, you will love to be here until you feel purified. Even if they say, 'Your time is over; you can go,' you may say, 'I am still not purified. I want to be here for some more time.'" In fact, many such prisoners continued to lead a Yogic life even after they left prison, and they were even thankful for their prison life. That means they took it in the right way.

So, if you can have control over the thought forms and change them as you want, you are not bound by the outside world. There's nothing wrong with the world. You can make it a heaven or a hell according to your approach. That is why the entire Yoga is based on *citta vṛtti nirodhaḥ*. If you control your mind, you have controlled everything. Then there is nothing in this world to bind you.

तदा द्रष्टुः स्वरूपेऽवस्थानम् ॥३॥

3. Tadā draṣṭuḥ svarūpe'vasthānam.

Tadā = then; **draṣṭuḥ** = the Seer; **sva** = own;
rūpe = in (Itself) color, in (Itself) nature;
avasthānam ('vasthānam) = abides.

Then the Seer (Self) abides in Its own nature.

You are that true Seer. You are not the body nor the mind. You are the Knower or Seer. You always see your mind and body acting in front of you. You know that the mind creates thoughts; it distinguishes and desires. The Seer *knows* that but is not involved in it.

But to understand that eternal peaceful You, the mind must be quiet; otherwise, it seems to distort the truth. If I explain this through an analogy, it will probably be easier to understand. You are the Seer who wants to see Itself. How? Even in the case of your physical face, if I ask if you have ever seen it, you have to say no, because it is the face that sees. The face itself is the seer or the subject. What it sees in the mirror is its image, the seen or the object. If the mirror is corrugated, curved, concave or convex, will you be able to see your true face? No. It will appear to be awful—too big or too high or full of waves. Will you be worried seeing this? No. You will immediately know something is wrong with the mirror. You are seeing a distorted reflection. Only if the mirror is perfectly smooth and clean will it give you the true reflection. Only then can you see your face as it is.

In the same way, the Seer, or true you, reflects in the mind which is your mirror. Normally, you can't see the true Self because your mind is colored. If the mind is dirty, you say, "I am dirty." If it's all polished and shining, "I am beautiful." That means you think you are your reflection in the mind. If the mind has a lot of waves like the surface of a lake, you will be seeing a distorted reflection. If the water of the mental lake is muddy or colored, you see your Self as muddy or colored. To see the true reflection, see that the water is clean and calm and without any ripples. When the mind ceases to create thought forms or when the *citta* is completely free from *vṛttis,* it becomes as clear as a still lake and you see your true Self.

Hearing this analogy, you might turn around and ask me, "Does that mean the Seer misunderstands Itself or has forgotten Itself?" No. The Seer can never misunderstand nor forget Itself. But we are talking on the level of the reflection. The reflection is distorted, so the Seer *appears* to be distorted. The true you is always the same, but you appear to be distorted or mixed up with the mind. By making the mind clean and pure, you feel you have gone back or you appear to have gone back to your original state.

वृत्तिसारूप्यमितरत्र ॥४॥

4. Vṛtti sārūpyam itaratra.

Vṛtti = modification; **sārūpyam** = assumes form, identification; **itaratra** = at other times.

At other times [the Self appears to] assume the forms of the mental modifications.

You seem to have lost your original identity and have identified with your thoughts and body. Suppose I ask you who you are. If you say, "I am a man," you have identified yourself with a masculine body. If you say, "I am a professor," you are identifying with the ideas gathered in your brain. If you say, "I am a millionaire," you are identifying with your bank account;

if "a mother," with a child; "a husband," with a wife. "I am tall; I am short; I am black or white" shows your identification with the shape and color of the body. But without any identifications, who are you? Have you ever thought about it? When you really understand that, you will see we are all the same. If you detach yourself completely from all the things you have identified yourself with, you realize yourself as the pure "I." In that pure "I" there is no difference between you and me.

This is true not only with human beings, but with everything. You call something a dog because it has a dog's body. The spirit in a dog and a human is the same. The same is true even with inanimate objects; there is the same spirit in a stone or a wall. If I use the term "spirit," or "Self," you might hesitate to believe me, but if the physicist says the wall is nothing but energy, you will believe that. So, using the scientist's language, there is nothing but energy everywhere. Even the atom is a form of energy. The same energy appears in different forms to which we also give different names. So the form and name are just different versions of the same energy. And, according to the Yogic scientists such as Patañjali—and even many modern scientists—behind the different forms of energy is one unchanging consciousness or spirit or Self.

That is why, if we could calm our minds and get to the basis of all these modifications, we would find the unity among everything. That is the real Yogic life. That does not mean we are indifferent to the changes and become useless to the world. Instead, with this experience of universal unity, we function better. We will have happy and harmonious lives. Only then can we love our neighbors as our own Self. Otherwise, how is it possible? If I identify myself with my body, I will also see another person as a body and the two bodies cannot be one—they are always different. If I identify myself with my mind, nobody can have a mind exactly like mine. No two individuals have the same body or mind, even twins. Even to the extent of the half-inch-square thumb, we are not the same. Ask the fingerprint experts; they will tell you no two fingerprints are the same.

But behind all these differences, in the Self, we never differ. That means behind all these ever-changing phenomena is a never-changing

One. That One appears to change due to our mental modifications. So, by changing your mind, you change everything. If only we could understand this point, we would see that there is nothing wrong outside; it is all in the mind. By correcting our vision, we correct things outside. If we can cure our jaundiced eye, nothing will look yellow. But without correcting the jaundice, however much we scrub the outside things, we are not going to make them white or blue or green; they will always be yellow. That's why Yoga is based on self-reformation, self-control and self-adjustment. When this reformation is accomplished we will see a new world, a harmonious and happy world. That's why we should always keep ourselves free from these wrong identifications.

वृत्तयः पञ्चतय्यः क्लिष्टाक्लिष्टाः ॥५॥

5. Vṛttayaḥ pañcatayyaḥ kliṣṭākliṣṭāḥ.

Vṛttayaḥ = modifications; **pañcatayyaḥ** = fivefold; **kliṣṭa** = painful; **akliṣṭāḥ** = painless [are].

There are five kinds of mental modifications which are either painful or painless.

Patañjali says there are five kinds of *vṛttis,* and again these are grouped into two major categories. One variety brings us pain; the other does not. Notice that he does not divide the thoughts into painful and pleasurable. Why? Because even a so-called pleasurable thought might ultimately bring us pain. And, again, we cannot easily know in the beginning whether a particular thought will bring pain or not. Some thoughts begin with pain but end leaving us at peace. Others appear to be pleasurable but bring pain. For example, our pity at another's suffering certainly causes us pain, but ultimately it expands our hearts and minds, gives us more understanding and leaves us in peace.

Instead of these terms, "painful" and "painless," we might be able to understand this point better if we use two other words. Call them "selfish" thoughts and "selfless" thoughts. The selfish thoughts ultimately bring pain. For example, to love something or somebody is pleasurable. But many of you have experienced how the very same love brought you a lot of unhappiness, pain, hatred, jealousy and so on. Why? Because that love was not just a pure love but was based on some expectation in return. There was selfishness in it. The expectation may be anything: a little financial comfort, some publicity or a little physical pleasure. With this expectation, love seldom lasts long. So love, though it appears to be a painless thought, ultimately ends in pain if it is based on selfishness.

On the other hand, a thought like anger might bring pain in the beginning. The anger of a selfless person has no personal motive behind it. Although that anger may cause somebody to feel bad in the beginning, ultimately it helps that person to correct himself or herself and to lead a better life. For example, a little strictness on the part of the classroom teacher is needed to reform the children and make them understand their responsibilities. Whatever the thought is, if there is no selfishness behind it, it can never really bring pain to the person concerned. The result is neither pain nor pleasure, but peace. Seeing this truth, we should analyze all our motives and try to cultivate selfless thoughts. That is our first and foremost duty.

Some people say, "I thought that in the name of meditation and Yoga, we were supposed to make the mind blank and without thoughts." But you can't make the mind thoughtless immediately. Many people try, but it is impossible. Once you make the mind thoughtless you have attained the goal. But it is not that easy. Many people say, "I have made my mind vacant." How did they know the mind was vacant? They were aware of it. Is not that type of awareness a thought? You have removed all other thoughts and retained this one thought of having made the mind vacant. That is not the real thoughtlessness.

That is why we use the trick of developing certain positive thoughts while removing negative ones. We say to the mind, "All right. If you want to create some thought forms, go ahead. But if you create thoughts that will bring you pain, you are the one who will suffer. If you are selfish, you will suffer later on. I don't want to kill you. I am your friend. I am interested in your welfare and peace, so please listen to me: do not create thoughts that will rebound on you. Forget your selfishness, make others happy, and you will be the happiest person." By seeing others happy, you can't be unhappy. But by making everybody unhappy, you can never be happy yourself. So, at least for your happiness, bring happiness to others. If you really want to be selfish, be selfish in the idea of retaining your peace. There is no harm in that selfishness because by that you are not going to harm anybody. Instead, you will be bringing the same peace to others also. If the mind says, "I can't be selfless; I must be selfish," tell it, "All right. Go to the other extreme and be selfish in refusing to disturb your own peace."

In our daily lives we always work with these two categories of thoughts. Now we know that selfish thoughts will bring misery and selfless ones leave us in peace. How are we to know whether our thoughts are selfless or not? We have to watch carefully the moment a thought-form arises in the mind. We become analysts. This itself is Yoga practice—watching our own thoughts and analyzing them.

प्रमाणविपर्ययविकल्पनिद्रास्मृतयः ॥६॥

6. Pramāṇa viparyaya vikalpa nidrā smṛtayaḥ.

Pramāṇa = correct or right knowledge;
viparyaya = misconception, incorrect knowledge;
vikalpa = verbal delusion, imagination; **nidrā** = sleep;
smṛti = memory; (**ayaḥ** = plural grouping these five).

They are right knowledge, misconception, verbal delusion, sleep and memory.

Here Patañjali names the five types of *vṛttis* and explains them one after the other.

प्रत्यक्षानुमानागमाः प्रमाणानि ॥७॥

7. Pratyakṣānumānāgamāḥ pramāṇāni.

Pratyakṣa = direct perception; **ānumāna** = inference; **āgamāḥ** = scriptural testimony; **pramāṇāni** = (are) the source of right knowledge; (**ani** = the three are).

The sources of right knowledge are direct perception, inference and scriptural testimony.

One example of what Patañjali calls valid knowledge is what you understand by seeing something yourself—direct perception. If you see something face-to-face, you don't have any doubt. That is one way to get valid knowledge. Another is by inference. Seeing smoke, you infer there is fire, because without fire there can't be smoke. When you see a cow giving milk, you infer that cows give milk. You have not seen them all, but you assume.

And there is one more way. You may not have seen anything personally and may not have anything from which to infer, but a reliable authority, or person who has really understood something, tells you.

Here we normally mean the holy scriptures, which we believe because they are the words of the sages, saints and prophets. They have seen the truth and have expounded upon it, so we believe them. That's why in the East, if anybody asks you to do some practice, it is expected that the scriptures also recommend it. You should not do something just because I say so. Everybody who has gone the same road should approve it, and the ancient scriptures should also approve it because the truth is the same. It is not something to be newly invented. All our present-day inventions can easily go wrong. What is the best thing today will be the worst thing tomorrow. They are still not finalized. The words of the prophets given through the holy scriptures are finalized. They can't just be modified.

But even in this, we have to understand the difference between the basic truth and the presentation. Truth can be presented only through some form or vehicle. We should always remember that the truth of the Self is the same, but when presented to you through words and forms and modes, it may appear in different ways to suit the individual or the trend of the age. That means rituals can be modified, language can be modified. But the truth can never be changed because truth is always the same. The rites are just the skeletal structures that uphold the outside building, but the foundation of all the rites should be the same. That is why, whatever be the scripture, whether from the East, West, South or North, the basic truth should be in agreement.

It's something like remaining the same while changing your clothing to suit the occasion. When you go skiing, you don't wear your business suit. When you go to the office, you don't come with ski boots on. Both these outfits are useless at a fancy wedding, and all three are ruled out if you go to the beach. But the person wearing the clothes remains the same. In the same way, the truth in all the scriptures is the same. But the presentation will vary.

If a teacher says, "Concentrate and meditate," or "Analyze your mind and develop virtuous qualities in your life," all the scriptures of the world should also say that. If I say, "In the name of Yoga, you can tell ten lies every day. That is the modern Yoga. Believe me," you can always ask, "Where is the proof?" I should be able to give a scriptural authority. If I cannot, there is something wrong with me. That's why you need not just believe and follow someone or something blindly. If you have any doubt, refer to any holy book. "Has the Holy Scripture approved it?" If you find it there also, then follow it.

So, by all these three ways we get valid knowledge. Of course, whether it is valid or invalid, ultimately you have to set it aside to find your peace. But before we push out all thoughts, we try to analyze them and eliminate one set after another. We can't just throw everything into one garbage pail. When I tried to do that once, the ashramites asked me not to. They said, "Gurudev, you have to put the vegetables in one, the papers in another and the bottles in still another one."

"Why?"

"The papers can be recycled but the vegetables go into the compost pile for the garden." So, even in throwing out garbage, you can't just throw it into one pail. You have to sort it so that later on it will be easier to dispose of.

It is the same way with the mind. You are going to dispose of all the thoughts as garbage, no doubt, whether they are good or bad, right or wrong, so that the mind will be free from modifications. But before we come to that, it makes it easier to dispose of them if we sort them first. Why? Because we still have a little clinging. We can't just throw everything away so easily. For example, when your wardrobe is too full you may say, "I'll give these dresses to somebody." But by the time you take it to the door, your mind will say, "I think I should keep just this one." See? First it's, "I'll throw out everything; I don't want these things." Then, when your friend comes to take them, you say, "Wait, wait, just leave this one for me. I can use it for another year. Let it be."

So we have to make use of this attitude. Your mental wardrobe is also full. You want to throw something out, but you don't feel like just dumping out everything. So you analyze, "This is painful. It's not necessary. But these things seem to be nice. Let them be." For the satisfaction of the mind, we are trying to analyze how many kinds of thoughts there are. "Oh, you are not going to empty me completely. At least you are giving something back to me." The mind has to be tricked like that.

I still remember when I was a young boy, my mother used to feed me, and I would make a fuss: "No. I don't want it all."

"Oh, is this too much, son? All right, I won't give you all of it." She would form all the rice into a flat disk and then cut a line across and say, "See, I'm taking away half; you only have to eat the other half." So, the other half would be pushed aside on the plate, and she would feed me, and I would be satisfied. But while I was eating, she would start telling me nice stories, and before long the other half would also have vanished.

If by any chance I looked down at the plate before the whole thing was empty and said, "Mother, you are feeding me more, I don't want it," she would say, "All right, son, I'll take away this half." She said she would take away half, no? She always took half from the remaining portion. That is a trick in feeding a child.

The same trick can be used in emptying the mind of thoughts. Tell the mind, "All right, you have that much, and I'll take the rest away." After a while say, "This also seems to be unwanted; let's take this away also." You remove them little by little. That's why Patañjali is so careful in forming the thoughts into different groups.

विपर्ययो मिथ्याज्ञानमतद्रूपप्रतिष्ठम् ॥८॥

8. Viparyayo mithyājñānam atadrūpa pratiṣṭham.

Viparyayaḥ (viparyayo) = misconception (is);
mithyā = false, mistaken; **jñānam** = knowledge;
atad = not on that; **rūpa** = form; **pratiṣṭham** = based.

Misconception occurs when knowledge of something is not based upon its true form.

In the twilight you see a coiled rope and mistake it for a snake. You get frightened. There is no snake there in reality. There is a false understanding. But still it created a terror in your mind. It is not only valid knowledge that creates thought waves, but erroneous impressions also.

शब्दज्ञानानुपाती वस्तुशून्यो विकल्पः ॥९॥

9. Śabdajñānānupātī vastu śūnyo vikalpaḥ.

Śabda = word, sound; **jñāna** = knowledge (here, based on words);
anupātī = arises; **vastu** = reality, real object;
śūnyaḥ (śūnyo) = without any; **vikalpaḥ** = verbal delusion.

An image that arises on hearing mere words without any reality [as its basis] is verbal delusion.

You hear something, but really there is nothing like that. In *viparyayaḥ* (misconception), at least there is a rope to be mistaken for a snake. But in *vikalpaḥ* (verbal delusion), there is nothing there. Yet you still create some opinion about it. Suppose I say, "John took his car to the garage and on the way all the tires got punctured, so he had to remove the wheels and give them to the mechanic to be repaired. He drove home very fast and got into an accident." You say, "Oh, was it a terrible accident?" You are only hearing my words. You haven't taken the time to think. If you thought about it, you would say, "If he gave all four wheels to be repaired, he couldn't drive it back." It didn't happen, but you take it seriously. Another example would be, "His mother was a barren woman." It's verbal delusion, but it may still create an impression in your mind.

अभावप्रत्ययालम्बना वृत्तिर्निद्रा ॥१०॥

10. Abhāva pratyayālambanā vṛttir nidrā.

Abhāva = nothingness; **pratyaya** = cognition; **ālambanā** = support; **vṛttiḥ** = modification of the mind; **nidrā** = sleep.

That mental modification supported by cognition of nothingness is sleep.

This is the fourth type. Normally, we say we do not have any thought in the mind during sleep. But actually we have the thought of having no thought. That is why when we wake up we say, "I slept very well; I knew nothing." You knew nothing, but you *know* that you knew nothing. Don't think there is no thought in sleep. If there were no thought and you were completely unconscious, you would not even feel that you had slept. All other thoughts are temporarily suspended except this one thought of emptiness in the mind, which leaves its impression upon waking.

अनुभूतविषयासंप्रमोषः स्मृतिः ॥११॥

11. Anubhūta viṣayāsaṁpramoṣaḥ smṛtiḥ.

Anubhūta = experienced; **viṣaya** = objects; **asaṁpramoṣaḥ** = not forgotten; **smṛtiḥ** = memory.

When a mental modification of an object previously experienced and not forgotten comes back to consciousness, that is memory.

Memories create impressions in the mind and at a later time come to the surface, either when we want them or sometimes even when we do not want them. Memories come in two ways: dreams are memories that come to the surface when we sleep; daydreams are memories that arise during the day. Both are impressions which, when formed, slowly descend to the bottom of the mind and come to the surface when they are rekindled for some reason.

So these are the five kinds of *vṛttis*, or thought forms, that must be controlled to make the mind void and to allow the inner peace to shine through. Knowing this, our next question is, "How can we control these *vṛttis?*" It is easy to say, "Control the mind." But, in reality, the mind seems to be controlling us.

अभ्यासवैराग्याभ्यां तन्निरोधः ॥१२॥

12. Abhyāsa vairāgyābhyām tannirodhaḥ.

Abyāsa = practice; **vairāgya** = non-attachment; (**abhyām** = by both); **tad** (tan) = they; **nirodhaḥ** = restrained.

These mental modifications are restrained by practice and non-attachment.

On the positive side, you practice. On the other side, you detach yourself from the cause for these modifications. Patañjali gives both a positive and negative approach to thought control, which he proceeds to elucidate in the following *sūtras.*

तत्र स्थितौ यत्नोऽभ्यासः ॥१३॥

13. Tatra sthitau yatno'bhyāsaḥ.

Tatra = of these; **sthitau** = in steadiness; **yatnaḥ** (yatno) = effort; **abhyāsaḥ** ('bhyāsaḥ) = practice.

Of these two, effort toward steadiness of mind is practice.

Here Patañjali means continuous practice, not just for one or two days. You have to always be at it, not just for a few minutes a day and then allowing the mind to have its own free time all the other hours. It means you become eternally watchful, scrutinizing every thought, every word and every action. How? Patañjali gives three qualifications:

स तु दीर्घकालनैरन्तर्यसत्कारासेवितो दृढभूमिः ॥१४॥

14. Sa tu dīrgha kāla nairantarya satkārāsevito dṛḍhabhūmiḥ.

Saḥ (Sa) = this; **tu** = and; **dīrgha** = long; **kāla** = time; **nairantarya** = without break, continuous; **satkāra** = earnestness; **asevito** = well attended to; **dṛḍha** = firm; **bhūmiḥ** = ground.

Practice becomes firmly grounded when well attended to for a long time, without break and in all earnestness.

The first qualification for the practice is that it should be done for a long time. Unfortunately, we just want the result immediately. If I ask you to repeat a *mantra* and tell you that you will become more peaceful and realize beautiful things within, you will go back home, repeat it for three days and then call me: "I've repeated it for three days but nothing happened. Maybe this is not a suitable *mantra* for me. Can you give me a different one?" See? So Patañjali says, "for a long time." He doesn't say *how* long.

And then it should be without break. I often hear, "Oh, I've been practicing Yoga for the past ten years but I'm still the same." "How often?" "Oh, off and on." So it must be continuous practice also.

And the last qualification is "in all earnestness." That means with full attention, with the entire application of your mind and with full faith in your achievement. Even when you want something or somebody on the worldly level, you will be after it day and night. You don't sleep, you don't even eat—you are always at it. If this quality is necessary to achieve even worldly success, how much more so for success in Yoga. So let us not be like little children who sow a seed today and dig it up tomorrow to see how much the root went down. We need all these three qualities: patience, devotion and faith.

This reminds me of a small story given in the Hindu scriptures. In the *Deva Loka,* or the heavenly plane where the divine beings live, there is a great *maharṣi* (sage) called Nārada. Just as there are great Yogis here, so there are also among the gods. So Nārada travels all over and sometimes comes to earth to see how we are doing. One day, he was passing through a forest and saw a Yoga student who had been meditating for so long that the ants had built an anthill around his body.

The Yogi looked at Nārada and said, "Nārada, Sir, where are you going?"

"To Heaven, to Lord Śiva's place."

"Oh, could you please do something for me there?"

"Sure, what can I do?"

"Could you find out from the Lord for how many more births I must meditate? I have been sitting here for quite a long time, so please find out."

"Sure."

Then Nārada walked a few miles farther and saw another man,but this one was jumping and dancing and singing with all joy: "Hare Rāma Hare Rāma Rāma Rāma Hare Hare; Hare Kṛṣṇa Hare Kṛṣṇa Kṛṣṇa Kṛṣṇa Hare Hare!"

When he saw Nārada, he said, "Hi, Nārada! Where are you going?"

"To Heaven."

"Oh, that's great. Could you please find out for how long I have to be here like this? When will I get final liberation?"

"Sure, I will."

So, after many years Nārada happened by the same route again and saw the first man. The Yogi recognized Nārada. "Nārada, I haven't had any answer from you. Did you go to Heaven? What did the Lord say?"

"I asked, but the Lord said you have to take another four births."

"Another . . . FOUR . . . births!? Haven't I waited long enough!?" He started shouting and lamenting. Nārada walked further and saw the second man still singing and dancing.

"Hi, Nārada. What happened? Did you get some news for me?"

"Yes."

"Well, tell me."

"Do you see that tree there?"

"Sure."

"Can you count the leaves on it?"

"Sure, I have the patience to do it. Do you want me to count them right away?"

"No, no, no. You can take your time to count."

"But what has that got to do with my question?"

"Well, Lord Śiva says you will have to take as many births as the number of leaves of that tree."

"Oh, is that all? So at least it's a limited number then. Now I know where it ends. That's fine. I can quickly finish it off. Thank God that he didn't say the leaves of the entire forest!"

Just then, a beautiful palanquin came down from Heaven, and the driver said, to the second man, "Come on, would you mind getting in? Lord Śiva has sent for you."

"I'm going to Heaven now?"

"Yes."

"But just now Nārada said I have to take so many more births first."

"Yes, but it seems that you were ready and willing to do that, so why should you wait? Come on."

"And what about the other man?"

"He's not even ready to wait four more births—let him wait and work more."

This is not a mere story. You can easily see the truth behind it. If you are that patient, your mind is more settled, and what you do will be more perfect. If you are unsettled and anxious to get the result, you are already disturbed; nothing done with that disturbed mind will have quality. So, it is not only how long you practice, but with what patience, what earnestness and what quality also.

दृष्टानुश्रविकविषयवितृष्णस्य वशीकारसंज्ञा वैराग्यम् ॥१५॥

15. Dṛṣṭānuśravika viṣaya vitṛṣṇasya vaśīkāra saṁjñā vairāgyam.

Dṛṣṭa = seen, experienced; **anuśravika** = heard, revealed; **viṣaya** = object; **vitṛṣṇasya** = of him who is free from cravings; **vaśīkāra** = mastery; **saṁjñā** = consciousness, clear knowledge; **vairāgyam** = non-attachment.

The consciousness of self-mastery in one who is free from craving from objects seen or heard about is non-attachment.

Normally, the mind gets attached by seeing or hearing something. It is mainly through the eyes and ears that the mind goes out and gathers things to satisfy its desires. Before the mind is attracted to something it sees or hears, you should have discrimination to see whether that object is good for you or not. The mind should not just go and grasp as it wants.

Non-attachment should not be misunderstood to be indifference. *Vairāgya* (non-attachment) literally means "colorless." *Vi* is "without;" *rāga* is "color." Every desire brings its own color to the mind. The moment you color the mind, a ripple is formed—just as when a stone is thrown into a calm lake, it creates waves in the water. When the mind is tossed by these desires one after the other, there won't be peace or rest in the mind. And with a restless mind you can't have steady practice. When you want to do something constantly, your mind should not be distracted by other desires. That's why this sort of dispassion or non-attachment must always go with the practice. Any practice without this non-attachment can never be fulfilled.

Many times people say, "Oh, I have been practicing meditation for so many years. I pray daily, morning and evening." Yes, they do that; we have to accept it because we see them sitting in meditation every day or going to the church or temple. Sometimes they sit in front of the altar for hours and hours. There are people who read the whole *Bible* every day. There are people who repeat the *Bhagavad Gītā* every day—they won't even eat until they do that. The moment they get up, they go in front of the altar and repeat the entire *Gītā* before even drinking a glass of water! But still they remain in the same state. The reason is that their minds are still dissipated because of the different desires. How many people stand in front of the altar and think of their business or allow their eyes to wander about to see how many of their friends are there? Temples and churches have become social centers. They have lost their original purpose because the minds of the people are more attracted to worldly things than to prayer. The lips may repeat the prayer mechanically like a phonograph record, but the mind wanders to other places. That's why you can't collect and compose the mind unless it is free from distracting desires. Meditation is possible only when the mind is free from attachment. In fact, you need not even practice meditation if your mind is completely free from all selfish desire. You will see that you are always at ease; you will never become restless and never disappointed. So we need the practice and the non-attachment; and, of these two, the non-attachment is the more important.

Immediately somebody will ask, "If you are unattached, won't you lose all incentive and become dull?" No. When we say unattached, it means without personal desires. If you really want to be greedy, be greedy in serving others. Try to remove the suffering of other people. Once you are unattached in your personal life, you can serve others, and by doing that you will find more and more joy. That's why sometimes I say that the selfless person is the most selfish one. Why? Because a selfless person doesn't want to lose his or her peace and happiness.

Even with God, do not have personal desire or attachment. Many people approach God and say, "God, give me this; give me that; help me win this campaign," or "If you help me pass this examination, I will light ten candles." We try to do business with God. It only shows our own ignorance. Those very candles were given to us by God, so what is the idea of giving them back to God as if we have created something? Our desirous mind deludes us, and we become ignorant. The discrimination of a desirous person gets completely faded. His or her interest is to achieve things, that's all; the desirous person doesn't bother to wait and think.

The *Vedantic* scriptures say: "Even the desire for liberation is a bondage." "*Mokṣabhekṣo bandhaḥ.*" Even if you desire liberation, you are binding yourself. Every desire binds you and brings restlessness. To get the liberation you have to be completely desireless.

Is it possible to be desireless? No. Actually, it is not possible. As long as the mind is there, its duty is to desire. It seems to be contradictory. But the secret is that any desire without any personal or selfish motive will never bind you. Why? Because the pure, selfless desire has no expectation whatsoever, so it knows no disappointment no matter what the result. But though it expects nothing, it has its own reward. When you make someone happy, you see his or her happy face and feel happy yourself. If you have really experienced the joy of just giving something for the sake of giving, you will wait greedily for opportunities to get that joy again and again.

Many people think that by renouncing everything, by becoming selfless and desireless, there is no enjoyment. No. That is not so. Instead, you become the happiest man or woman. The more you serve, the more happiness you enjoy. Such a person knows the secret of life. There is a joy in losing everything, in giving everything. You cannot be eternally happy by possessing things. The more you possess, the more sad you become. Haven't we seen millionaires, people of high position, prime ministers, presidents? Are they happy? No. The higher the position, the greater the trouble. Only a saint, a renunciate, is always happy because there is nothing for a saint to lose. Because you don't have anything, you have your Self always. That is the secret. That's why we say, "Have *vairāgya*, have dispassion, have non-attachment." By renouncing worldly things, you possess the most important sacred property: your peace.

There is another aspect, or benefit, of non-attachment. It is mainly a person with a detached mind who can do a job perfectly. As an example, the other day I received a letter from a disciple who runs one of my centers. Another Yoga teacher visited this center and asked, "Don't your students ask for something more? In my classes, if I don't teach something new each class, they say, 'What is this? We paid you and got this yesterday. You are teaching us the same thing today; why should we pay more? Unless you give us something new, we won't pay you more.' So I carefully arrange my lessons in such a way that every day I can add something new, so that I can ask for more money. But here, I see the same old stuff every day, and people are coming more and more—and nobody seems to be disappointed."

Then my child said, "We don't sell Yoga; we just teach for our joy. The people contribute as they want. There's no business here, but rather the heart is working. Probably in your case you expect money, and so you are interested in teaching something new every time to get more people and more money."

It is a fact. The same thing is happening in our other hatha classes also. For years now, people have been coming to the classes and each class has been more or less the same. And every time they come, they contribute something without ever getting tired of it. They could practice the same thing at home, but still they come to the classes because they don't feel the vibration of business there, but the vibration of Yoga. That is what they don't want to miss.

Even in my lectures, I don't quote many scriptures or try to give something new every time. Probably if I were to play back tapes of my past talks, it would be the same ideas again and again. People might say, "The Swami says nothing new—the same old Swami, the same old stuff. Why do they listen again and again?" I feel happy and they all feel happy being there, so they make me happy and I make them happy. We just spend a little happy time together, that's all. We just talk about something or do something in the name of Yoga. Yes, that is the secret. There is a joy in being together, that's all. So that is the life of detachment. There is no expectation. We just come together. They don't feel that they are losing their money, and I don't feel that I am gaining their money. We are all as one family. We pool our money, our energy and our ideas. What else do we want in this life? And that is Yoga.

So, when the mind is free from personal interest, we do our work well and feel joyful. Our lives become meaningful. If our minds are free from selfishness and there is sacrifice in everyone's lives, the very world becomes a heaven, an abode of peace and bliss. Everything in this life gives. Sacrifice is the law of life. That is why we admire and adore people who have given their lives for the sake of humanity. Why do we worship Jesus and the cross? Because sacrifice is the meaning of that cross. He sacrificed himself, and we worship that quality; it is not the piece of wood we appreciate, but the sacrifice it represents. He gave his very life for the sake of humanity. It is because of that sacrifice that all the prophets, sages and saints are worshipped as divine beings or as God. It is not only saints, but everything in nature—trees, birds, animals— they all live for the sake of others. Why does a candle burn and melt away? To give light. Why does an incense stick burn to ash? To give fragrance. Why does a tree grow? To give fruit and flowers. Is there anything, sentient or insentient, in this world that lives for its own sake? No. When the entire nature sacrifices, why should we human beings alone lead selfish lives? We are here to give and give and give. What is due to us will come without our worrying about it.

Of course, even here we can wonder, "If I am to lead a sacrificial life, how can I eat, how can I clothe myself or have a house of my own?" You can have all these things to equip yourself to serve others. You must have a bed to rest in to feel refreshed in the morning, in order to go out to serve others. You must eat to have enough energy to serve others. So you do everything with the idea that you are preparing yourself to serve others. Even the practice of meditation is not done just for your own peace but is done because with a peaceful mind you can go out into the world and serve well. With that very idea you can meditate. So, even your Yogic meditation becomes a selfless action. That is what is meant by "Even with God do not have attachment." This *vairāgya*, or non-attachment, alone is enough to change your entire life into a joyful one.

तत् परं पुरुषख्यातेर्गुणवैतृष्ण्यम् ॥१६॥

16. Tat param Puruṣa khyāter guṇavaitṛṣṇyam.

Tat = that; **param** = supreme; **Puruṣa** = true self;
khyāteḥ (khyāter) = due to the realization;
guṇa = of any of the constituents of nature; **vairṛṣṇyam** = non-thirst.

When there is non-thirst for even the *guṇas* (constituents of Nature) due to the realization of the *Puruṣa* (True Self), that is supreme non-attachment.

In this *sūtra*, Patañjali goes on to explain the higher form of *vairāgya*. The detachment of the mind from its personal desires and enjoyment is the ordinary *vairāgya*. The mind might want something; but, having control, you tell the mind, "No," and it stays away. But in the higher non-attachment you don't even think of attaching yourself. In other words, with the ordinary *vairāgya* you may be completely free from new things coming in to tempt you. But what will you do with the impressions that are already in your mind? The memory of having experienced something will still be there.

For example, after many years of thievery, a robber decides not to steal any more. But still, the memory of having stolen so many things and enjoyed them remains in that robber's mind. In the Yogic term these memories are called "impressions," or *saṁskāras*. Now and then the *saṁskāras* will come up: "Oh, how nice it would be if I had just stolen that car. How I would have enjoyed it. But these people came and told me not to attach myself, and I accepted it and am staying away from this." Or, "I remember how much I enjoyed smoking and drinking. This Yoga business came in, and somehow I don't have those joys anymore." Many people feel like that because the *saṁskāras* are still there.

You can't just go into the mind and erase the impressions. But they get themselves erased at one point. When? When you succeed in going within and realizing the peace and joy of your own Self. The moment you understand yourself as the true Self, you find such peace and bliss that the impressions of the petty enjoyments you experienced before become as ordinary specks of light in front of the brilliant sun. You lose all interest in them permanently. That is the highest non-attachment.

Before that, you are in-between. You have not tasted that greatest joy, but you have experienced some mental peace. However, this peace is just the reflection of the true peace on your tranquil mind. We should understand this point well. To use the analogy of the mirror again, imagine a brilliant light reflecting on a mirror. If the mirror has a crooked or colored surface, the reflection gets distorted. The distorted or colored reflection is like the distorted happiness you enjoy from outside things. By detaching yourself from these things, you make the mental mirror steady and straight and see a steady image of your Self. But, still, the image is not the true original Self or Bliss Absolute. Once the mind becomes pure and steady, you experience a steady happiness. That is the result of the first detachment or lower *vairāgya*.

Although it is only the reflection, it is almost the same as the original. Once that steady reflection is achieved, the true experience will happen automatically. You need not do anything more to get it. The mind automatically ceases to exist, and all that remains is the original peace and joy which we call God or the Self.

If that supreme non-attachment comes even once, even for a second, you experience that joy. That's why we try to sit for a while in meditation every day. If we get even a glimpse of that, we will not try to go here and there to taste other things. If you find a delicious dish in one restaurant, you will never go to any other restaurant, is it not so? You will even walk ten or twenty blocks out of your way to get that dish you like. In the same way, we will just leave all these things saying, "How can these things compare to that?" You will not want to lose any opportunity to sit and enjoy that peace. And if you slowly get rooted in it, you can allow your hands and even your mind to work, but you will always be in peace.

In Hindi there is a saying, *"Man me Rām, hath me kām."* Literally, it means, "In the mind, Ram (God); in the hand, work." Or it could be said more clearly as, "Keep the heart in God and the head in the world." If you know how to put your heart in God, you can rest there always and still play in the world. It will no longer be a hell to you, but a beautiful playground. Nothing can bind you; you can enjoy everything as play. You can be an expert player.

If you don't know how to play, you sometimes get kicked. I still remember the first time I played cricket. I was just looking around and somebody hit me with the ball. I just threw down my racket and left. Cricket became a terrible game to me because I couldn't play well. But by knowing how to play, many thousands of people enjoy that game. How many people are always in the water from morning until night, whereas other people are dreadfully afraid of it. In the same way, we need never be afraid of the world if we learn how to enjoy it. We can really enjoy the world and even give all the pleasures to our senses. Nothing needs to be starved. But when? Only when we have found the source and connected one part of the mind there—then we can enjoy everything. Otherwise we will get lost. So, "Enjoy the world," doesn't mean immediately. Achieve supreme *vairāgya* first, and then enjoy. That is the secret of success in life. One who does this will always succeed. There can be no failure in his or her life. Everyone should do that. That is our goal and birthright—nothing less than that.

वितर्कविचारानन्दास्मितानुगमात् संप्रज्ञातः ॥१७॥

17. Vitarka vicārānandāsmitānugamāt saṁprajñātaḥ.

Vitarka = reasoning; **vicāra** = reflecting; **ānanda** = rejoicing; **asmita** = pure I-am-ness; **anugamāt** = due to the following, from accompaniment; **saṁprajñātaḥ** = distinguishing, discerning; [samādhi = contemplation].

***Saṁprajñāta samādhi* is accompanied by reasoning, reflecting, rejoicing and pure I-am-ness.**

In the first section of this portion, Patañjali gives the theory of Yoga. Now he speaks of the final practice called *samādhi*, or contemplation, and its variations. Patañjali is completely scientific in this respect. He sees Yoga as a rigorous science and never hesitates to give all the aspects of the practice and their ramifications. It is the duty of scientists to understand and explain every aspect of their discoveries. It is just as when chemists formulate medicine. They have to explain its proper usage as well as any adverse reactions that could occur if not used properly.

In case you might think you are ready to practice *samādhi* right away, you should know that the practice of *samādhi* only becomes possible after a person has achieved perfection in concentration and meditation. The mind must have acquired one-pointedness and have been brought completely under control, because the entire mind must be used in the practice of *samādhi.*

In this and the following *sūtra* Patañjali talks about two kinds of *samādhi: saṁprajñāta* (distinguished) and *asaṁprajñāta* (undistinguished). Patañjali further divides the *saṁprajñāta samādhi* into four forms. To understand them we have to understand the make-up of what he calls nature, or *Prakṛti.* According to Patañjali, *Prakṛti* also has four divisions: the very gross material; the subtle elements called the *tanmātras,* which ultimately express as the concrete forms which you see; the mind-stuff (*citta*), and the ego or individuality.

So, *samādhi* is practiced first on the gross objects (*savitarka samādhi*), then on the subtle elements (*savicāra samādhi*), then on the mind devoid of any objects except its own joy—in other words, on the *sattvic* mind *(sa-ānanda samādhi)*—and finally on the "I" feeling alone *(sa-asmita samādhi).* There is a gradation because you can't immediately contemplate the very subtle. First you have to train the mind to focus on something concrete. When the mind is focused on a concrete object, that is called *savitarka samādhi.* Remember that at this point the mind is already well under control. The moment the purely focused mind contemplates an object, it goes to the very depth of that object and understands every particle of it. A focused mind gains power, and when that powerful mind concentrates on an object, the entire knowledge of that object is revealed to it.

Knowing this, we can easily see that the scientists who probed the matter and discovered atomic energy were practicing *savitarka samādhi.*

They were practical and wanted to know; they focused their entire minds on that, and even that small particle of matter revealed itself. In getting the knowledge, we gained power over the atom. That is what is meant by *savitarka samādhi.*

So, the benefit of this contemplation is the understanding of the inner secrets and powers of your object of contemplation. But what will you do with this power? The danger can easily be realized by seeing how atomic energy has been used for destructive bombs instead of soothing balms. There is a danger in getting all the extraordinary powers. If this *samādhi* is practiced without the proper moral background, the result will be dangerous. But, as a scientist, Patañjali must explain it anyway.

In the next form, you contemplate the *tanmātras,* or subtle elements. Here there is no concrete object to see. You contemplate something abstract like white or red or love or beauty. Because they are abstract, a normal person cannot understand what redness or love is without the help of a concrete object. But if you are able to contemplate and understand the concrete objects well, your mind gets the capacity to understand the abstract things even without concrete objects. Then you rise above time and space also. This *samādhi* is called *savicāra,* or with reflection.

Further on, we go into the still subtler one in which even the discrimination or reflection is not there. You don't use the intellect here, but you contemplate just the tranquil mind itself. In that you get a joy which is called *sa-ānanda samādhi,* or the blissful *samādhi.* There is only joy there and no reasoning or reflection.

In the fourth *samādhi,* even that *ānanda* is not there but just awareness of individuality. You contemplate the "I-ness." You are just there and you are aware of nothing else. It's called *sa-asmita samādhi,* with egoity. It's impossible to visualize what that could be, but still, let us understand theoretically at least. In *sa-asmita samādhi,* the *saṁskāras* are still in the mind in their seed form. Even though you are only aware of the "I," the *saṁskāras* are still buried in the mind.

Saṁprajñāta samādhi is a process of going inward—not evolution, but involution. Originally, the world, or *Prakṛti,* was unmanifested, or *avyakta.* When it begins to manifest, the ego comes in first, then the individuality and then the mind. Then, from the mind you get into the *tanmātras,* then the gross elements. That is the natural evolution.

In Yogic meditation we experience the involution. It could be called the creation and destruction. But, actually, there is nothing created in you; nor is anything destroyed. As the *Bhagavad Gītā* explains, the unmanifest appears as manifest and then returns to the unmanifest. What we see outside is the manifested, the in-between. That is what we call the creation. That's why, according to Yoga, we don't say that God created anything. Yoga says God is just the pure consciousness. And *Prakṛti* is also there, its nature being to evolve and then dissolve.

Prakṛti in the unmanifested condition has both matter and force, which are inseparable like fire and heat. Without fire there is no heat; without heat there is no fire. When the nature is in an unmanifested condition, the force is dormant or static; for example, when a dynamo doesn't revolve, no electricity is produced. But the moment the motor starts rotating, it produces electricity.

This force, or *prāṇa,* has three constituents called the *guṇas: sattva, rajas* and *tamas*—tranquility, activity and inertia. When all three qualities are in equilibrium, they do not affect the matter. But once there is a little disturbance in the *guṇas,* it creates motion in the matter, which gives rise to all kinds of forms. That is how the entire universe appears; the sky, the earth, the fire, the air and all the elements are created. So the One that is unmanifested slowly evolves Itself and ultimately we see the concrete forms.

Now we are in the concrete world with *sattva, rajas* and *tamas* in full swing. We have to work from what we see now—from the known we work back toward the unknown. We can't just ignore the known and directly tackle the unknown. It is easier to do something with concrete things which we can see, feel, touch and taste. So that is why the mind is given a concrete object to contemplate first when it has been made tranquil by concentration. Once it understands that, then it goes a little deeper into the subtle elements, then the still subtler ones, until it reaches the original matter.

Unless you understand the *Prakṛti* very well, you can't get out of it. You can't just ignore it or set it aside. That's why the four stages of *saṁprajñāta samādhi* are to be practiced first, one after the other.

But there is a danger in *saṁprajñāta samādhi* also. It is to be practiced, but we have to face the danger of it. That is why you have to prepare yourself with purity and selflessness. Otherwise, you will be in danger with your new-found powers. Take, for example, Jesus, who was able to heal sick and crippled people. He used his powers to bring good to others, but he never used the same force to save himself when he was to be crucified. If he really wanted to, he could have done it, but he didn't. That means that these mysterious forces should not be used for selfish purposes.

विरामप्रत्ययाभ्यासपूर्वः संस्कारशेषोऽन्यः ॥१८॥

18. Virāma pratyayābhyāsa pūrvaḥ saṁskāraśeṣo'nyaḥ.

Virāma = complete cessation;
pratyaya = content of mind (mental modification);
abhyāsa = by the practice;
pūrvaḥ = of the previous; **saṁskāra** = impressions;
śeṣaḥ (śeṣo) = remain; **anyaḥ** ('nyaḥ) = the other [samādhi].

By the firmly convinced practice of the complete cessation of the mental modifications, the impressions only remain. This is the other *samādhi* [*asaṁprajñāta samādhi*].

In *saṁprajñāta samādhi* the buried seeds can still come into the conscious mind when the proper opportunity is given and pull you into worldly experience. That is why all these four stages should be passed and you should get into *asaṁprajñāta samādhi* where even the ego feeling is not there and the seeds of past impressions are rendered harmless. In that state, only the consciousness is there and nothing else. Once that is achieved, the individual is completely liberated and there is no more coming into the world and getting tossed. Although you appear to be in the world then, you are not involved. Having achieved this, the world is just a shadow from which you are completely free. That is what is meant by a liberated person. It is not that a liberated person just goes away from the world or dies. He or she is called a *jīvanmukta*—one who lives but at the same time is liberated.

So, you first understand the nature completely, then bring it under your control and then push it aside and get liberated. Sometimes people try to renounce the world by retiring to a forest or cave, thinking that otherwise they will get caught. But such people can never be free from the nature. They can never hide anywhere; wherever they go, Nature will follow. There is no other way except to understand it, handle it properly and then rise above it. That's why the *saṁprajñāta samādhi* with all its four varieties should be practiced. Then you can easily understand the *asaṁprajñāta samādhi,* because when you understand the *Prakṛti,* you can brush it aside and turn in to see yourself. You understand yourself to be the pure Self, or the *Puruṣa,* which seemed to have been entangled in *Prakṛti* and is now finally free.

भवप्रत्ययो विदेहप्रकृतिलयानाम् ॥१९॥

19. Bhavapratyayo videha prakṛtilayānām.

Bhava = existence, birth; **pratyayaḥ** (pratyayo) = content of mind (mental modification); **videha** = bodiless [gods and spirits]; **prakṛtilayānām** = merged into nature.

Those who merely leave their physical bodies and attain the state of celestial deities, or those who get merged in Nature, have rebirth.

Suppose you practice a little *saṁprajñāta samādhi* and then die. Do you lose all the benefit? Patañjali says no. Once you gain a certain mastery over nature but lose this body before attaining the highest goal of liberation, you go on to become one of the controllers of nature. Such people are called *videhas.*

Suppose you have mastered the gross elements without going into the subtler ones. You become the controller of the gross elements of nature.

If you had stopped at the practice of *sa-asmita samādhi,* having reached the very depth of nature, you would have become the Master of Nature. Such people are called the *siddha puruṣas,* or the gods who control the different phenomena—*Indra, Varuṇa, Agni,* and so on, according to the Hindu names. But, whoever they become, they have to come back to study further and get liberated. Temporarily they have dropped out of nature, but to get the final degree they have to enter the university again. We drop out temporarily, but if we are interested in getting the degree we have to go back to the university. *Prakṛti* is that "universe-ity." You go to a certain point and get into a higher abode and control nature, but still the seeds of desires and attachments are there. You are not completely liberated, so you come back again to fulfill the other practices and get the degree. That's why even the gods have to become human beings. It is only on the human level that there is a possibility of getting liberation. The gods are just human beings who have evolved a little further and learned to control nature and, by that control, have earned the enjoyment of certain pleasures in the heavens. But, after that, they come back. This coming and going will always be there until they burn all the seeds of desire and become completely liberated by knowing themselves.

श्रद्धावीर्यस्मृतिसमाधिप्रज्ञापूर्वक इतरेषाम् ॥२०॥

20. Śraddhāvīryasmṛtisamādhiprajñāpūrvaka itareṣām.

Śraddhā = faith; **vīrya** = vigor, power; **smṛti** = memory; **samādhi** = contemplation; **prajñā** = discernement, wisdom, insight; **pūrvakaḥ** = precedes; **itareṣām** = for the others.

For the others, this *asaṁprajñāta samādhi* could come through faith, vigor, memory, contemplation and/or by discernment.

These are some of the methods Patañjali gives that will be discussed further in Book Two—the portion on Yogic practice. Just briefly, faith must be there—or at least courage. You must be strong, and you should have a good memory of all the mistakes you have made and the lessons you've learned so as not to fall back into the worldly rut again. And, of course, there must be contemplation, or *samādhi*, as Patañjali has been talking about all along, and finally discernment or discrimination between the real (Self) and the unreal (*Prakṛti*).

तीव्रसंवेगानामासन्नः ॥२१॥

21. Tīvrasaṁvegānāmāsannaḥ.

Tīvra = keen intent; **saṁvegānām** = with great speed; **āsannaḥ** = sitting very close.

To the keen and intent practitioner this [*samādhi*] comes very quickly.

मृदुमध्याधिमात्रत्वात् ततोऽपि विशेषः ॥२२॥

22. Mṛdu madhyādhimātratvāt tato'pi viśeṣaḥ.

Mṛdu = mild; **madhya** = medium;
adhmātratvāt = from full, intense; **tataḥ** (tato) = thereupon;
api ('pi) = also; **viśeṣaḥ** = differentiation, distinction.

The time necessary for success further depends on whether the practice is mild, medium or intense.

ईश्वरप्रणिधानाद्वा ॥२३॥

23. Īśvarapraṇidhānādvā

Īśvara = Supreme God; **praṇidhānāt** = from dedicated devotion; **vā** = or.

Or [*samādhi* is attained] by devotion with total dedication to *Īśvara*.

Here he says that there is another way to get success: *Īśvara praṇidhāna*, or self-surrender to God. By the term *Īśvara*, Patañjali means the supreme consciousness—not the individual soul but the supreme soul. Patañjali goes on to explain who *Īśvara* is:

क्लेशकर्मविपाकाशयैरपरामृष्टः पुरुषविशेष ईश्वरः ॥२४॥

24. Kleśa karma vipākāśayairaparāmṛṣṭaḥ Puruṣaviśeṣa Īśvaraḥ.

kleśa = afflictions; **karma** = actions; **vipāka** = fruit of actions; **aśayaiḥ** = storehouse of impressions left by desires; **aparāmṛṣṭaḥ** = unaffected by; **Puruṣa** = self, soul; **viśeṣaḥ** = distinction; **Īśvaraḥ** = supreme God.

***Īśvara* is the supreme *Puruṣa*, unaffected by any afflictions, actions, fruits of actions or by any inner impressions of desires.**

This means *Īśvara* has no desire, thus no action and no need to reap the fruits of action. Then what is *Īśvara*?

तत्र निरतिशयं सर्वज्ञबीजम् ॥२५॥

25. Tatra niratiśayam sarvajñabījam.

Tatra = there [in *Īśvara*]; **niratiśayam** = unsurpassed manifestation, above the highest; **sarvajña** = omniscience; **bījam** = seed.

In *Īśvara* is the complete manifestation of the seed of omniscience.

In other words, *Īśvara* is all-knowing and is knowledge itself. The cosmic knowledge is called the Supreme Soul, or *Puruṣa.* How can we imagine or visualize it? Imagine a circle. You see the space within it and the space outside it. The inner space is finite and the outer is infinite. If you accept the existence of a finite space, automatically you have to accept an infinite one. Without infinite there can be no finite. The moment you say, "I am a man," there must be a woman. If you say "left," there must be a right. The thought of one implies the thought of the other. We feel that our minds and knowledge are limited and finite. So, there must be a source of infinite knowledge beyond that.

स पूर्वेषामपि गुरुः कालेनानवच्छेदात् ॥२६॥

26. Sa pūrveṣām api guruḥ kālenānavacchedāt.

Saḥ = He; **pūrveṣām** = of the ancients; **api** = even; **guruḥ** = teacher; **kālena** = by time; **anavacchedāt** = unconditioned, uncut from.

Unconditioned by time, *Īśvara* is the teacher of even the most ancient teachers.

Although all knowledge is within you and you need not get it from outside, somebody is still necessary to help you understand your own knowledge. That is why a teacher, or *guru,* is necessary. He or she helps you go within and understand yourself. To help you, your *guru* must know something him- or herself. From where did your *guru* get that knowledge? It must have been learned from somebody else. There must be a chain of *gurus*. Then who is the first *guru*? There may be hundreds of thousands of gurus, but there should be a primary one. There should be an infinite reservoir of knowledge from which all knowledge came in the beginning. That's why Patañjali says the supreme *Puruṣa*, or *Īśvara*, is the *Guru* of the *gurus*.

So *Īśvara praṇidhāna*, or devotion to the all-knowing *Īśvara*, is another method for obtaining *samādhi*. It is the emotional path which is easier than the other methods mentioned before. Just surrender yourself, saying, "I am Thine; all is Thine; Thy will be done." The moment you have resigned yourself completely, you have transcended your own ego.

We try to practice Yoga with our egos, "Oh, I can concentrate; I can penetrate this object; I can empty my mind." All these ideas of "I can" should become "I can'ts." We should become completely resigned. When we say, "I can," we are speaking as a part of nature. Once we say, "I can't do anything; it is You," we have risen above nature. That is a simple and safe shortcut if you can do it.

Ultimately, nobody can achieve eternal peace by doing something with the mind, which is part of nature. That supreme joy can only be acquired when you rise above nature by complete surrender. Then you transcend nature and understand God in the transcendental state. Once you transcend, you know that you were never involved in nature. Big or small, you are completely pure and free. Then you become one with the transcendent God. In that state, as Jesus said, "I and my Father are one." You can never say that as Mr. So-and-so with 150 pounds of flesh and bone and 5'6" height and curly hair. Which "I" can say, "I and my Father are One"? The pure "I" who is uninvolved and free from nature. That freedom comes once you surrender yourself completely to God.

In our ordinary lives we have Yoga (union) with nature but now we want Yoga with God. We have union always, but our union with *Prakṛti* should be changed to union with God. Union with God is the real Yoga. So now, you can see the connection between the devotional side of the religious teachings and Yoga. There is no difference between religion and Yoga. Yoga is the basis of all the religions. With the light of Yogic understanding you can walk into even the difficult corners of the scriptures and understand every religion well.

तस्य वाचकः प्रणवः ॥२७॥

27. Tasya vācakaḥ praṇavaḥ.

Tasya = of [Īśvara]; **vācakaḥ** = word, expressive, signifying; **praṇavaḥ** = mystic sound "OM."

The word expressive of *Īśvara* is the mystic sound *OM*. [*OM* is God's name as well as form.]

Because it is difficult to understand anything without a name, Patañjali wants to give the supreme *Puruṣa* a name. Even if *Īśvara* doesn't have a particular form, there should be a name. But "*Īśvara*" is a limited name; "God" is also limited because the very vibrations of the letters are limited. So Patañjali wants a name that can give an unlimited idea and vibration and which can include all vibrations, all sounds and syllables, because God is like that—infinite. So Patañjali says *Īśvara's* name is "Mmmm." We can't easily say "Mmmm," so it is written as *OM*. *OM* is called *praṇava*, which simply means "humming."

But you need not hum to feel God's presence. If you hum, it is as if you were trying to create God or bring God into you. There's no need to create God, but just to feel God in you. If you close your eyes and ears, sit quietly, allow the mind to be completely silent and then listen within, you will hear God humming. God talks to us always, but we talk so loud we fail to hear.

Here also, we have to understand why we should give a name to something. In Sanskrit there is a term "*padārtha.*" Colloquially, it means "thing," but literally it means the "*pada*" and "*artha*": the thing and its meaning. The name and form of a thing are inseparable. When you want to express a thought, you have to put it into words. Without words you can't convey what you are thinking. So every thought or substance should have a name to express it. That is why we have a name for everything in this world. But in the normal sense, a name may *mean* something but it can't convey the exact nature of that thing. For example, when I say "apple," we all know what an apple is so we are able to visualize the substance behind that name. But if you have never seen or heard of an apple, the word cannot convey anything. You cannot create a picture from the word itself. You may even wonder who this "apple" is! It has only become the name of that fruit through usage.

But God's designation should not be like that. There are hundreds and thousands of names for God but none of them conveys the exact idea of God. They may give a picture of one aspect of God, but not the fullness. God is, was and always will be—without beginning or end, infinite and omnipresent. For such a great One, there should be a name that conveys those same ideas. And not only that, but by repeating it, the very name should manifest God in you. The name "chair" can remind you of a chair, but you can't sit on it. "Sugar" can remind you of something sweet, but you can't taste it. But God's name should not only denote the fullness of God and itself represent God, it should also bring God to you. And such a name cannot be anything but *OM*.

Please do not think that I am a Hindu and the Hindu scriptures say this so that is why I am saying it. I don't belong to any particular religion. All the scriptures indicate this. The *Bible* says, "In the beginning there was the Word, and the Word was with God and the *Word was God.*" And the Hindu *Vedas* say, "The name of Brahman is *OM*, and *OM* is Brahman." Why do they say this *OM* is so rich, so deep, and capable of representing the omnipresent, endless and beginningless God?

Let us see why it is so. The name *OM* can be split into three letters: A, U, and M. That is why it is often written *AUM*. The entire *Māṇḍūkya Upaniṣad* expounds the meaning of *OM*. There it divides *OM* into four stages: A, U, M and *anahata*, or the one that is beyond verbal pronunciation. A is the beginning of all sounds. Every language begins with the letter A or "ah." A is pronounced by simply opening the mouth and making a sound. That sound is produced in the throat where the tongue is rooted. So audible sound begins with A. Then as the sound comes forward between the tongue and the palate up to the lips U or "oo" is produced. Then closing the lips produces the M. So the creation is A, the preservation is U and the culmination is M. So A-U-M includes the entire process of sound, and all other sounds are contained in it. Thus, *OM* is the origin, or seed, from which all other sounds and words come. So, in actuality, *OM* is dormant in all other words.

After the verbal sound ends there is still a vibration. That is the unspoken, or *anahata*, sound which is always in you, even before saying the A and after finishing M. There is always a sound vibration in you that can never be destroyed. You can always listen to that sound if you remain quiet. For that reason it is also called *ajapa*, or unrepeated. *Japa* means repetition, but the *ajapa* is that which need not be repeated; it is always going on within. It is heard only when all the other sounds cease. Even thinking creates a sound, because thought itself is a form of speaking. By thinking you distort the original sound which transcends the beginning, continuation and end of the *OM* sound. To listen to that sound you have to keep your mind quiet, stop the thinking process and dive within. Then you will be able to listen to that hum.

That hum is called *praṇava* because it is connected with *prāṇa*. *Prāṇa* is the basic vibration which always exists whether it is manifesting or not. It is never-ending. It is something like when we think, speak and act during our waking state, whereas in the sleeping condition the mind seems to keep quiet. But actually, even in the sleeping state, movement is still there. Vibration is still there in the mind in an unmanifested condition. Scientifically, we can say that when manifested objects are reduced to their unmanifested condition, they go back to the atomic vibration. Nobody can stop that atomic vibration. We say that animate objects move while inanimate ones do not, because it appears that way to our eyes. We can't see any motion in a stone, but that does not mean it is motionless. We need not go to the scriptures. The scientists themselves have proven that.

Similarly, even without your repeating it, the basic sound is always vibrating in you. It is the seed from which all other sounds manifest. That is why *OM* represents God in the fullest sense. It has the power to create everything. If you make an apple out of clay, paint it beautifully and put it on a table with a real apple, an ordinary person cannot see the difference between the clay apple and the real one. They look alike and have the same name. But if you plant them both, your clay apple will not create an apple tree, but the real one will. The true apple has that creative capacity within itself because the seed is there.

Likewise, other words are just like the clay apple, while the seed word *OM* has the creative capacity to manifest the entire world. The entire world evolves from that and goes back into that again. That is why God's name should be *OM*. No other name can be more adequate to represent God.

We should also understand that *OM* was not invented by anybody. Some people didn't come together, hold nominations, take a vote, and the majority decided, "All right, let God have the name OM." No. God manifested as *OM*. Any seeker who really wants to see God face to face will ultimately see God as *OM*. That is why it transcends all geographical, political or theological limitations. It doesn't belong to one country or one religion; it belongs to the entire universe.

It is a variation of this *OM* that we see as the "Amen" or "Ameen," which the Christians, Muslims and Jews say. That doesn't mean someone changed it. Truth is always the same. Wherever you sit for meditation, you will ultimately end in experiencing *OM* or the hum. But when you want to express what you experienced, you may use different words according to your capacity or the language you know.

For example, if some children hear somebody fire a gun and come running to their mama, one may cry, "Mama, Mama, I heard a big sound 'Doomm.'" Another child will say, "No, Mama; it went 'Dooop.'" "Oh, Mama, I heard a big 'bang.'" The third child will say, "Is it 'doomm,' or 'dooop' or 'bang'?" These are all different versions of the same sound as heard by the different children. Likewise, if you sit and meditate and go deep into the cosmic sound, you may say, "Oh, I heard it as 'Amen.'" Another will say, "I heard 'Ameen.'" A third will say "*OM*;" a fourth "Mmmm." That is why the *Upaniṣads* say, "*Ekam sat, viprahā bahudha vadanti.*" "Truth is one; seers express it in many ways."

So, here we have learned the greatness of that basic seed word *OM*. No other name can be more suitable than this for the Supreme. And now, having expressed its greatness, Patañjali continues by saying:

तज्जपस्तदर्थभावनम् ॥२८॥

28. Tajjapas tadartha bhāvanam.

Tad (taj) = that (OM); **japaḥ** = repetition; **tad** = that (OM); **artha** = meaning; **bhāvanam** = reflection.

To repeat it with reflection upon its meaning is an aid.

Here we come to the practice of *japa*. It's a very powerful technique and, at the same time, it's the easiest, simplest and the best. Almost every religion advocates the repetition of God's name because all the prophets, sages and saints experienced and understood its greatness, glory and power.

That's why in the Hindu system, a mystic word, or *mantra*, is given to the student to repeat. The meaning of *mantra* is "that which keeps the mind steady and produces the proper effect." Its repetition is called *japa*. So Japa Yoga is communion with God through the repetition of holy name. In the Catholic religion you see the *japa* of Hail Mary practiced with the aid of the rosary. And in the Greek Orthodox Church I was surprised to see that *japa* is their constant practice also. They repeat, "Lord Jesus, have mercy on me," continuously. And in Tibetan Tantric Buddhism, *japa* is a predominant practice.

We say it is the easiest because you need not go to a particular place nor have a particular time for it. It is not somewhere outside you, but always within. Wherever you are, your *mantra* is with you. To worship a form you have to have a picture or image and a place to keep it. But in *mantra* practice it is always in your heart, the most sacred place, because it is your beloved. And that's why your *mantra* is to be kept sacred and secret. You don't even reveal it to others, lest you lose the reverence for it.

By repeating it constantly, a part of the mind gets linked to that. It is like going down into a tunnel with a life-rope tied around the waist and one end of the rope fixed to a peg outside the tunnel. Whenever there is any danger, you can just shake the rope and get pulled out. In the same way, a part of your mind is tied to God through your *mantra* while the other part is engaged in worldly pursuits. You dive deep to get all the pearls you want to gather: name, fame, money, position, friends, anything you want. You need not stay away from anything as long as you do not lose hold of the rope. Sensible climbers see to that first, and even pull it a few times to see whether it is strong enough. Only after making sure do they begin to climb. But, alas, many people do not bother about any rope. It is a golden cord between you and God or the cosmic force.

Do not bother about the meaning in the beginning. Let the repetition become a constant habit. When it becomes a firm habit, then you can think, "What am I repeating?" Then you will be able to think of the meaning without forgetting the repetition itself because it has become a habit already. Most things happen by habit in our lives. Twelve o'clock means lunch; six o'clock, dinner. Just by the clock, things have become habits. Because we repeat something so often, it becomes second nature to us. In the same way, God's name can also be mechanically or habitually created in the beginning until finally it absorbs you and you become that. If you repeat, "war, war, war," one day you will be at war. Think, "monkey, monkey, monkey," and probably within a week or two you will be jumping here and there. Yes, "As you think, so you become." Knowingly or unknowingly, you imbibe the qualities of the thing named.

That is why the right name has to be selected. Any word could help you keep the mind focused, but some names might lead you into difficulty later on. A holy name which will elevate your mind should be taken as a *mantra*. For a special benefit, a special *mantra* is called for, but the basis of them all is *OM*, just as cotton is the basis for cloth, which is then cut in different designs according to its purpose—a pillowcase, a bedsheet, a tablecloth or a napkin. *OM* is the basic seed. For different purposes you use different *mantras* which are all part and parcel of the original cosmic sound vibration *OM*.

You can use the same sound power to bring harm or good. The people who do voodoo and black magic are also using *mantric* power. So you can make or break, bless or curse, with your words. In fact, at no other time has the power of the word been more exhibited than in this century. Politicians get elected by the power of their words. The power of words can be clearly seen in the present-day advertisements. Even a worthless product can be made to seem the best by clever words. So the power of the word can be misused also. That is why even before you handle these words, you should have purity of mind. So in *japa*, you repeat the word and later on feel the meaning also.

ततः प्रत्यक्चेतनाधिगमोऽप्यन्तरायाभावश्च ॥२९॥

29. Tataḥ pratyak cetanādhigamo 'pyantarāyābhāvaś ca.

Tataḥ = from this; **pratyak** = inner; **cetana** = Self;
adhigamaḥ (adhigamo) = knowledge; **api** (apy) = also;
antarāya = obstacles; **abhāvaḥ** (abhāvaś) = disappear; **ca** = and.

From this practice all the obstacles disappear and simultaneously dawns knowledge of the inner Self.

You get in tune with the cosmic power. By that tuning you feel that force in you, imbibe all those qualities, get the cosmic vision, transcend all your limitations and finally become that transcendental reality. Normally, the mind and body limit you, but by holding something infinite, you slowly raise yourself from the finite objects that bind you and transcend them. Through that you get rid of all the obstacles and your path is made easy. This probably reminds Patañjali of the different obstructions on the way, so he goes on to explain them next.

व्याधिस्त्यानसंशयप्रमादालस्याविरति
भ्रान्तिदर्शनालब्धभूमिकत्वानवस्थितत्वानि
चित्तविक्षेपास्तेऽन्तरायाः ॥३०॥

30. Vyādhi styāna saṁśaya pramādālasyāvirati bhrāntidarśanālabdha-bhūmikatvānavasthitatvāni cittavikṣepāste'ntarāyāḥ.

Vyādhi = disease; **styāna** = dullness; **saṁśaya** = doubt; **pramāda** = carelessness; **ālasya** = laziness; **avirati** = sensuality, intemperance; **bhrānti** = false; **darśana** = perception; **alabdhabhumikatva** = failure to reach firm ground; **anavasthitatva** = slipping down from the ground gained; (**ani** = an ending to the nine words indicating them as a group); **citta** = mind-stuff; **vikṣepāḥ** (vikṣepās) = distraction; **te** = these; **antarāyāḥ** ('ntarāyāḥ) = obstacles.

Disease, dullness, doubt, carelessness, laziness, sensuality, false perception, failure to reach firm ground and slipping from the ground gained—these distractions of the mind-stuff are the obstacles.

They are more or less like a chain. The first obstacle is physical disease. Disease makes you dull, and a dull mind will doubt everything because it doesn't want to penetrate into a thing to understand it. When doubt is there, there is a carelessness, a sort of lethargic attitude or laziness. And when the mind loses the interest and alertness toward the higher goal, it has to do something else so it will slowly descend to the sensual enjoyments. Actually, all these things could be summed up as the qualities of *tamas*, or inertia, dullness.

Another obstacle is slipping down from the ground one has gained. This puzzles many people. Beginners, for example, will practice with intense interest. Every day they will feel more and more interested and feel they are progressing steadily. They may even be proud of their progress. All of a sudden one day they will find that they have lost everything and slipped down to rock bottom.

It happens to many people. If we know it is a common occurrence on the spiritual path, we won't get disheartened. Otherwise, we will say, "Oh, I lost everything. There is no hope for me," and we lose all our interest. Let us know that this is common in the case of every aspirant. The mind can't function on the same level always—it has its heights and depths. If there is going to be steady progress always, there will be no challenge, no game in it.

Remember, Yoga practice is like an obstacle race; many obstructions are purposely put on the way for us to pass through. They are there to make us understand and express our own capacities. We all have that strength, but we don't seem to know it. We seem to need to be challenged and tested in order to understand our own capacities. In fact, that is the natural law. If a river just flows easily, the water in the river does not express its power. But once you put an obstacle to the flow by constructing a dam, then you can see its strength in the form of tremendous electrical power.

दुःखदौर्मनस्याङ्गमेजयत्वश्वासप्रश्वासा
विक्षेपसहभुवः ॥३१॥

31. Duḥkha daurmanasyāṅgamejayatva śvāsa praśvāsā vikṣepa sahabhuvaḥ.

Duḥkha = distress; **daurmanasya** = despair; **aṅgam** = the body; **ejayatva** = trembling of; **śvāsa** = disturbed inhalation; **praśvāsā** = disturbed exhalation; **vikṣepa** = distraction, confusion; **saha** = accompany; **bhuvaḥ** = arising, existing.

Accompaniments to the mental distractions include distress, despair, trembling of the body and disturbed breathing.

These are symptoms that we all sometimes experience which prevent concentration and meditation. That is where we have to take care of our day-to-day activities, movements, associations and diet. We shouldn't allow the body and mind to be *tamasic.* They should always be in a *sattvic* (tranquil) condition. That cannot be created all of a sudden by meditation alone, so we have to take care of all these things in our daily life. A sickly body can never be fit to sit; it will not allow the mind to meditate quietly. Weak nerves will always create tremors. When some people meditate, they tremble and perspire. These are symptoms of physical weakness. But such things will not happen if we keep our body in proper condition by right diet, exercise, proper rest and if we do not allow it to be lazy or dull.

तत्प्रतिषेधार्थमेकतत्त्वाभ्यासः ॥३२॥

32. Tat pratiṣedhārthamekatattvābhyāsaḥ.

Tat = their; **pratiṣedha** = prevention; **artham** = for the sake of; **eka** = one, single; **tattva** = subject, true principle, reality; **abhyāsah** = practice.

The practice of concentration on a single subject [or the use of one technique] is the best way to prevent the obstacles and their accompaniments.

The point here is that we should not keep changing our object of concentration. When you decide on one thing, stick to it whatever happens. There's no value in digging shallow wells in a hundred places. Decide on one place and dig deep. Even if you encounter a rock, use dynamite and keep going down. If you leave that to dig another well, all the first effort is wasted and there is no proof you won't hit rock again. Before you start digging, analyze well and find out which spot is good. Then, once you decide and begin, you should not question it further. Go right at it, because it will be too late then to think whether it is worthwhile or not; you should have done that before.

Even if it is a long route, your perseverance will make it short. Our aim is to make the mind steady, so it is immaterial what object we take.

Anything can take you to the goal, because you are not concentrating on the object for the sake of the object but for the sake of your goal. The object is only a symbol of that. We should always remember this. All our ideas, objects or even *mantras* are just symbols to hold onto as aids toward the goal. Behind the objects you should always remember the goal.

Tastes, temperaments and capacities differ, so you should not criticize other people's objects of meditation because you have selected another. They are approaching the same goal through their objects. Just as you have confidence in your object, they too have that confidence in their way. We should not disturb other people's faith, nor let ourselves get disturbed from our faith. Stick to one thing and forge ahead with that. Why do you want to have this one-pointed concentration? To make the mind clear so you can transcend it. You are not going to cling to the object but just use it as a ladder to climb up. Once you have reached the roof you leave the ladder behind.

Now, in the following *sūtras* Patañjali gives certain suggestions for attaining and maintaining this one-pointedness. We can easily see what a broad outlook he has. He is interested in the goal and not in the paths. He doesn't try to squeeze you into one particular path. He only gives you a few suggestions and ultimately says that if none of these satisfy you, select whatever you want. He is that liberal. That is why Yoga is appreciated by everyone. Nobody can deny the Yoga philosophy because it has something to suit everyone.

मैत्रीकरुणामुदितोपेक्षाणां सुखदुःखपुण्यापुण्य
विषयाणांभावनातश्चित्तप्रसादनम् ॥३३॥

33. Maitrī karuṇā muditopekṣāṇām sukha duḥkha puṇyāpuṇya viṣayāṇam bhāvanātaś citta prasādanam.

Maitrī = friendliness; **karunā** = compassion; **mudita** = delight;
upekṣa = disregard; (**aṇām** = of these four);
sukha = happy; **duḥkha** = unhappy; **puṇya** = virtuous;
apuṇya = wicked; **viṣaya** = in the domain;
(**aṇām** = of the four, with respect to the previous four);
bhāvanātaḥ (bhāvanātaś) = cultivating the attitudes;
citta = mind-stuff; **prasādanam** = undisturbed calmness.

By cultivating attitudes of friendliness toward the happy, compassion for the unhappy, delight in the virtuous and disregard toward the wicked, the mind-stuff retains its undisturbed calmness.

Whether you are interested in reaching *samādhi* or plan to ignore Yoga entirely, I would advise you to remember at least this one *sūtra.* It will be very helpful to you in keeping a peaceful mind in your daily life. You may not have any great goal in your life, but just try to follow this one *sūtra* very well and you will see its efficacy. In my own experience, this *sūtra* became my guiding light to keep my mind serene always.

Who would not like serenity of mind always? Who would not like to be happy always? Everybody wants that. So Patañjali gives four keys: friendliness, compassion, delight and disregard. There are only four kinds of locks in the world. Keep these four keys always with you, and when you come across any one of these four locks, you will have the proper key to open it.

What are those four locks? *Sukha, duḥkha, puṇya* and *apuṇya*—the happy people, unhappy people, the virtuous and the wicked. At any given moment, you can fit any person into one of these four categories.

When you see happy people, use the "friendliness" key. Why should Patañjali say this? Because even four thousand years ago there must have been people who were not happy at seeing others happy. It is still the same way. Suppose some people drive up in a big car, park in front of a huge palatial home and get out. Some other people are standing on the pavement in the hot sun getting tired. How many of those people will be happy? Not many. They will be saying, "See that big car? Those people are sucking the blood of the laborers." We come across people like that; they are always jealous. When a person gets name, fame or high position, they try to criticize that person. "Oh, don't you know, that person's brother is so-and-so. Some strings must have been pulled." They will never admit that the person might have gone up by his or her own merit. By that jealousy, you will not disturb the other person, but you disturb your own serenity. Those people simply got out of the car and walked into the house, but you are burning up inside. Instead, think, "Oh, such fortunate people. If everyone was like that how happy the world would be. May God bless everybody to have such comfort. I will also get that one day." Make those people your friends. That response is missed in many cases, not only between individuals but even among nations. When some nation is prospering, the neighboring country is jealous of it and wants to ruin its economy. So we should always have the key of friendliness when we see happy people.

And what of the next lock, the unhappy people? "Well, Swami said people have their own *karma*; they must have done some wretched thing in their last birth. Let them suffer now." That should not be our attitude. Maybe they are suffering from previous bad *karma*, but we should have compassion. If you can lend a helping hand, do it. If you can share half of your loaf, share it. Be merciful always. By doing that, you will retain the peace and poise of your mind. Remember, our goal is to keep the serenity of our minds. Whether our mercy is going to help others or not, by our own feeling of mercy, at least we are helped. Then comes the third kind, the virtuous people. When you see virtuous people, feel delighted. "Oh, how great they are. They must be my heroes. I should imitate their great qualities." Don't envy them; don't try to pull them down. Appreciate the virtuous qualities in them and try to cultivate them in your own life.

And, lastly, the wicked. We come across wicked people sometimes. We can't deny that. So what should be our attitude? Indifference. "Well, some people are like that. Probably I was like that yesterday. Am I not a better person now? They will probably be all right tomorrow." Don't try to advise such people because wicked people seldom take advice. If you try to advise them, you will lose your peace.

I still remember a small story from the *Pañca Tantra* which I was told as a small child. One rainy day, a monkey was sitting on a tree branch getting completely drenched. Right opposite on another branch of the same tree there was a small sparrow sitting in its hanging nest. Normally a sparrow builds its nest on the edge of a branch so it can hang down and swing around gently in the breeze. It has a nice cabin inside with an upper chamber, a reception room, a bedroom down below and even a delivery room if it is going to give birth to little ones. Oh yes, you should see and admire a sparrow's nest sometime.

It was warm and cozy inside its nest and the sparrow peeped out and, seeing the poor monkey, said, "Oh, my dear friend, I am so small; I don't even have hands like you, only a small beak. But with only that I built a nice house, expecting this rainy day. Even if the rain continues for days, I will be warm inside. I heard Darwin saying that you are the forefather of human beings, so why don't you use your brain? Build a nice, small hut somewhere to protect yourself during the rain."

You should have seen the face of that monkey. It was terrible! "Oh, you little devil! How dare you try to advise me? Because you are warm and cozy in your nest you are teasing me. Wait, you will see where you are!" The monkey proceeded to tear the nest to pieces, and the poor bird had to fly out and get drenched like the monkey.

This is a story I was told when I was quite young and I still remember it. Sometimes we come across such monkeys, and if you advise them they take it as an insult. They think you are proud of your position. If you sense even a little of that tendency in somebody, stay away. He or she will have to learn by experience. By giving advice to such people, you will only lose your peace of mind.

Is there any other category you can think of? Patañjali groups all individuals in these four ways: the happy, the unhappy, the virtuous and the wicked. So have these four attitudes: friendliness, compassion, gladness and indifference. These four keys should always be with you in your pocket. If you use the right key with the right person you will retain your peace. Nothing in the world can upset you then. Remember, our goal is to keep a serene mind. From the very beginning of Patañjali's *Sūtras* we are reminded of that. And this *sūtra* will help us a lot.

प्रच्छर्दनविधारणाभ्यां वा प्राणस्य ॥३४॥

34. Pracchardanavidhāraṇābhyām vā prāṇasya.

Pracchardana = exhale, expulsion; **vidhāraṇa** = retention; (**abhyām** = by these two); **vā** = or; **prāṇasya** = of the breath.

Or that calm is retained by the controlled exhalation or retention of the breath.

Here Patañjali talks about *prāṇāyāma*, or the control of the movement of the *prāṇa*, which we experience as our breathing. Some *prāṇāyāma* specialists say Patañjali meant that we should retain the breath outside. Instead of breathing in and holding the breath, breathe out and hold. But Patañjali didn't go that deeply into the different kinds of breathing exercises, and he probably meant that we should just watch and regulate the breath. You can begin with a deep exhalation, then watch the breath come slowly in and out. This is also given in the Buddhist meditation called *ana-pana sati. Ana-pana* is similar to the *prāṇa-apāna* of Hatha Yoga. The force that moves upward is the *prāṇa*, the force that moves downward is the *apāna.* The aim is to bring together the *prāṇa* and *apāna.* In fact, Haṭha Yoga is based mainly on the equilibrium of these two forces. "Haṭha" means the "sun" and "moon." The two opposites must be blended together in a gentle way. So here he says that to bring peace to the mind, watch and regulate the breath.

We should always remember that the mind and the *prāṇa*, or breathing, have close connections. The great South Indian saint, Thirumular, said, "Where the mind goes, the *prāṇa* follows." We see that even in our daily life. If your mind is agitated, you will be breathing heavily. If you are deeply interested in reading something or thinking seriously and break the concentration to watch your breath, you will notice that you are hardly breathing. That is why after deep thinking, you sigh heavily or take a deep breath. This proves that when the mind is concentrated and made still, the breath stops. That is called *kevala kumbhaka,* or the automatic retention of breath without your effort. People who go into deep meditation will discover this.

So, in the reverse way, if you regulate the *prāṇa* you regulate the mind automatically also. That's why, whenever you are agitated, worried or puzzled, you should take a few deep breaths, putting your entire mind on the breath. Within a few minutes you will find that the mind is completely serene. It's a very useful hint for our daily lives. Suppose, all of a sudden, you are getting into a fit of anger. Take a few deep breaths, watch the breath and the anger will go away. Whatever be the agitation in the mind, regulating the breath will help.

विषयवती वा प्रवृत्तिरुत्पन्ना मनसः
स्थितिनिबन्धनी ॥३५॥

35. Viṣayavatī vā pravṛttirutpannā manasaḥ sthitinibandhanī.

Viṣayavatī = having object of sense perception
(sound, tangibility, form, savor and odor); **vā** = or;
pravṛttiḥ = refined activity, subtle sense perception;
utpannā = uprising; **manasaḥ** = of the mind; **sthiti** = steadiness;
nibandhanī = bind, fix upon.

Or the concentration on subtle sense perceptions can cause steadiness of mind.

At certain points during the initial practice of concentration, various extraordinary sense perceptions occur. They themselves could become the helpful objects for further concentration to make the mind steady. If you practice Yoga and do not see any benefit, you might lose interest and begin to doubt its efficacy. So to make yourself more confident, you can concentrate on the extraordinary sense perceptions that come after some continuous practice. In this way you understand that you are progressing in one-pointedness. It is something like a litmus paper test.

One example is to concentrate on the tip of the nose. Do not strain or you will cause a headache. Do not actually stare at the nose; it's as if you are looking at it. Keep the mind on that. If the mind is really one-pointed, after some time you will experience an extraordinary smell. You may even look around to see if there is any flower or perfume nearby. If that experience comes, it is a proof that you have made the mind one-pointed. It will give you confidence. But in itself, it will not help you to reach the goal. It's just a test, that's all. Don't make concentrating on the nose and getting nice smells your goal.

Another example is to put your mind on the tip of the tongue. If the concentration is deep enough, you will get a nice taste without eating anything. If you do not get it, you still have a long way to go. There are many suggestions like that: concentrate on your palate, or on the middle or back part of the tongue or on the throat region, and you get certain other extraordinary experiences. Those experiences will give you confidence and make you feel you are on the way—they are useful only for that.

विशोका वा ज्योतिष्मती ॥३६॥

36. Viśokā vā jyotiṣmatī.

Viśokā = blissful (sorrow-less); **vā** = or;
jyotiṣmatī = the internal Supreme Light.

Or by concentrating on the supreme, ever-blissful Light within.

You can imagine a brilliant divine light which is beyond all anxieties, fear and worry—a supreme Light in you. Visualize a brilliant globe in your heart representing your Divine Consciousness. Or imagine your heart to contain a beautiful glowing lotus. The mind will easily get absorbed in that, and you will have a nice experience. In the beginning one has to imagine this Light, which later becomes a reality.

वीतरागविषयं वा चित्तम् ॥३७॥

37. Vītarāgaviṣayam vā cittam.

Vīta = free (from); **rāga** = attachment;
viṣayam = objects of the senses; **vā** =or; **cittam** = mind-stuff.

Or by concentrating on a great soul's mind which is totally freed from attachment to sense objects.

Many people do not have that much confidence in their own hearts. "Oh, how could I have such a wonderful heart with all this rubbish inside?" In that case, you can think of the heart of a noble person. Meditate on a heart that has given up all attachments to sense objects, on a heart that has realized the goal. If you can't imagine that your heart is full of that Light, at least you can imagine it in his or her heart. The mind should be allowed to dwell on something high, something serene; that is the main idea.

स्वप्ननिद्राज्ञानालम्बनं वा ॥३८॥

38. Svapnanidrājñānālambanam vā.

Svapna = dream; **nidrā** = deep sleep; **jñāna** = becoming acquainted; **alambanam** = to hold attention; **vā** = or.

Or by concentrating on an experience had during dream or deep sleep.

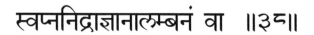

Sometimes when we sleep, we have dreams of divine beings or feel we are elevated to a higher plane. If you have such dreams, remember them and let your mind dwell on them. It will also bring the same serenity and one-pointedness. Or, if you have not had any dream like that, imagine the peace of deep sleep. Everybody goes into a very peaceful state when they sleep. Of course, you are not conscious at that time, but when you wake up you say, "Oh, I slept very soundly." Imagine that peace. Sleep itself is *tamasic*, or inert; so you should imagine the peace of that sleep, not the sleep itself. If you start imagining the sleep itself, you know where you will go!

So, these are a few suggestions of techniques to keep the mind serene. But Patañjali knows that people have their own individuality and that not everybody is going to listen to him. "Well, suppose I don't like any of these things? Does that mean I can't get anything?" someone may ask. So Patañjali concludes this section by saying:

यथाभिमतध्यानाद्वा ॥३९॥

39. Yathābhimata dhyānād vā.

Yathā = as, in which manner; **abhimata** = per choice or desire, agreeableness; **dhyānāt** = from meditating; **vā** = or.

Or by meditating on anything one chooses that is elevating.

It should not just appeal to you but should appeal as elevating and good. Many people ask, "On what should I meditate? Where should I get initiation? Is there just one way to meditate?" Here Patañjali clearly says, "No, you can meditate on anything that will elevate you."

If you can select for yourself, go ahead. If you can't, then ask for a suggestion from somebody in whom you have faith. It is only then that a teacher or initiation comes in; otherwise it is not necessary. But there is this advantage in it; instead of your trying this and that and wasting time, you ask a person who already knows the way. Otherwise, it will be like my driving in Manhattan. Suppose I want to go to 96th Street from 84th Street. I might go downtown, roam around and waste the whole day. Instead, if I just ask somebody where it is, I'll get the directions and go directly there. A teacher helps you in that way. He or she can give you the right way easily. A teacher also gives you his or her blessings, which are even more important because they give you momentum. Normally our batteries are weak; the teacher's battery is always fully charged, so he or she brings the car close to yours and uses a jumper cable, puts a little current in your battery and you go ahead. That is the sort of help we get from the teacher. But if you can crank yourself and put a little current into the battery, go ahead. There is more than one way to start a car.

परमाणुपरममहत्त्वान्तोऽस्य वशीकारः ॥४०॥

40. Paramāṇu paramamahattvānto'sya vaśīkāraḥ.

Paramāṇu = primal atom, smallest; **parama** = greatest; **mahattva** = magnitude; **antaḥ** (anto) = end, extension; **asya** ('sya) = his (her); **vaśīkāraḥ** = mastery.

Gradually, one's mastery in concentration extends from the primal atom to the greatest magnitude.

That means you can attract the entire universe, from the minutest atom to the unlimited vastness. *Anu* in Sanskrit means "atom." They had discovered the atom even several thousand years ago. And here, Patañjali not only uses the term "atom," but he says the primal atom: the atom of the atoms, or the minutest particle. There will be nothing that is unknowable by you. You can attract anything and everything by the meditations explained in the previous *sūtras*.

It is only if one achieves that meditation that he or she becomes a Yogi, not just a person who sits for a while in the name of meditation and then goes to the movies! No. Once you have established yourself in deep meditation, using any one of the foregoing methods or anything selected by you, and have gained mastery over the mind, nothing is difficult for you to meditate upon. It is simply for you to choose on what to meditate—from an atom to the entire universe.

क्षीणवृत्तेरभिजातस्येव मणेर्ग्रहीतृग्रहणग्राह्येषु तत्स्थतदञ्जनता समापत्तिः ॥४१॥

41. Kṣīṇa vṛtter abhijātasyeva maṇer grahītṛ grahaṇa grāhyeṣu tatstha tadañjanatā samāpattiḥ.

kṣīṇa = totally weakened, waned or dwindled;
vṛtteḥ (vṛtter) = modifications;
abhijātasya = of natural pureness, of flawless; **iva** = like, as if;
maṇeḥ (maṇer) = crystal; **grahītṛ** = knower;
grahaṇa = knowledge; **grāhyeṣu** = in knowledge (and);
tad = by that; **stha** = similar, being on or in; **tad** = on that;
añjanatā = assuming the color of any near object;
samāpattiḥ = samādhi, balanced state, coincidence.

Just as the naturally pure crystal assumes shapes and colors of objects placed near it, so the yogi's mind, with its totally weakened modifications, becomes clear and balanced and attains the state devoid of differentiation between knower, knowable and knowledge. This culmination of meditation is *samādhi*.

"The mind of the Yogi with its totally weakened modifications" means that the Yogi has cultivated one thought form at the cost of all others. When you cultivate one alone, all the other impressions become weaker and finer. To give a physical example, if you concentrate on the development of the brain alone, you are apt to ignore the other parts of the body.

This reminds me of a story by H.G. Wells where the future generation is described as having only a big head with little limbs like the roots of a potato. Because the people will not use the limbs, there will be no need for the limbs. These people will just think, "I must have food," and the food will come. No need even to use a hand to flip a switch, because the switch will be activated by thought.

In fact, science is devising cars now where you sit in the car and say, "All right, start. Go ahead. Be quick. Hold on. Stop." And even that seems to be unnecessary now that they have printed circuits. If you want to go to Boston, take the Boston card, put it into the car's computer, sit quietly and soon you are in Boston! All you will have to do is buy those cards. Wherever you want to go, put the card into the machine and just do anything you want in the car—talk business, chat or watch television. Then the car will remind you, "Sir, we are in Boston." That's all. No part of the body will be put into use; so it will slowly reduce in size.

That is not only true of the physical body; the same is true of the mind. If you develop one idea through constant meditation, all other thoughts and desires will gradually die away. In our daily lives we see that. If you are interested in someone, you think of that person day and night. If you open a book, your mind will not go into the subject but instead will think of that person. You will gradually lose interest in all other people and things. The same is true in Yoga practice. Our concentration and meditation should be like that.

In the ancient Hindu scriptures, we come across stories which illustrate this point. For example, there's the story of Vālmīki, the highwayman. Sage Nārada was passing by, and, as usual, Vālmīki accosted him and said,

"Hey, what do you have in your pockets?!"

"Oh, I don't even have pockets, sir."

"What a wretched man. I've never seen a man with nothing. You must give me something, otherwise I won't spare your life."

Then Nārada said, "All right, I will try to get something for you; but don't you think it's a sin to harm innocent people?"

"Oh, you *swamis* talk a lot about sin. You have no other business, but I have to maintain my wife, children and my house. If I just sit and think of virtue, our tummies are not going to be satisfied. I have to get money somehow, by hook or crook."

"Well, all right, do it. If that's your policy, I don't mind. But you say that you must feed your wife and children by hook or crook. You should know that it is a sin and you will have to face the reactions of it."

"Well, I don't bother about that."

"*You* may not bother, but since you are committing sins to provide for your wife and children, you'd better ask them whether they are willing to share the reactions of the sins also."

"Undoubtedly they will. My wife always says we are one and my children love me like anything; so, naturally, all I do for their sake will be shared by them."

"Well, maybe so, but don't just tell *me*. Go find out for sure."

"Will you run away?"

"No."

"Okay. You stay here. I will run there and find out."

So he ran to his house and said, "Hey, this man asked me a funny question just now. He says that I am committing sins, and certainly there's no doubt about that. But I am doing it for your sake. When you take a share of the food, will you take a share of the sin also?"

The wife answered, "It is your duty as a husband and father to maintain us. It is immaterial to us how you do it. We are not responsible. We didn't ask you to commit sins. You could do some proper work to bring us food. Anyway, that's your business and your duty. We are not going to bother whether it's right or wrong. We won't take a share of your sins."

"My God! My beloved children, how about you?"

"As Mommy says, Dad."

"What a dirty family. I thought you were going to share everything with me. You are going to share only the food and nothing else. I don't even want to see your faces!"

He ran back and fell at Nārada's feet. "Svāmiji, you have opened my eyes. What am I to do now?"

"Well, you have committed a lot of sins. You have to purge them all."

"Please tell me some way."

So Nārada gave Vālmīki *mantra* initiation. "All right. Can you repeat, 'Rāma, Rāma'?"

"What's that? I've never heard of it; I'm just an illiterate person. I can't repeat it. Can you give me something easier?"

"Oh, what a pity. Let's see, look at this." He pointed at a tree.

"What is it?"

"It's a *marā* (tree)."

"All right. Can you repeat it?"

"Sure. That's easy."

"Fine. Sit in a quiet place and just go on repeating: '*Marā, marā, marā...*'"

"Is that all? That will save me from all my sins?"

"Certainly."

"Well, sir. I believe you. You have already enlightened me quite a lot. You seem to be a good *swami*. I'll begin right here and now. I don't want to waste any time."

So he just sat under a tree and went on repeating, "*Marā, marā, ma rā ma rāma,* Rāma, Rāma ..." See? *Marā marā* soon became Rāma, Rāma. He sat for years like that until at last an anthill was formed completely covering his body. Yes; because he was so deeply interested in that, he forgot everything else. Even his body became benumbed, as if the fuse were blown in the main power house. This is what happens in *samādhi*. So, after a long, long time somebody just passed and happened to disturb the anthill, and the saint Vālmīki emerged. Later, he got the divine vision of Lord Rāma's life and wrote the entire epic story of the *Rāmāyana*. Even now you can read Vālmīki's *Rāmāyana*.

What is to be learned from this story? He just concentrated on that *mantra* and forgot everything else. All the sins slowly dried up for want of nourishment and died away. If you do not pour water on your plant, what will happen? It will slowly wither and die. Our habits will also slowly wither and die away if we do not give them an opportunity to manifest. You need not fight to stop a habit. Just don't give it an opportunity to repeat itself. That's all you have to do. Any kind of habit can be easily removed this way. And that is possible by cultivating one proper habit. The mind must have something to hold onto, so you stick to one thing and all the other things die.

Now to finish the *sūtra*, "... the mind of the Yogi with its totally weakened modifications attains ... a state in which there can be no differentiation between the knower, knowable and knowledge." The Yogi whose *vṛttis* have thus become powerless by the cultivation of one particular *vṛtti* ceases to distinguish between the knower, knowable and knowledge (or meditator, meditated upon and meditation). In meditation you are conscious of all three—subject, object and process of meditation. But at this point, the three become one; either the object becomes subject or subject becomes object. And when there is no subject-object separation, there is no process either. The mind is completely absorbed and loses itself in the idea or object of meditation. Patañjali gives the example of an object near a crystal. If you put a red flower near a crystal, the crystal itself appears to be red like the flower. It becomes one with that; it accepts that. Likewise, the mind accepts the idea of your meditation and takes that form.

तत्र शब्दार्थज्ञानविकल्पैः संकीर्णा
सवितर्का ॥४२॥

42. Tatra śabdārtha jñāna vikalpaiḥ saṁkīrṇā savitarkā.

Tatra = there; **śabda** = sound, word, name;
artha = meaning, object, form; **jñāna** = knowledge, idea;
vikalpaiḥ = assumptions, concept (these three);
saṁkīrṇa = mixed up; **savitarkā** = with deliberation.

The *samādhi* in which name, form and knowledge of them is mixed is called *savitarkā samādhi*, or *samādhi* with deliberation.

From this *sūtra* on, Patañjali tries to define the different kinds of *samādhi* again. We remember the four kinds of *saṁprajñāta samādhi*—*savitarkā, savicāra, sa-ānanda* and *sa-asmita*—explained in *Sūtra* 17. He once again reminds us about them.

In this *sūtra* he says that in *savitarkā samādhi*, you can actually understand the sound, the meaning and the resulting knowledge of an object. Normally, every time we hear a sound, we simultaneously do all these three things: hear the word, try to understand the object denoted by the sound, and gain the knowledge of that object. For example, if you hear the word "dog," the sound goes into the brain and then tries to find a similar groove there. If it finds such a groove, made by hearing "dog" before, you understand: "Yes, the word 'dog' which I hear now is the same that I heard before." And then you know what "dog" means. So the word, the object and the knowledge, or *śabda, artha* and *jñāna*, happen simultaneously. But in this *samādhi* we can separate them one after the other; we can arrest the process wherever we want.

स्मृतिपरिशुद्धौ स्वरूपशून्येवार्थमात्रनिर्भासा निर्वितर्का ॥४३॥

43. Smṛti pariśuddhau svarūpa śūnyevārtha mātra nirbhāsā nirvitarkā.

Smṛti = memory; **pariśuddhau** = upon utmost purification; **svarūpa** = its own nature, own form; **śūnya** = empty; **iva** = as if; **artha** = object; **mātra** = only; **nirbhāsā** = shining; **nirvitarkā** = without deliberation.

When the memory is well purified, the knowledge of the object of concentration shines alone, devoid of the distinction of name and quality. This is *nirvitarkā samādhi*, or *samādhi* without deliberation.

When the memory is purified or devoid of qualities, then there is only the knowledge of the object meditated upon. Ignoring the *sabda* and *artha*, you get the *jñāna* alone. In a way it gives you the knowledge of the Knower also.

एतयैव सविचारा निर्विचारा च सूक्ष्मविषया व्याख्याता ॥४४॥

44. Etayaiva savicārā nirvicārā ca sūkṣmaviṣayā vyākhyātā.

Etayā = in the same way; **iva** = indeed; **savicārā** = reflective; **nirvicārā** = super non-reflective; **ca** = and; **sūkṣma** = subtle; **viṣayā** = objects; **vyākhātā** = are explained.

In the same way, both *savicārā* (reflective) and *nirvicārā* (super or non-reflective) *samādhi*, which are practiced upon subtle objects, are explained.

In the previous two *sūtras* we looked at *savitarkā* and *nirvitarkā samādhi*. Here are two other kinds of *samādhis* which are more or less practiced in the same way but which have the finer elements for their objects.

सूक्ष्मविषयत्वं चालिङ्गपर्यवसानम् ॥४५॥

45. Sūkṣma viṣayatvam cāliṅga paryavasānam.

Sūkṣma = subtle; **viṣayatvam** = objectiveness; **ca** = and; **aliṅga** = without mark, undefinable, unmanifest prakṛti; **paryavasānam** = end only at, all the way up to.

The subtlety of possible objects of concentration ends only at the undefinable.

In other words, the finer objects [*tanmātras*, *citta* and ego] ultimately end in the primal force called the *Prakṛti*, or the primordial basic substance in its unmanifested condition. In that condition there is no name, no form and no thought, only the fully balanced, tranquil unmanifested state of nature. So the mind has the power to go to the very root of the unmanifested nature.

ता एव सबीजः समाधिः ॥४६॥

46. Tā eva sabījaḥ samādhiḥ.

Tāh = they; **eva** = indeed; **sabījaḥ** = with seed; **samādhiḥ** = contemplation.

Each of the above kinds of *samādhi* are *sabīja* (with seed), which could bring one back into bondage or mental disturbance.

In all these *samādhis*, the goal has not yet been reached. Even after acquiring all these states, you can come back as an ordinary person because the impressions are still there. All your desires are still in the seed form, not completely fried, because you have not completely purified the mind.

That is why you should make the mind pure before you practice deep meditation. "Blessed are the pure; they shall see God." That does not mean the impure cannot see God. If they work for it, they can, but their God will appear as a demon to them because of their impurity. Their vision is colored; they can't see God's pure nature. They see God from the wrong angle. If you write God as G-O-D and read it from the right angle, it is "God"; read it from the wrong angle: D-O-G, it is "dog." The impure mind reads it from the wrong angle. So the mind must be pure. It is all well and good to learn the different methods of meditation and the experiences that could come to you. But if you are really serious about this business and really want to go deep into meditation, take care to have a clean mind. Otherwise, you are not going to get it.

Even the so-called scientific discoveries and inventions are a result of concentration and meditation. The scientists meditated on the material side, on the gross elements, and found out many things, created many machines and we are all enjoying the benefits. They went deeper and deeper and ultimately went into the atom itself. It's all meditation. They're

Yogis, no doubt. They were able to plumb the secrets of the atom, but what is happening now with those secrets? It has become a terrifying force. Is there anything wrong with atomic force? Nothing. We can't blame it, nor need we condemn or stop the atomic research. What is to be condemned? The minds of the people using those forces. That is why the entire world is terrified. If we are going to go into the secrets of life and the universe and gain control over them, we should have pure minds to make the proper use of them. Otherwise, we will bring destruction on the entire humanity. The purification of the mind is very necessary.

निर्विचारवैशारद्येऽध्यात्मप्रसादः ॥४७॥

47. Nirvicāra vaiśāradye 'dhyātma prasādaḥ.

Nirvicāra = non-reflective; **vaiśāradye** = pure, lucid;
adhyātma ('dhyātma) = supreme Self; **prasādaḥ** = shine, clear.

In the purity of *nirvicārā samādhi*, the supreme Self shines.

ऋतम्भरा तत्र प्रज्ञा ॥४८॥

48. Ṛtambharā tatra prajñā.

Ṛtam = absolute truth; **bharā** = bearing; **tatra** = there;
prajñā = wisdom consciousness.

This is *ṛtambharā prajñā*, or the absolute true consciousness.

After attaining the pure, non-reflective *samādhi*, the Yogi gets "wisdom-filled-with-truth." This is the meaning of *ṛtambharā*. What is this actually? Patañjali continues by saying:

श्रुतानुमानप्रज्ञाभ्यामन्यविषया
विशेषार्थत्वात् ॥४९॥

49. Śrutānumāna prajñābhyām anya viṣayā viśeṣārthatvāt.

Śruta = study of scriptures (scriptures are heard);
anumāna = inference; **prajñābhyām** = from the knowledge of both;
anya = different (totally); **viṣayā** = domain (truth); **viśeṣa** = special;
arthatvāt = from its significance, from its purposefulness.

This special truth is totally different from knowledge gained by hearing, study of scripture or inference.

When you achieve that *ṛtaṁbharā prajñā* you understand everything without study. When you transcend the mind through proper concentration, you feel the cosmic force or God. You can check your experience with the scriptures or through the word of sages and saints, but it is known by you through your own experience. Until then, all you have heard and read and visualized will be by your own mind. Experiencing God is something that is genuine and comes only when you transcend the mind. God cannot be understood by the mind, because mind is matter; and matter cannot possibly understand something more subtle than matter.

Western psychology talks only about the mind, saying, "Unless you understand by your mind, you can't know something." At the same time it says, "But you cannot know everything by the mind." That is all; it stops there. But Yoga tells you that you can know something without the mind. There is a higher knowledge which can only be understood without the mind. As the *Māṇḍūkya Upaniṣad* says, "*Nantaḥ-prajñām, na bahis-prajñām, nobhayataḥ-prajñām, na prajñāna-ghanam, na prajñām, naprajñām.*" "Not inside knowledge, not outside knowledge, not knowledge itself, not ignorance." It's all expressed in the negative: you can't grasp it, you can't think of it, you can't mark it with a symbol; it has no name or form, and you can't explain it. Hundreds of people might sit in front of a speaker who might talk for hours and hours about God. They might sit and listen for hours and hours, but it's all nonsense. Yes. The speaker has said nothing about God, and they have heard nothing about God. The lecturer has only said something about God that he or she could fit into his or her own mind, and the audience has only understood the God that they could grasp with their own minds. That's all. Nobody has said anything about the real God and no one has understood the real God. It's unexplainable.

So, in that *ṛtaṁbharā prajñā* you transcend the mind and gain a knowledge that is realization. For that, the mind must be completely silent. That is why in Hindu mythology there is one form of God called *Dakṣiṇāmūrti*, who sat with four disciples in front of him. They were all learned people; they had read all the *Vedas* and *Upaniṣads* and heard all that was to be heard, but they still couldn't realize the truth. So they came to *Dakṣiṇāmūrti* and requested him to explain the highest *Brahman* (the unmanifested God). He just sat there in silence. After a while they got up, bowed down and said, "Swamiji, we have understood." And they went away, because only in silence can it be explained.

"*Mauna vākya Prākṛtita Parabrahma tattvam.*" "The *Parabrahma tattvam,* or unmanifested supreme principle, can only be explained by silence, not by words." In not only the physical silence, but in the real mental silence, the wisdom dawns.

तज्जः संस्कारोऽन्यसंस्कारप्रतिबन्धी ॥५०॥

50. Tajjaḥ saṁskāro'nya saṁskāra pratibandhī.

Tad = that; **jaḥ** = born of, produced by;
saṁskāraḥ (saṁskāro) = subliminal impression;
anya ('nya) = other; **pratibandhī** = wipes out, replaces.

The impression produced by this *samādhi* wipes out all other impressions.

The impression that results from the *samādhi* by which you get *ṛtaṁbharā prajñā* will obstruct all other impressions. Everything dies away and there is no more coming back as an ordinary person, ignorant of your true nature. When you come to this stage you always retain this knowledge. In this state you become a *jīvanmukta*, a realized saint. *Jīvan* means one who lives; *mukta* means liberated, so such a person is a liberated living being. You live, eat and talk like anybody else, even do business like anybody else, but still you are liberated.

A *jīvanmukta* may be doing anything. He or she need not be sitting in *samādhi* in some cave; this person may be in Times Square, but is still a *jīvanmukta*. A *jīvanmukta* is involved in the world for the sake of humanity without any personal attachment.

And nothing is exciting to a *jīvanmukta*. As a beautiful Tamil verse says, "If he sees the cool rays of the moon in the broad daylight, or a three-day-old corpse getting out of its coffin to walk, he will not wonder, 'Oh, how could that be?'" Nothing will be exciting to the *jīvanmukta* because he or she knows it is all phenomena of nature, or *Prakṛti*. In the universe many things happen, so the liberated ones won't worry about that. They will just take the golden present in hand and, prompted by the Higher Will, just do what they can and pass by. They will not be attached to anything. In that state no impressions, no old thought, will bring them back into ordinary life. Although they appear to be normal, the seeds of all mental impressions are completely burnt out and they always live in that unattached state.

तस्यापि निरोधे सर्वनिरोधान्निर्बीजः
समाधिः ॥५१॥

51. Tasyāpi nirodhe sarva nirodhān nirbījaḥ samādhiḥ.

Tasya = of that; **api** = even (also);
nirodhe = upon being wiped out, upon the restraint;
sarva = all; **nirodhān** = from being wiped out, due to restraint;
nirbījaḥ = seedless; **samādhiḥ** = contemplation.

When even this impression is wiped out, every impression is totally wiped out and there is *nirbīja* [seedless] *samādhi.*

Only now does Patañjali describe the highest *samādhi.* Even with the *ṛtaṁbharā prajñā* the subtle mind is there. There is still a division between the *prajñā,* or wisdom, and the owner of that wisdom. Even the feeling, "I have realized God," should go. Then you are completely free. You have attained *nirbīja samādhi.* There is no more birth or death for you; you realize your immortality.

Book Two

Sādhana Pāda

Portion on Practice

This second book, *Sādhana Pāda,* is concerned with the practice of Yoga. Patañjali begins with instructions in Kriyā Yoga. You might have heard the term "Kriyā Yoga" as propagated by Sri Swami Yogananda Paramahansa, but that should not be confused with Patañjali's Kriyā Yoga. Yogananda speaks of it as a special combination of breathing and *mantras.* Patañjali refers to certain practical hints to be followed in our daily lives to prepare us for the more subtle practices to follow.

In the *Samādhi Pāda,* Patañjali gives us the aim of Yoga in a theoretical way, explaining it as the control of the *citta vṛtti,* or thought forms. Then the rest of the *sūtras* in Book I could be classified into several groups: the different kinds of thought forms, the practices to control them, and the different kinds of superconscious experience culminating in the highest experience of *nirbīja samādhi,* the seedless contemplation. But it is not that easy to get into *samādhi,* so in this book he tells the student not to get frightened but to prepare himself or herself by laying the proper foundation, then gradually build until that level is reached. For this Patañjali gives a number of simple directions.

तपः स्वाध्यायेश्वरप्रणिधानानि क्रियायोगः ॥१॥

1. **Tapaḥ svādhyāyeśvarapraṇidhānāni kriyā yogaḥ.**

Tapaḥ = accepting pain as purification;
svādhyāya = study of spiritual books; **Īśvara** = Supreme Being;
praṇidhāna = surrender, to place before;
ani = indicating the three as a group;
kriyā = in action/in practice; **yogaḥ** = yoga.

Accepting pain as help for purification, study of spiritual books and surrender to the Supreme Being constitute Yoga in practice.

Using the Sanskrit terms, Kriyā Yoga comprises *tapas, svādhyāya* and *Īśvara praṇidhāna. Tapas* is often misunderstood, because it gets translated as "mortification" or "austerity," when it actually stands for something different here. *Tapas* means "to burn or create heat." Anything burned out will be purified. The more you fire gold, for example, the more pure it becomes. Each time it goes into the fire, more impurities are removed.

But how can this burning process be effected with our mental impurities? By accepting all the pain that comes to us, even though the nature of the mind is to run after pleasure. We will actually be happy to receive pain if we keep in mind its purifying effects. Such acceptance makes the mind steady and strong because, although it is easy to give pain to others, it is hard to accept without returning it. Such self-discipline obviously cannot be practiced in our meditation rooms, but only in our daily lives as we relate with other people.

Tapas also refers to self-discipline. Normally the mind is like a wild horse tied to a chariot. Imagine the body is the chariot; the intelligence is the charioteer; the mind is the reins; and the horses are the senses. The Self, or true you, is the passenger. If the horses are allowed to gallop without reins and charioteer, the journey will not be safe for the passenger. Although control of the senses and organs often seems to bring pain in the beginning, it eventually ends in happiness. If *tapas* is understood in this light, we will look forward to pain; we will even thank people who cause it, since they are giving us the opportunity to steady our minds and burn out impurities.

In the seventeenth chapter of the *Bhagavad Gītā,* Lord Kṛṣṇa [Krishna] talks about *tapasya.* He says, "Those who practice severe austerities not enjoined by the scriptures; who are given to hypocrisy and egoism, impelled by the forces of lust and attachment; who are senseless; who torture all the elements in the body and Me also who dwells in the body; know thou these to be of demoniacal resolves." In the name of *tapasya* people sometimes practice all sorts of self-torture. In the East there are *sādhus* (ascetics) who lie on beds of nails or keep one arm raised in the air so the arm gets thinner and thinner and finally decays. These are all just forms of self-torture. Lord Kṛṣṇa himself says these people are demons because they disturb the pure Self who dwells within their bodies. Self-discipline is an aid to spiritual progress, whereas self-torture is an obstacle.

Lord Kṛṣṇa divides the true austerities into three groups: physical, verbal and mental. He classifies worship, purity, straightforwardness, celibacy and non-injury as the austerities of the body. Many people immediately come to the conclusion that physical *tapasya* is not suitable for them. The moment they hear the word "celibacy" they become dismayed. But *brahmacarya,* or celibacy, means control, not suppression, of the sex desire or sex force. If the mind can be filled with sublime thoughts by meditation, *mantra* repetition, prayer, study of scriptures and contemplation of the sexless, pure Self, the sex desire will be devitalized by the withdrawal of the mind. On the other hand, suppression of sexual desire will attach you to it again and again, producing wet dreams, irritability and mental restlessness. So the mind should be purified first; then it is easy to control the senses. Strict control over the senses alone will lead to difficulties instead of spiritual progress.

The next *tapas* is austerity of speech. Speech should bring tranquility and be truthful, pleasant and beneficial. As the *Vedic* teaching goes, "*Satyam bruvat priyam bruvat.*" "Speak what is true, speak what is pleasant." And one should not speak what is true if it is not pleasant, nor what is pleasant if it is false. If something is true and unpleasant, we should make it more pleasant by presenting it in a proper way. And mental austerity is described by Śrī Kṛṣṇa as serenity of mind, goodheartedness, self-control and purity of nature.

Next comes *svādhyāya*, or study. This means study that concerns the true Self, not merely analyzing the emotions and mind as the psychologists and psychiatrists do. Anything that will elevate your mind and remind you of your true Self should be studied: the *Bhagavad Gītā, the Bible, the Koran,* these *Yoga Sūtras* or any uplifting scripture. Study does not just mean passing over the pages. It means trying to understand every word—studying with the heart. The more often you read them, the more you understand. For thousands of years, so many people have been studying the *Bible*. Every day, thousands of people read this same book. On the other hand, we have millions and millions of books that, after we read them once, we throw away as trash. We don't exhaust the *Bible* even after reading it hundreds of times. Each time we read it we see it in a new light. That is the greatness of the holy scriptures. They are that way because they were created by holy prophets who experienced the truth. Each time we read these works we elevate ourselves to see a little more.

It is something like going to the Empire State Building. When you look out of a first floor window you see something. From the second floor, you see a little more; from the third floor, still more. But when you finally reach the hundred and first floor and look over the balcony, you see something completely different.

Similarly, in reading the scriptures, we slowly rise up, expanding and enlarging the mind. The more we elevate the mind, the better our understanding is. But only when we become prophets ourselves will we fully understand the scriptures. That is nature's law. If you want to understand me fully, you must become me. Otherwise, you can understand me only according to your own capacity. In the same way, God cannot be understood by books alone. God can only be understood when you become God. A Tamil proverb says, "Only a saint knows a saint. Only a snake knows the leg of another snake." You cannot exactly understand how a snake crawls unless you become a snake. We can hear things, study, form our own opinions, use our imagination, but nothing can equal experience.

Many people simply become walking libraries. They have thousands of books recorded in their brains like computers, but that doesn't mean they have actually experienced the Self. The Self cannot be known by theory alone. By merely thinking, no one has ever understood the One that is beyond the mind. Only when you transcend the mind can you understand it. This is where Yoga differs from most other psychological approaches. They usually believe you have to understand everything with the mind and that beyond it you cannot understand anything. They stop there, but Yoga claims there is a knowledge possible without the mind. All that you know through the mind is limited and conditioned. How is the limited mind to understand the Unlimited One? Only by transcending it and getting into the unlimited.

Study is all right—but not for mere logic, quoting or fighting. Actually, it is only when you "quote" from your own experience that your words have weight. Sri Ramakrishna Paramahamsa used to say, "Forget all you have learned; become a child again. Then it will be easy to realize that wisdom." Sometimes, learning becomes an obstacle if you don't know what and how much to learn. So, limit your reading and put into practice what you read. Just select one or two books—anything that will remind you of your goal.

The last part of Kriyā Yoga is simple but great. It is surrendering to the Supreme Being. I understand this to mean dedicating the fruits of your actions to God or to humanity—God in manifestation. Dedicate everything—your study, your *japa*, your practices—to God. When you offer such things, God accepts them but then gives them back many times magnified. You never lose what you have given. Even virtuous, meritorious deeds will bind you in some form or other if you do them with an egoistic feeling. Every time you do something, feel, "May this be dedicated to God." If you constantly remember to do this, the mind will be free and tranquil. Try not to possess anything for yourself. Temporarily keep things but feel you are just a trustee, not an owner.

Be like the mother who receives a soul, nourishes it for nine months and then lets it come out into the world. If the mother were always to keep the baby in her womb, what would happen? There would be great pain. Once something has ripened, it should be passed on. So dedication is true Yoga. Say, "I am Thine. All is Thine. Thy will be done." Mine binds; Thine liberates. If you drop "mines" all over, they will "undermine" your life—or blow up in your face. But if you change all the "mines" to Thines, you will always be safe.

Let us all dedicate our lives for the sake of the entire humanity. With every minute, every breath, every atom of our bodies we should repeat this *mantra*: "dedication, dedication, giving, giving, loving, loving." That is the best *japa*, the best Yoga which will bring us all permanent peace and joy and keep the mind free from the disturbances of the *citta vṛttis*.

समाधिभावनार्थः क्लेशतनूकरणार्थश्च ॥२॥

2. Samādhi bhāvanārthaḥ kleśa tanūkaraṇārthaś ca.

Samādhi = contemplation;
bhāvana = conception, act of producing or effecting;
arthaḥ = to strive, to obtain, ask for;
kleśa = afflictions, troubles, obstacles; **tanū** = to diminish;
karaṇa = causing, making;
arthaḥ (arthaś) = to strive, to obtain, ask for; **ca** = and.

They help us minimize obstacles and attain *samādhi*.

Here, Patañjali explains why Kriyā Yoga should be practiced: to minimize obstacles and to get into *samādhi*. He puts everything in very simple terms, but we should know and remember the vital importance of Kriyā Yoga. Without it we can never overcome the obstacles and reach *samādhi*. Mainly, all we do in the name of Haṭha Yoga, Japa Yoga, living in Yoga institutes and *āśrams* is all part of our Kriyā Yoga—our preparation for meditation and *samādhi*.

अविद्यास्मितारागद्वेषाभिनिवेशाः क्लेशाः ॥३॥

3. Avidyāsmitā rāga dveṣābhiniveśāḥ kleśāḥ.

Avidyā = ignorance; **asmitā** = ego sense, egoism, I-ness;
rāga = attachment; **dveṣa** = hatred;
abhiniveśaḥ = clinging to bodily life; **kleśāḥ** = obstacles, afflictions.

Ignorance, egoism, attachment, hatred and clinging to bodily life are the five obstacles.

Here he gives the obstacles (*kleśas*) which will then be explained one by one in the following *sūtras*. The order is also significant: because of ignorance of the Self, egoism comes. Because of egoism, there is attachment to things for the ego's selfish pleasure. Because sometimes the things we are attached to do not come or are taken away, hatred for those who get in our way comes in. And, finally, because we are attached to things and afraid of death, there is clinging to life in the body.

अविद्या क्षेत्रमुत्तरेषां प्रसुप्ततनु
विच्छिन्नोदाराणाम् ॥४॥

4. Avidyā kṣetram uttareṣām prasupta tanu vicchinnodārāṇām.

Avidyā = ignorance; **kṣetram** = field; **uttareṣām** = for the others;
prasupta = dormant; **tanu** = feeble; **vicchinna** = intercepted;
udārāṇām = sustained, fully active.

Ignorance is the field for the others mentioned after it, whether they be dormant, feeble, intercepted or sustained.

In a baby we see an example of the first category. The baby's obstacles are completely dormant. When you see a baby, you feel, "How innocent it is!" That seems to be so, but as the baby matures, the inborn disposition will emerge; it will not remain innocent. Ignorance and the other obstacles dormant in the mind will come to the surface at the proper time.

The mind of an advanced Yoga practitioner is an example of the second type: the feeble, or attenuated, stage. Such a person is not completely free of the *kleśas*, but they are there in his or her mind in very subtle trace form. They have sunk to the bottom of the mental lake and out of disuse have become very weak.

The third state of intercepted development is seen in the mind of a beginning practitioner. The obstacles are temporarily pushed down by the constant practice of virtuous qualities such as love, truthfulness, discipline, cheerfulness, etc. If such a seeker is not careful to cultivate these qualities, even for a few days, the obstacles will immediately come to the surface.

The fourth type is seen in the case of average people. The *kleśas* constantly manifest. Every minute their minds are affected by the obstructions. They have no say over them because they are not exerting any force to control them.

By analyzing our minds we can probably see, "Do I have completely dormant *kleśas*? Do traces remain, but buried? Am I controlling them by the cultivation of good qualities? Or am I completely ruled by them?"

Here is an example of the different stages in operation. Imagine there is a nice performance at a nightclub. A friend is going and invites you to come. Let's say you feel drawn to go, but finally you decide, "I have seen hundreds of shows like that; what can I gain by another one? No, I'm going to a Rāja Yoga lecture instead." The obstacle is there but you overpower it. That is the "intercepted" stage.

If you continue with such discipline, the obstacle will sink to the bottom, but since a trace will still be there, occasionally you'll be reminded of it. "Why shouldn't I go to a club?" A gentle trace will arise, which you can easily overpower. "No, I'm not going." It just comes up to remind you, "I'm still here." That is the "feeble" stage.

In the case of average people, the moment a nightclub is thought of, both legs immediately go toward it, and the people simply follow. From there, they probably go to an adjoining bar and so on. In their case the obstacles are "sustained."

अनित्याशुचिदुःखानात्मसु
नित्यशुचिसुखात्मख्यातिरविद्या ॥५॥

5. **Anityāśuci duḥkhānātmasu nitya śuci sukhātmakhyātir avidyā.**

Anitya = impermanent; **aśuci** = impure; **duḥkha** = painful; **anātma** = non-Self; (**su** = in these); **nitya** = permanent; **śuci** = pure; **sukha** = pleasant; **Ātma** = Self; **khyātir** = cognition; **avidyā** = ignorance.

Ignorance is regarding the impermanent as permanent, the impure as pure, the painful as pleasant and the non-Self as the Self.

Now Patañjali explains what ignorance is. If I show you a nice piece of fruit that you have never seen before, you will say, "I am completely ignorant of this; I don't know what it is." That is just normal ignorance, not knowing something. What Patañjali speaks of in this *sūtra* is something different. He mentions last the basic ignorance: "regarding the non-Self as the Self."

What is Self and what is non-Self? The Self is the eternal, never-changing One. It is always everywhere as the very basic substance. All things are actually nothing but the Self, but in our ignorance we see them as different objects. Thus, we take the changing appearances to be the unchanging truth. When something changes, it can't be the Self. For example, our own bodies are changing every second. Yet we take the body to be our Self; and, speaking in terms of it, we say, "I am hungry" or "I am physically challenged"; "I am black" or "I am white." These are all just the conditions and qualities of the body. We touch the truth when we say, "My body aches," implying that the body belongs to us and that therefore we are not that.

Unfortunately, we often add, "I am very, very sick." Who is actually sick? If the body aches, then the body is sick, not you. Whenever we forget this truth, we are involved in the non-Self, the basic ignorance.

We make the same ignorant mistake in regard to the mind, saying, "I am happy," or "I am ignorant." Feeling happy, fearful or angry, or knowing a lot or knowing nothing are all modifications or feelings of the mind. Once that is understood, there is nothing that can disturb us in this world. Things will come near us or go away from us, but we will know we are not connected with them—we will know we are not that. Under all conditions we can sing, "Knowledge bliss, knowledge bliss, bliss is absolute; in all conditions I am knowledge, bliss is absolute!"

Well, who is practicing Yoga then? Who does *japa*, who meditates? It is the mind along with the body. "You" need not do any practice. When you fully realize this, even *japa* will become an ignorant business. But for now we can get rid of ignorance with ignorance. Take a better ignorance to get rid of a worse one. In the final analysis, only the light of understanding will remove the darkness of ignorance.

There is a story, given in the scriptures, that illustrates this. Once a man walked into the backyard of his house during twilight. All of a sudden, in a dark corner, he saw a coiled snake. Frightened, he yelled, "Snake! Snake!" His voice roused a number of people who came running with sticks. They advanced slowly toward the corner, and one bold fellow with a particularly long, pointed stick gave the snake a hard blow. Nothing happened.

Suddenly, an old man arrived with a lantern. He brought the lantern near the corner where the snake was. The light revealed nothing but a coiled rope. The old man laughed, "Look at all of you blind people groping in darkness. There's nothing but a rope there, and you took it for a snake." In order to understand the rope as a rope, a light was necessary. We, too, need a light—the light of wisdom, *jñāna*. With such a light, the world is no longer a world and all the qualities we call the non-Self appear in their true nature.

We can use this analogy to understand another point also. Twilight is the most dangerous time. Why? Because in total darkness neither a rope nor a snake could be seen. In broad daylight the rope would obviously be a rope. Only in a dull light could the man mistake the rope for a snake. If you are completely ignorant, groping in darkness, you will not even see the "rope"—the pains of this world—and want to understand the truth. So, Yoga is neither for a person who has gained the light nor for the totally ignorant person who doesn't bother to know anything. It is for the person in between. It is to dispell this ignorance that Yoga is practiced.

दृग्दर्शनशक्त्योरेकात्मतेवास्मिता ॥६॥

6. Dṛg darśana śaktyor ekātmatevāsmitā.

Dṛk (dṛg) = Seer; **darśana** = instrument of seeing;
śaktyoḥ (śaktyor) = power of both; **eka** = one; **ātmata** = identity;
iva = as if; **asmitā** = ego sense, egoism, I-ness.

Egoism is the identification, as it were, of the power of the Seer (*Puruṣa*) with that of the instrument of seeing [body-mind].

In this *sūtra* Patañjali explains egoism. The ego is the reflection of the true Self on the mind. The two appear to be the same, but one is the original, the other a reflected duplicate. The Self will always be falsely represented by the ego until our ignorance is removed. I often refer to these two "I's" as the little "i" and the capital "I." What is the difference? Just a small dot, a little blemish of ego. The capital "I" is just one pure stroke, just as the highest truth is always simple and pure. What limits us and makes us little? Just the dot. Without the dot, we are always great, always the capital "I."

All the practices of Yoga are just to remove that dot. How simple it is. All the difficulties and turmoils can be removed from our lives in no time just by taking away that dot. But preparation for that is what takes time. Many times we climb up only to slip down. Sometimes we get all the way up there only to find we have forgotten to take along an eraser to wipe off the dot. So we have to come down again.

सुखानुशयी रागः ॥७॥

7. Sukhānuśayī rāgaḥ.

Sukha = pleasure; **anuśayī** = follow with; **rāgaḥ** = attachment.

Attachment is that which follows identification with pleasurable experiences.

दुःखानुशयी द्वेषः ॥८॥

8. Duḥkhānuśayī dveṣaḥ.

Duḥkha = pain; **anuśayī** = follow with; **dveṣaḥ** = aversion.

Aversion is that which follows identification with painful experiences.

Attachment to pleasure, or *rāga*, is another pain-bearing obstacle. We attach ourselves to pleasure because we expect happiness from it, forgetting that happiness is always in us as the true Self. When we expect joy from outside things, we become attached to those things. If we find these things make us unhappy, we create an aversion toward them (*dveṣa*). So *rāga* and *dveṣa*, likes and dislikes, are impediments on the spiritual path. One we like because it seems to bring happiness; the other we dislike because it seems to bring unhappiness.

Everyone wants to be happy. Is there anything we can think of that doesn't? Even a small worm put in the sun immediately rolls toward the shade. If we put a plant indoors, it will slowly turn its face toward the light, because it too wants to be happy. Happiness seems to be the basic need of everything in this world; yet rarely does anybody find it. Why? Because happiness is like the musk deer. The ancient scriptures have a fable about this animal which has a scented spot above its forehead that gives off the musk fragrance. This deer runs here and there in search of the scent, not knowing the scent comes from its own forehead.

Just like that, happiness is already in us. Wherever we go we reflect our happiness onto people and things. When we see a smiling face and feel happy, it is because the smiling face *reflects* our happiness. Just as a pure, clean mirror reflects our face beautifully, certain pure, clean faces reflect our happiness. Then we say, "This person gives me happiness." In other faces, our happiness reflects in a distorted way and we say, "I don't like that person." It's absolute nonsense. No one can ever give us happiness or unhappiness but can only reflect or distort our own inner happiness.

स्वरसवाही विदुषोऽपि तथा रूढोऽभिनिवेशः ॥९॥

9. Svarasavāhī viduṣo'pi tathā rūḍho'bhiniveśaḥ.

Sva = its own; **rasa** = potency; **vāhī** = flowing;
viduṣaḥ (viduṣo) = in the wise; **api** ('pi) = even; **tathā** = thus;
rūḍhaḥ (rūḍho) = rooted, established;
abhiniveśaḥ ('bhiniveśaḥ) = intentness for life.

Clinging to life, flowing by its own potency [due to past experience], exists even in the wise.

The next obstacle is the clinging to life: *abhiniveśa.* Here we can get a clue to the nature of rebirth also.

Many Westerners don't believe in reincarnation. They feel, "It's all over once we die." But the Yoga philosophy reminds us that all our knowledge comes through experience. Without experience we cannot understand or learn anything. Even books can only remind us of something we have experienced in the past. They help kindle a fire that is already in us. That fire must be there first for the kindling stick to kindle it.

For example, have you ever experienced a sapadilla fruit? It is abundant in Mumbai, India, in certain seasons and is very soft and tasty. But even if I spend three hours explaining a sapadilla fruit and how it tastes, you are not going to understand it because you have never experienced it. Knowledge comes only through experience. If you allow a baby to crawl on a tabletop, as it comes to the edge and is about to fall, it will yell. Why? Out of fear of falling and dying. How can fear of death come into the mind of a baby? The baby can only fear death if it has died before.

Some might say, "That's just instinct." But what does instinct mean? Yoga says instinct is a trace of an old experience that has been repeated many times, and the impressions have sunk down to the bottom of the mental lake. Although they go down, they aren't completely erased. Don't think you ever forget anything. All experiences are stored in the *citta*; and, when the proper atmosphere is created, they come to the surface again. When we do something several times, it forms a habit. Continue with that habit for a long time, and it becomes our character. Continue with that character, and eventually, perhaps in another life, it comes up as instinct.

Many of you might play the guitar. When you first learned, you might have even marked the notes right on the guitar to get the proper finger position. Each time you played, you checked to see which string should be manipulated. But after a few months, you became proficient and could even talk to someone and play at the same time without looking or thinking about it. How? The experience became habit, and eventually the habit became your character. Probably, in another birth, you might easily pick up guitar-playing without much effort. Don't people say, "Oh, So-and-so is a 'born' guitarist?"

In the same way, all of our instincts were once experiences. That's why the fear of death exists. We have died hundreds and thousands of times. We know well the pang of death. And so, the moment we get into a body, we love it so much that we are afraid to leave it and go forward because we have a sentimental attachment to it.

Some people have old, old cars, say a 1943 Dodge. Even if you offer them the latest model Dodge, they wouldn't want it. You may even say, "Your car is no good anymore. You are blocking the road by driving it at ten miles an hour when everybody else is going fifty-five. You need to get a new one." The motor vehicles department may even take it away by force and throw it in a junkyard, but the owner will sit by it, crying and lamenting. Attachment to the body is like attachment to that car.

God's government regulations say that if your old body is taken away by force, they must give you a new one. Many people do not know this and cling to the body even when it gets old and dilapidated. That constant clinging, breaking away, clinging again, breaking away is why we are mortally afraid of death. It is another *kleśa* based on ignorance of our true nature. So all these *kleśas*, whether dormant, feeble, intercepted or sustained should slowly be gotten rid of. Only then are we ready to go further.

ते प्रतिप्रसवहेयाः सूक्ष्माः ॥१०॥

10. Te pratiprasavaheyāḥ sūkṣmāḥ.

Te = these; **pratiprasava** = resolving back into their cause; **heyāḥ** = destroyed, avoided; **sūkṣmāḥ** = subtle.

In subtle form, these obstacles can be destroyed by resolving them back into their primal cause [the ego].

ध्यानहेयास्तद्वृत्तयः ॥११॥

11. Dhyānaheyāstadvṛttayaḥ.

Dhyāna = by meditation; **heyāḥ** (heyās) = destroyed, avoided; **tad** = those; **vṛttayaḥ** = active modifications.

In the active state, they can be destroyed by meditation.

The hindering thoughts come in two stages: the potential form, before they come to the surface and get converted to action, and the manifesting ones which are being put into action. It is easier to control manifested things first; then from the more gross, we can slowly get into the more subtle. Thought forms in a potential state (*saṁskāras*) cannot be removed by meditation. When you meditate on these impressions, you bring them to the surface. You can't destroy them by this means, but you can see and understand them well and gain control over whether or not they should manifest in action. You can trace them back into their subtle form and see directly that the ego is the basis for all these obstructing thoughts. Then, when you transcend the mind in the higher *samādhi*, even the ego is lost. When you let go of the ego, all the impressions in it will be lost also. But until that occurs, the impressions will not go away .

It is something like using the herb *asafoetida. Asafoetida* is a product that aids digestion and helps control gas. In India it is used in curries and kept in a mud pot. But it smells so much that even if you clean the pot hundreds of times, the smell will stay. How can you get rid of the smell? The only way is to break the pot. The ego has the "smell" of your thoughts in a very subtle form. But you can only understand the smell and see that the thoughts are there when they manifest. To get rid of the impressions completely, you have to break the ego. So, first you clean the superficial things, and ultimately you break the pot. By meditation you can understand the thought forms and clean them up. Then when you have gotten a glimpse of where and how they are, you can slowly trace them to their root and finally cut it out. When you want to uproot a tree, you cut the branches first and then dig to the very root.

क्लेशमूलः कर्माशयो दृष्टादृष्टजन्मवेदनीयः ॥१२॥

12. Kleśa mūlaḥ karmāśayodṛṣṭādṛṣṭa janma vedanīyaḥ.

Kleśa = obstacles; **mūlaḥ** = root; **karma** = reactions;
āśayaḥ (**āśayo**) = reservoir, womb; **dṛṣṭa** = seen [present];
adṛṣṭa = unseen [future]; **janma** = birth; **vedanīyaḥ** = experienced

The womb of *karmas* (actions and reactions) has its root in these obstacles, and the *karmas* bring experiences in the seen [present] or in the unseen [future] births.

Here Patañjali tries to explain what *karma* is, how it is stored and how it functions. The Sanskrit term "*karma*" can mean two things: action and/or the result of action. When you do *karma*, you reap *karma*. But, generally, when we say *karma*, we are referring to the reactions to past actions. Every action will leave its result; every cause will bear its effect. It is impossible to say which comes first. For instance, how does a tree grow? You sow a seed. But where do you get the seed? From another tree. Which comes first, the tree or the seed? Which comes first, the chicken or the egg? It's impossible to find out. Likewise, it is impossible to know the origin of *karma*. No one knows where and how it started. But it is here, we see it and we should try to put an end to it.

So, no action goes without its reaction, and these don't go away but are stored. The receptacle for the *karmas* is called the *karmāśaya*, or womb of *karmas*. The *karmas* wait for an opportunity to come to the surface and bring their reactions. The *kleśas* cause these *karmas*, which may bear fruit now or in a future life; in other words, they are seen or unseen. According to the number of our *karmas*, we will have births.

But there need not be a separate birth for every *karma*. *Karmas* may group together. One strong *karma* may call for a body, and all other similar *karmas* that can make use of that particular vehicle to bring their reactions will join in. It's something like a taxi driver collecting a number of people at the airport and bringing them into the city instead of picking up just one person. First, one person hails the cab, and then a few others who want to go the same way will jump in and then drop out along the way to the city. In the same way, one very strong and powerful *karma* will say, "I must have a body. I have to express myself." When such a *karma* brings a new body and starts working through it, all the other *karmas* that can take advantage of that body join in. When that *karma* is over, there will be many more waiting in line.

Even your present body can be changed if you have an intense desire. If your mind is consumed with intense anger, for example, the whole face and body will change to express that emotion. If your present body can't change enough to fulfill the purpose of a particular thought, the body will be disposed of and you will get a new one. *Karmas* are that powerful.

Just imagine how many actions you perform, how many have brought forth reactions, and how many reactions must be pending. Good and bad actions bring either meritorious or demeritorious reactions. So, when you take a birth, you are not only enjoying the reactions to previous actions or purging *karma*, but you may be creating new *karma* also. There are, then, three kinds of *karmas*: those being expressed and exhausted through this birth (*prārabdha karma*); new *karmas* being created during this birth (*āgami karma*); and those waiting in the *karmāśaya* to be fulfilled in future births (*sañjīta karma*). These are something like the paraphernalia of an archer. There are a number of arrows in the quiver. A really expert archer can take one arrow, fit it into the bow, aim and release it, and immediately take up a second arrow to fit. The arrows would then be in three different stages: one has already left the bow and is on its way. You have no more say over it. You can neither stop it now nor draw it back. This is like the *prārabdha karma* which has caused this birth. As long as the body stays, the *karma* allotted to it will continue. Even a person who has transcended the mind and realized the Self still appears to be doing something because the momentum created by his or her birth is still continuing.

The second arrow, ready to be aimed, is like the new *karma* you create at each moment. You have full control over it. And the quiver represents the *karmāśaya*. If you want, you can aim the arrows from the quiver. Otherwise, you can take them out. It is in your hands. They are called the *sañjīta karma*. We control the *āgami* and the *sañjīta*, but we can't do anything about the *prārabdha*; we just have to accept it. So this cycle continues until Self-realization comes.

सति मूले तद्विपाकोजात्यायुर्भोगाः ॥१३॥

13. Sati mūle tad vipākojātyāyur bhogāḥ.

Sati = existence; **mūle** = upon root; **tad** = that;
vipākaḥ (vipāko) = fruit maturation; **jāti** = birth in a species of life;
āyuḥ (ayur) = life span; **bhogāḥ** = experiences.

With the existence of the root, there will be fruits also: namely, the births of different species of life, their life spans and experiences.

Here you might think about what species you may belong to in your next birth. You need not get a human body. If your thoughts are animalistic, the *karmas* may call for an animal's body. If someone is always cunning in this life, the reactions will bring forth more cunning actions which might be better expressed through a fox's body. Or a person who wants to eat excessively might take a pig's body so he or she can enjoy that more. But don't think that this contradicts the theory of evolution. The individual soul always continues to evolve. Even though the individual may get various bodies, which are evolved to a greater or lesser degree and which experience things through these different forms, he or she continues to progress. Remember that the body is not the experiencer. Life is experienced by the mind through the body. The body is only a vehicle or instrument.

When a flower is fragrant, it is not the nose that experiences the fragrance, but the mind through the nose. If the mind doesn't want to function through the nose because it is occupied elsewhere, it won't experience the fragrance even if the flower is placed right up next to the nose. When we are concentrating on a book, we won't hear our friend even if he or she shouts to us, not because our ears are closed, but because the mind is not connected to the ears at this point. So it is the mind that experiences and enjoys everything, not the organs of the body. Even in an animal's body, the mind experiences and undergoes things. And whenever we gain experience we progress, we purge and we eventually reach our destination.

In our life's journey toward realization, each body is a different vehicle. A dog on the road may have once been a saint who by a small mistake got into that body. A fox may once have been a miserly, cunning businessperson; a scorpion might have been a big employer always "stinging" his or her employees. So, we can't say they are merely animals. Within each form lies a soul on its evolutionary path toward realization.

The *sūtra* also tells us that the span of each life (*āyuḥ*) and experiences of pleasure and pain (*bhogā*) are determined by *karma*, which in turn is the fruit of the obstacles mentioned before.

ते ह्लादपरितापफलाः पुण्यापुण्यहेतुत्वात् ॥१४॥

14. Te hlāda paritāpa phalāḥ puṇyāpuṇya hetutvāt.

Te = they; **hlāda** = pleasure, delight; **paritāpa** = pain, distress; **phalāḥ** = fruits, results; **puṇya** = merit; **apuṇya** = demerit; **hetutvāt** = from having cause.

The *karmas* bear fruits of pleasure and pain caused by merit and demerit.

If you have done something meritorious, you experience pleasure and happiness; if wrong things, suffering. A happy or unhappy life is your own creation. Nobody else is responsible. If you remember this, you won't find fault with anybody. You are your own best friend as well as your worst enemy.

परिणामतापसंस्कारदुःखैर्गुणवृत्ति विरोधाच्च
दुःखमेव सर्वं विवेकिनः ॥१५॥

15. Pariṇāma tāpa saṁskāra duḥkhair guṇa vṛtti virodhāc ca duḥkham eva sarvaṁ vivekinaḥ.

Pariṇāma = transformation, alteration, consequence; **tāpa** = anxiety, anguish; **saṁskāra** = subliminal impression; **duḥkhaiḥ** (duḥkhair) = due to pain from the above three; **guṇa** = qualities; **vṛtti** = functioning; **virodhāt** (virodhāc) = contradiction; **ca** = and; **duḥkham** = painful; **eva** = indeed; **sarvam** = all; **vivekinaḥ** = to the man of discrimination.

To one of discrimination, everything is painful indeed, due to its consequences: the anxiety and fear over losing what is gained; the resulting impressions left in the mind to create renewed cravings; and the constant conflict among the three *guṇas*, which control the mind.

Here, Patañjali gives a very important *sūtra* and a great truth in the spiritual field. If we could only contemplate this for at least a little while daily, our lives would be completely transformed. All experiences are painful for the person of spiritual discrimination. In this world, all experiences that come from outside through the world, through nature or material things, are ultimately painful. None can give everlasting happiness. They may give temporary pleasure, but they always end in pain. Even the enjoyment of our present pleasures is usually painful because we fear its loss.

Imagine you have a high position, appreciated by hundreds of people. Everybody says you're a great person. Gradually you learn to love that position. "Isn't it nice to be admired by everybody, to have hundreds of devotees around, thousands of disciples across the country? This is really fine." But a fear might simultaneously come in. "Suppose I lose this position? If my disciples leave me one after another, what will happen to me?" Where is the pleasure in the position then?

Or perhaps you accumulate money. I have seen people who rush to the stock market page as soon as they see a newspaper. If their stocks rise just one percent over the previous day, they're ecstatic until they see the next day's paper. Toward evening their tension will build up; all night they are restlessly waiting to see the morning's paper. Do they really enjoy their money? No, because they want to possess it. All our so-called pleasures bring in the fear of losing them. We might lose our position, our money or our beauty. There are even people who insure their eyes, noses, earlobes, even fingers and toes. They become anxious about even touching things. They are always tense. It's all right to have a beautiful face; it's all right to have *anything*, as long as you don't let these things bring you anxiety and fear. If they come to you, let them come; enjoy their presence. But when they go, enjoy their departure too. When they come, they come alone, so allow them to go alone without losing your mind along with the external object. Past pleasures are painful because renewed cravings arise from the impressions they leave in the mind. "Once I had a beautiful car; I don't know when I'm going to get another one like it." Whenever you see someone with such a car, it will make you unhappy. You'll be reminded of all your old high times.

In reality, nothing is bad in this world. But the three *guṇas* are forever tossing the mind. What you enjoy one minute, you hate the next. When you are in a good mood, your children may come and play with you. But when you are in a terrible mood, you say, "Get out. Don't disturb me." Real pleasure comes from detaching ourselves completely from the entire world, in standing aloof—making use of the world as a master of it. Only in that can we have pride.

I am not saying that because everything is painful, we should run from it. That doesn't work. Wherever we go, the world follows. If you don't understand the world and attempt to run away, you can never succeed. I have seen people who cannot run their own homes or cooperate with their families say, "I'm disgusted. I renounce. I don't want anything. I am going into the spiritual field to meditate and practice Yoga." You try to run away from family life, but once you come to an *āśram*, you face a whole new home and family. At least in the original family you knew the people, and those people probably had a little consideration for you. In an *āśram* all the faces are new. In the beginning there isn't much affection. Each person may have his or her own problems. So when you can't adapt yourself to your known family, how can you expect to adapt to an unknown group? A known devil is much better than an unknown one.

Wherever we are, we have to learn to handle things properly. We can't always change environments, running here and there. But once we know how to handle one small family, we can handle a larger group. A family life is a training place for public life. If you can't face a sharp word from your mate, how can you face such words from a stranger? The world is a training place where we learn to use the world without getting attached. Instead of saying, "To one of discrimination, everything is painful," it becomes, "To one of discrimination, everything is pleasurable." A person with such an understanding has the magic wand to convert everything into happiness. Pleasure and pain are but the outcome of your approach. The same world can be a heaven or a hell.

The way to begin, though, is with the feeling, "It is all painful. Let me detach myself. Let me not become involved in it. Let me not approach the world with selfish motives." Once this is accomplished, you see with a different vision. You begin to use the world for a different purpose, and you experience happiness. Before you learn to swim, water seems to be a dreadful place. "Suppose I drown? What will happen to me?" But once you learn to swim, you love the water. The world is like that. You have to learn to swim in this ocean of *saṁsāra*—to become a master swimmer.

हेयं दुःखमनागतम् ॥१६॥

16. Heyaṁ duḥkham anāgatam.

Heyam = avoid, prevent; **duḥkham** = pain;
anāgatam = not yet come, future.

Pain that has not yet come is avoidable.

द्रष्ट दृश्चयाः संयोगो हेयहेतुः ॥१७॥

17. Draṣṭṛ dṛśyayoḥ saṁyogo heya hetuḥ.

Draṣṭṛ = the Seer; **dṛṣyayoḥ**. = the seen;
saṁyogaḥ (saṁyogo) = union; **heya** = avoidable; **hetuḥ** = cause.

The cause of that avoidable pain is the union of the Seer (*Puruṣa*) and the Seen (*Prakṛti* or Nature).

First, Patañjali tells us the reason for this pain. Its cause is the union of the Seer and the seen. Yoga philosophy speaks of two important things: one is the *Puruṣa*, the other is the *Prakṛti*. The *Puruṣa* is the true Self. It is the *Puruṣa* who sees. The *Prakṛti* is everything else. All other things besides you are the seen. But it seems we always identify ourselves with what is seen, with what we possess. As the Self, all things are possessed by us. That's why we say, "my body, my mind, my language, my knowledge." Everything we call ours cannot be us. We speak of ourselves in two ways. One is, "Look at my body. Isn't it slim?" The other is, "Look at how slim *I* am." Who is slim? Is it you or the body? This identification with other things is the cause of all our pain. Instead, if we are just ourselves always, things may change or stay as they are, but they will never cause us pain because the changes will be in the things we possess and not in us.

Stay in your true Self. You are the knower. You know everything. When you are happy, you know you are happy. When you suffer, you know you suffer. That knowing is permanent. You know you have a headache, but at the same time you say, "*I* am aching." This identification should be avoided. If you feel you have suffered a loss, ask, "Who is the loser?" You'll find that *you* are still here, that you didn't lose yourself, but just something you had. That will greatly reduce your sorrow. When you mix yourself up with your possessions, pull yourself out of the mire, and your feelings will change greatly. You'll be a different person.

प्रकाश क्रिया स्थितिशीलं भूतेन्द्रियात्मकं भोगापवर्गार्थं दृश्यम् ॥१८॥

18. Prakāśa kriyā sthitiśīlaṁ bhūtendriyātmakaṁ bhogāpavargārthaṁ dṛśyam.

Prakāśa = illumination; **kriyā** = activity; **sthiti** = inertia; **śīlam** = nature, characteristic; **bhūta** = elements; **indriya** = sense organs; **ātmakam** = consists of, having that nature; **bhoga** = experience; **apavarga** = liberation; **artham** = purpose; **dṛśyam** = the seen.

The seen is of the nature of the *guṇas*: illumination, activity and inertia; and consists of the elements and sense organs, whose purpose is to provide both experiences and liberation to the *Puruṣa*.

Now Patañjali talks about the *dṛśya*, or seen. *Ātma* or *Puruṣa* or the Seer all denote the same entity, the true you. You become a knower because there is a known. You become a seer because there is something to see. Here Patañjali tries to analyze what this "seen" is that gives us experience. He says it is a combination of different elements and organs controlled by the three *guṇas*. He uses the terms *prakāśa kriyā sthiti*. *Prakāśa* means illumination and stands for *sattva*. *Kriyā* is action and represents *rajas*. *Sthiti* is inertia, or *tamas*. Why are there these outside things which we see? Why does *Prakṛti* exist?

Nature is here to give you experience and, ultimately, to liberate you from its bondage. Even if people do not want to be liberated, it educates them gradually so that one day they will come to feel, "I'm tired of the whole thing. I don't want it anymore. I've had enough." When will we feel this way? Only after we've gotten enough kicks and burns. The purpose of *Prakṛti* is to give you those knocks. So, we should never condemn nature.

Nature is a combination of elements and organs. The organs include the intellect, mind, senses and the body. Normally, we think of nature as being something other than our own bodies, but when we feel we are the true Self even the body becomes part of the nature because it, again, is merely a composition of the elements. If we don't eat, there will be no body. A baby comes out as six or seven pounds of flesh, and even that weight is built up in the womb by the mother's food. The food materials which create the body are just part of nature. Even the mind, senses and intellect are part of nature, although a very subtle part. They are matter, and that's why they change. Anything that is matter, or nature, changes. The body changes every second. Cells die; more are born. Likewise, there is continuous change in the mind and intellect.

Nothing in nature can bring the mind continuous, unchanging happiness, because the mind itself changes constantly. Although we have the same stomach, we don't want to eat the same food every day. Although we wear the same shape, we don't wear the same outfit every day.

The secret of our wanting changes is that the mind changes. If it were always the same, why would it look for change? If we know that, we can just allow things to change without clinging to them. If something changes, we should let it go—something else will come. We should watch the changes like passing clouds. But, normally, we don't want to merely watch them. We want to hold onto a section without letting go. Then the tension comes in. Changes are like flowing water. If you just allow water to flow, it is very pleasant to sit and watch. But if you want to arrest the flow and keep the water for yourself, you will have to construct a dam. Then the water will resist the dam and try to escape. There will be a terrible struggle. Although you may stop some of the water, another portion will overflow. So you must allow for spill-out or the dam will certainly break.

All life is a passing show. If we want to hold it, even for a minute, we feel tension. Nature will try to run away; we will try to pull it back and keep it. When we want to keep it, we put up barriers which ultimately cause us pain.

Even with our own bodies, if we don't want them to change, trouble will come. We will buy all kinds of make-up, creams and wigs to retain our "youth." If only we learn to enjoy each change, we can recognize the beauty even in aging. A ripe fruit has its own beautiful taste. When we just allow things to pass, we are free. Things will just come and go while we retain our peace.

Swami Vivekananda tells a story from Hindu mythology. At one time Indra, the king of the gods, was forced to descend from his high position and take the body of a pig. Pigs, as you know, live in mud. So Indra got into the mire, rolled around and eventually found a female pig with whom he mated. The outcome of their love was a number of young piglets. They were all very happy. But the gods in heaven, seeing the plight of their king, were horrified. When the gods could no longer tolerate it, they came down and said, "You are Indra, our king. What are you doing here? We are ashamed of your present habits."

Indra replied, "Who says I am unhappy like this? You live up there and say I don't have a happy life here. What fools you are. You should become pigs. Then you'd really appreciate the joy of it. Come on. Don't waste another minute. Get into pigs' bodies. Then you'll see how wonderful it is."

"Sir," the *devas* (gods) said, "we can't let you go on like this. You must come out."

"Don't disturb me," Indra replied. "I have to take care of my young ones. They are waiting for me to play with them."

The *devas* went wild. "All right," they decided. "Since he's so attached to his children, we'll have to take them all away." One after another they killed the piglets. Indra began crying and wailing.

"What are you doing?" When he calmed down, he went to the she-pig and clung to her, saying, "All right. I'll just have more babies." But the *devas* were adamant. They pulled the she-pig from Indra and killed her. When Indra continued to moan and cry, they decided to get rid of his body as well. As soon as they pierced open his pig body, Indra's soul came out and looked in amazement at the dead body on the ground.

"Not only were you in that body, sir, but you wanted to stay there."

"I don't want any more of this," Indra said. "Come. Let's go back."

That is how nature works. As long as we enjoy experiencing nature, no matter what those who understand the truth tell us, we will answer, "Oh, you just don't know how to enjoy the world. You don't have enough education, enough money, enough power. You people come from your poor country and tell us nonsense. You want us to become beggars also. Get out. We want to enjoy all our luxuries." And because the enlightened can't tear out your pig's body, rip up your checkbooks and finish up your bank balance, they say, "We'll wait. One day you'll learn your lesson." When all the entanglements tie you down, when you see you have no room to move about any longer, then you will realize the truth of their words.

All these entanglements are like the life of the silk moth. Silk yarn is a sort of fleshy, pulpy substance that comes out of the silk moth. When the moth is just a day old, it is the size of a hair. You can have more than a hundred worms within the space of a thumb. The next day, you'll need the palm of your hand to accommodate them. On the third day, you'll need a large tray. Within thirty days, each worm is thicker than a thumb and over three inches long. They grow so big within such a short time because they do nothing but eat mulberry leaves.

The first day, all hundred worms can feed on a single leaf. The second, a basketful of leaves is needed. The third, a cartload. The fourth, a truckload. Day and night they consume the leaves. The more they are given, the more they take. After thirty or forty days they are so tired they can no longer eat. Then they sleep, as anyone who overeats does. When people go to sleep on a full stomach, they roll about, this way and that, as digestion is carried on. So the worms roll, and while they roll, a juicy type of saliva comes out of their mouths. All that the worms ate comes out as a stream of thick paste, which forms silk thread. While the worms rotate they become bound up in the thread—the silk cocoon. When all the thread has come out, the worms go into a deep sleep wherein they know nothing.

Finally, they awaken to see themselves caught in the tight cage created by their own saliva. "What is this?" the worms think. "Where am I? How did this happen?" Then they remember. "We ate and ate and ate. We enjoyed everything we could, without exception. We overindulged and became completely exhausted, then totally unconscious. We rolled around and around, binding ourselves up in this cocoon. What a terrible thing. We should have at least shared what we had with others. We were completely selfish. People of wisdom spoke a lot about a selfless life of sacrifice, but we never listened, nor followed their advice. The moment they stopped speaking, we started eating again. All those wise words came in one way and out the other. We are paying for our mistakes now. Well, we repent for all our sins."

The worms repent, pray and fast. In their deep meditation they resolve all their unconscious impressions and decide not to live a selfish life again; in the future, they will discriminate before accepting anything. At this decision two wings appear on either side of each worm—one named *viveka* (discrimination), the other *vairāgya* (dispassion). These are combined with a sharp, clear intellect, which turns into a sharp nose to pierce open the cocoon. With that, the worms—now silk moths—slip out and fly up high with their fantastically colored wings and look back to see their discarded prisons. "We are leaving and we'll never come back to that again."

There is a beautiful lesson in this story. We should ask ourselves, "Where are we now? Are we still eating? Are we in the cocoon? Are we meditating? Are we growing wings?" Let us ask that question, and if we find ourselves still in the process of consuming, it is better to stop and dispose of what we have already taken in. The more we enjoy, the more we are bound. While enjoying, we are not going to listen to wisdom unless we have extraordinary intelligence. If we don't want to listen, nature teaches us her lesson by putting us into a tight corner. She binds us tight to reveal her nature so we will no longer cling to that. In other words, she liberates us.

After liberation, although we are still in nature, we are no longer bound by it. It is as if we acquire nice thick rubber gloves which allow us to touch any voltage without damage. Like the silk moth's wings, these gloves are *viveka* and *vairāgya*. When you possess them, you can touch anything and no harm will come to you.

When you've learned nature's lessons, she no longer has any business with you, but she continues to exist to teach the many others who have not yet learned. You have passed out of the university. You might still go in as an alumnus, just to see how the people are faring, but you are no longer attached. A liberated person can come into the world and be useful to it but is not affected by it.

विशेषाविशेषलिङ्गमात्रालिङ्गानि गुणपर्वाणि ॥१९॥

19. Viśeṣāviśeṣa liṅgamātrāliṅgāni guṇa parvāṇi.

Viśeṣa = specific; **aviśeṣa** = non-specific; **liṅga** = mark, defined;
mātra = only;
aliṅgāni = without mark, undefinable, primary, undetectable matter;
guṇa = qualities; **parvāṇi** = stages.

The stages of the *guṇas* are specific, non-specific, defined and undefinable.

Here, Patañjali analyzes *Prakṛti* a little more. He divides all of nature into four stages. Going in reverse order from the way Patañjali expresses them, first there is the unmanifested, or *avyakta*, stage which is nature in a static or undefinable condition. A slightly manifested stage (defined) is next. The third is a more developed stage where nature forms into the subtle senses, *buddhi* and mind. And the fourth stage is the gross objects, which we can hear, feel, see, touch, smell and taste.

Normally, we only understand things we can see. However, if we develop a subtler perception we can also see the subtler things. For instance, we can see a flower, but we can only sense the smell, rather than see it. Even the smell is matter, although very subtle; and, if we have developed subtle enough perception, we can see it emanating like a magnetic force. Although each individual has an aura, we normally see bodies but not their auras, the colors of their astral bodies. But we can develop the subtle senses to see them.

द्रष्टा दृशिमात्रः शुद्धोऽपि प्रत्ययानुपश्यः ॥२०॥

20. Draṣṭā dṛśimātraḥ śuddho'pi pratyayānupaśyaḥ.

Draṣṭā = the seer; **dṛśi** = power of seeing; **mātraḥ** = only;
śuddhaḥ (śuddho) = pure; **api** ('pi) = although;
pratyaya = contents of mind, assumption, belief;
anupaśyaḥ = perceive, seeing.

The Seer is nothing but the power of seeing which, although pure, appears to see through the mind.

After discussing *Prakṛti*, Patañjali talks about the Seer, or *Puruṣa.* Even though the light is pure and never-changing, it appears to change because of the medium of nature. The sun's rays appear to bend when they pass through a section of water although they do not actually bend. A filament gives pure light but appears to be red because of the red glass that surrounds it. Likewise, we are all the same light; but we do not look alike, act alike or think alike because of the nature of our bodies and minds. If the mind accumulates some ideas of law, we become lawyers; some knowledge of medicine, we become doctors. If we have no ideas, we are called fools. So, although the original substance is the same, we appear to be different.

Through Yogic thinking we can see the entire humanity as our own. We can embrace all without any exceptions. Even the worst sinner will be loved by us because we ourselves were once sinners. Today's sinner is tomorrow's saint. We will never criticize a sinner if we realize that we were once in the same boat. Instead, we can give the so-called sinner a helping hand. If a baby dirties its diaper, you take it out of the crib, clean it and put on a new diaper. You don't criticize it. If you wish to criticize it, you have no business being with that child.

So Yoga helps in every aspect of our lives, from the White House to the outhouse. It's not something to be experienced only after sixty years of practice, but something that can benefit everyone now.

तदर्थ एव दृश्यस्यात्मा ॥२१॥

21. Tadartha eva dṛśyasyātmā.

Tad = that, its; **arthaḥ** = purpose; **eva** = only; **dṛśyasya** = of the seen; **ātmā** = the Seer.

The seen exists only for the sake of the Seer.

As we saw in the previous *sūtras*, nature is here to give experience to the *Puruṣa* and so we think the *Puruṣa* is doing the experiencing. In reality, the *Puruṣa* isn't experiencing anything. It is just a witness. But since it appears to be experiencing, we must try to understand it from that level. Once we go further, we will realize that the *Puruṣa* is neither the doer nor the enjoyer and we will change our vision and attitude; but, for now, we start from where we are.

The very word "understanding" is a combination of two words: "under" and "stand." To understand, we should stand under. But stand under what? Under where we now stand. We should know where we stand first and then try to "under" stand, to go a little deeper. When we try to understand, we will find we are not all on one "stand" but at different levels, with different capacities, tastes and temperaments.

Each individual has his or her own stand. My understanding is completely different from yours. One and the same scripture appears differently to different people as each one tries to interpret it from where he or she stands. So, here Patañjali is saying we are now under the impression that the true Self is experiencing something, but one day we will know that the Self never does anything nor will it ever enjoy anything.

कृतार्थं प्रति नष्टमप्यनष्टं
तदन्यसाधारणत्वात् ॥२२॥

22. Kṛtārtham prati naṣṭam apyanaṣṭam tad anya sādhāraṇatvāt.

Kṛta = done, accomplished; **artham** = purpose [here: liberation]; **prati** = upon, towards; **naṣṭam** = destruction [the seen]; **api** = even though; **anaṣṭam** = not destroyed; **tad** = that [the seen]; **anya** = others; **sādhāraṇatvāt** = from commonality, universal.

Although destroyed for one who has attained liberation, it [the seen] still exists for others, being common to them.

According to the *Vedantic* term, nature is called *māyā*, or illusion. To whom is it *māyā*? To the person who has understood it. To others it is still real. The entire world is a sort of factory. In a factory we can see raw materials come in: timber, iron, etc.; but as they pass through different processes and various machines, they come out as finished products, which go to the showroom, the sales section and finally to the consumer. These products don't return to the workshop again. But the workshop continues to function as raw materials keep passing through it.

The world is our factory. As we pass through we are shaped every minute by different experiences. We become refined as our knowledge develops. Eventually, we understand the world completely and have no business being in the factory any longer. Then we can say, "Once I thought all this was real: money, name, position, beauty. But now I understand that none of this is permanent. I have watched millionaires become paupers, famous beauties become wrinkled." When that understanding comes, we no longer trust the worldly pleasures nor run after them. When we stop running after the world, the world says, "All right, I won't bother you any more. But whenever you wish to make use of me, I'm ready to serve you." Then the world runs after you. But we can't shape ourselves without the factory's help. We should know nature first. That is why nature is called the Mother. Only through the

Mother can we know God. Nobody on this earth has understood who his or her father is without the mother's help. She alone can tell us who the father is.

Know nature well. Don't try to run from it. Let there be no running away or dropping out. Escapism never helps us. If we try to leave something now, we will have to face it in a more difficult form later on.

Another thing is: we must always be alert and aware with *māyā*. The world will try to cheat us in every way. It will attempt to come through every nook and corner. We must have thousands of eyes all over in order to face the world. But we must face it, understand it, analyze it and solve its tests.

Many people are afraid of knowing what their problems are. They just want to swallow a pill and forget everything. Instead, they wake up with several new problems. They want to become ostriches. When there is a danger in sight, they want to bury their heads in the sand. But that doesn't mean they have solved their problems. Once we solve and understand our problems, we become masters. Once we are masters, we are no longer bound by nature. It becomes our slave.

स्व स्वामि शक्त्योः स्वरूपोपलब्धिहेतुः
संयोगः ॥२३॥

23. Sva Svāmi śaktyoḥ svarūpopalabdhihetuḥ saṁyogaḥ.

Sva = being owned (Prakṛti), one's; **Svāmi** = the owner (Puruṣa);
śaktyoḥ = of the powers; **sva** = one's; **rūpa** = nature;
svarūpa = one's true nature, essence;
upalabdhi = recognition, apprehension;
hetuḥ = cause; **saṁyogaḥ** = union.

The union of the Owner (*Puruṣa*) and Owned (*Prakṛti*) causes the recognition of the nature and powers of them both.

Saṁyoga (union) is necessary for the *Puruṣa* to realize itself with the help of nature. *Saṁyoga* means perfect union or junction. And here it doesn't mean the union of the individual self with the higher Self, but the union of the *Puruṣa* and *Prakṛti*, Self and nature. When they are completely apart, they don't express themselves. Their connection, however, lets us know them both. They help each other. It is something like if you want to print with white letters, you must have a black background for contrast. You can't write white letters on a white background. Through the *Prakṛti*, we realize we are the *Puruṣa*. If not for the *Prakṛti*, we could not know ourselves. So *Prakṛti* isn't just bondage as many people think. It is necessary.

तस्य हेतुरविद्या ॥२४॥

24. Tasya heturavidyā

Tasya = its; **hetuḥ** (hetur) = cause; **avidyā** = ignorance.

The cause of this union is ignorance.

Here, Patañjali laughs at the idea he has just expressed. The cause of the *saṁyoga* is ignorance. This may seem a bit confusing, but if we understand it properly there's no puzzle. You see, in the previous *sūtra*, we're still in the world and wondering about the reason for nature. Once the *Puruṣa* understands itself, it thinks, "How did this union come about? It's because I've forgotten myself. What an ignorant person I was. Because of my ignorance I created this union." Such a person laughs at it, but this attitude comes only *after* realization. It's like a dreaming person who, upon waking, laughs at his or her own frightening dream. The understanding behind this *sūtra* is a result of realization. Once we realize, we can advise others: "I was ignorant. I had terrible experiences. I thought nature was real, happiness was real. I ran after them. But now I know what they are. I learned the hard way. Do you also want to have to learn the hard way? Why don't you take my advice?"

These *sūtras* are reminiscent of the Four Noble Truths of the Buddha: the misery of the world, the cause of misery, the removal of that misery and the method used to remove it. Patañjali tells us that pain can be avoided. He further tells us that its cause is ignorance. In *sūtra* 26, he gives us another word, *hāna*, the removal of this misery, and then *hāno-pāya*, the method to remove it. We can really see the similarity between the Four Noble Truths and the Yoga Sutras. We needn't search for who copies whom. Truth is the same always. Whoever ponders it will get the same answer. The Buddha got it. Śri Patañjali got it. Lord Jesus got it. Prophet Muhammad got it. The answer is the same, but the method of working it out may vary this way or that.

तदभावात् संयोगाभावो हानं तद् धृशेः
कैवल्यम् ॥२५॥

25. Tad abhāvāt saṁyogābhāvohānam tad dṛśeḥ kaivalyam.

Tad = that [ignorance];
abhāvāt = from the absence, from the disappearance;
saṁyoga = union; **abhāvaḥ** (abhāvo) = absent, dissolution;
hānam = removal, cessation; **tad** = that;
dṛśeḥ = of the Seer, of seeing; **kaivalyam** = absolute independence.

Without this ignorance, no such union occurs. This is the independence of the Seer.

More simply, once the junction created by ignorance is removed, the Seer rests in Its own true nature. The *Puruṣa* is always like that; although temporarily it appears to be bound by *Prakṛti*. We should not only understand this theoretically but should remember this point in all our experiences, all our actions, all our ups and downs. Ask, "Am I tainted by this?" "Who am I?" "Who is happy?" "Who is unhappy?" If we continually ask these questions and do this kind of meditation, we will find that we are only the knower. We know that many different things happen, but there is no difference in the knowing.

The Vedantins say, "*Aham sakṣiḥ.*" "I am the eternal witness." Even if we know this only theoretically, it will help us out on many occasions.

When we are worried over a loss we should ask, "Who is worried? Who knows I am worried?" Along with the answer, the worry will go away. When we analyze the worry, it becomes an object, something we are no longer involved with.

We can have that attitude even with pain. If we burn a finger, instead of saying, "Oh, I'm burning!" we should ask ourselves, "Who says, 'I am burning?' Who feels the burn?" The burn will become a nice object of meditation. This method is only a matter of changing the mind, taking it away from a certain object.

I used to treat people for scorpion stings. These stings create a lot of pain. The easiest and quickest way to relieve someone from the pain was to put a few drops of a salt solution in their eyes. This has nothing to do with curing the sting, but it would cause the patient to cry, kick and weep, taking the entire mind from the sting to the eye. By the time the sore eye was relieved, the pain from the sting would have been forgotten and would have gone away. If we are sad over a minor discomfort and all of a sudden receive a telegram saying our business has suffered a tremendous loss, we immediately forget the small problem. The attention is instantly transferred. So everything is relative. Every experience in the world is mental. We might put our minds onto something and think, "This is really great," but once our attention goes somewhere else, that thing becomes nothing to us. That is the reason for the Sanskrit expression, "*Mana eva manuṣyanam,*" "As the mind, so the person."

The cause of *bandha* and *mokṣa* (bondage and liberation) is our own minds. If we think we are bound, we are bound. If we think we are liberated, we are liberated. Because you think you are living, you are living. If you applied your mind one hundred percent to the thought that you were dying, you would die. It is only when we transcend the mind that we are free from all these troubles.

The mind is the agent of *Prakṛti* and a subtle part of that same *Prakṛti.* We should realize we are completely different from the mind. We are eternally free, never bound. That doesn't mean we should simply become idle; but once we realize our freedom we should work for the sake of others who are still bound. When a strong person crosses a turbulent river, he or she will not walk away after crossing but will stand on the bank and help pull out everyone else. There are many sages and saints who are involved in the world even with the knowledge that there is no happiness in it. They work for the sake of others.

विवेकख्यातिरविप्लवा हानोपायः ॥२६॥

26. Vivekakhyātiraviplavā hānopāyaḥ.

Viveka = discrimination, discernment; **khyātir** = pristine perception; **aviplavā** = uninterrupted; **hāna** = removal; **upāyaḥ** = method.

Uninterrupted discriminative discernment is the method for its removal.

This is called *viveka* in Sanskrit. You try to understand and see the permanent aspect in everything and ignore the impermanent aspect. The entire world has these two aspects: permanent and impermanent, or the never-changing and the ever-changing. The essence of everything is the same, but it appears in many forms and names. On the level of form, you are not the same person now as you were last week. Even a minute ago you were different. Every minute the body is changing: some part is dying, and some part is being born. According to the Yogic system, the entire body changes in a period of twelve years; in other words, you do not have even one cell that was there twelve years ago.

Discrimination does not mean to discriminate what is salt and what is sugar. That is just ordinary understanding. The real discrimination is to tell the original basic Truth from the ever-changing names and forms It assumes. If we could remember that basic Truth, we would never face disappointment nor get upset over the changes in the forms and names. Our minds would remain steady. It is for this understanding that we say the prayer, "Lead us from unreal to real, from darkness to light, from death to immortality." What is it that dies? A log of wood dies to become a few planks. The planks die to become a chair. The chair dies to become a piece of firewood, and the firewood dies to become ash. You give different names to the different shapes the wood takes, but the basic substance is there always. If we could always remember this, we would never worry about the loss of anything. We never lose anything; we never gain anything. By such discrimination we put an end to unhappiness.

Next, Patañjali goes on to explain the *Puruṣa's* different stages of attainment as it gradually goes upward to rest in its own true nature. This is called *saptadhā bhūmi*, or the seven planes of understanding.

तस्य सप्तधा प्रान्तभूमिः प्रज्ञा ॥२७॥

27. Tasya saptadhā prāntabhūmiḥ prajñā.

Tasya = it has; **saptadhā** = sevenfold; **prānta** = final, ultimate; **bhūmiḥ** = stage, ground; **prajñā** = wisdom.

One's wisdom in the final stage is sevenfold. [One experiences the end of 1) the desire to know anything more; 2) the desire to stay away from anything; 3) the desire to gain anything new; 4) the desire to do anything; 5) sorrow; 6) fear; 7) delusion.]

The first stage is where we come to the conclusion that by running here and there, by looking to externals, we are not going to gain the knowledge we seek. Knowledge is a thing to be obtained from within by tuning in. "Tuning in" means to go in, to understand ourselves, to "know thyself" first. If we do not know ourselves, we will make mistakes in knowing other things. We should know with what glasses we are viewing the outside. Are they clean or colored? If they are colored, naturally we will see a colored world outside. We can't blame the world for this color. A scale should be correct itself before trying to give the correct weight of objects placed on it. If the scale is wrong, the weight will certainly be wrong. We must see if the mind is in a neutral position so it can judge things properly.

The second understanding is that all experiences of pleasure and pain come not from the outside but are the interpretation of our own mind. The mind makes these experiences and creates these feelings. If this understanding comes, all miseries and pains are over; we will see we are not pained by any externals and that nothing can make us unhappy. When we know that our mind is the cause of these pains, we will try to correct it rather than blaming the outside world or other people. We will feel no need to seek after things, nor to avoid them.

The third position comes once you understand the mind fully and, with that neutral mind, attain cosmic understanding. You need not study anything for that. No books can give it. Many saints were illiterate. They never even knew what a school was. But we read their ideas even now. None of the *Upanishadic* seers went to colleges or universities. They merely sat under trees and watched nature. But their words are crest jewels now. Where did their learning come from? It came from within. There is a wealth of knowledge inside. The scriptures say, "Know the One by knowing which you will know everything." This understanding without learning is the third level of consciousness.

The fourth step comes once we understand nature and its workings. We feel there is no longer anything to be done. If we understand the cosmic plan, we rise above all doership. There is no particular duty for us, no do's or don'ts. At that time, we are prompted to do things only because our minds are linked to the cosmic mind; there is no personal action. As we are prompted, we just do. We do not know why we are doing things and will not bother about whether they are good or bad. The scriptures ask, "*Ko vidhi ko niṣedaḥ?*" "What is a must and what is not?" There are no musts, nothing one must do, nothing one should or should not do. Whatever we do is part of the cosmic plan. That means, even though such a person appears to be doing something, really he or she is not doing anything and becomes the *akartā*, the non-doer. A Tamil saint put that idea into a poem. "Oh Lord, I gave You my entire personality, body, mind and life—and You have accepted it. If there is anything happening through my body or mind, am I responsible? Good might happen. Bad might happen. But You are responsible. You make me do this. People may say, 'He is a bad man. He is doing bad things.' But You know that it is not I who do it; it is You working through me."

These words will come only when we realize we are completely in the hands of a higher will. It is very easy to stand in front of the altar and say, "I am Thine. All is Thine. Thy will be done." But do we really feel that way? Have we really completely given up? In such a state there are no duties for us. All our duties are God's duties. We are not responsible. But this state cannot be merely an intellectual understanding. If that is the case, we can even slap someone on the face and say, "It is all God's will. I gave God everything. Even my hand has been given to God who is using it to slap you."

Some people, when their businesses do well, say, "We really know how to do business. We bought this at the right time. Now see the ten percent increase in sales?" And if their businesses do badly, they say, "My goodness. Every day we burn candles for God who has no eyes at all. There is no point in my believing in God. If God were merciful why should we have such a great loss?" When profit comes, *they* are responsible. When loss comes, God is responsible. Our attitude should be constant: either we are responsible for everything or God is. We should always blame it on the big "I" or the little "i" but not on whichever is convenient at the time. If we want to be egoistic, we should be egoistic for everything. Even if someone abuses us, we should feel responsible for that abuse. Either we should surrender completely to God's will or use only our will.

The fifth plane is actually an after-effect of that understanding. Once we come to know there is nothing to be done, the *citta* is completely free of impressions. It is liberated. Because it had the tinge of ego, it acted as it wanted. Once that is separated, it just becomes a humble, simple mind, completely free of impressions; and, although old impressions remain, they lose their capacity to disturb the mind.

In the sixth level, the *citta* loses itself. That is called *mano-nāsa* or *citta-nāśa* and means the mind is completely chucked off. When the mind gets totally dissolved, the seventh and last plane remains. This is when the *Puruṣa* alone remains, resting in its own *svarūpa*. Here, the *Puruṣa* rests in itself for there is nothing else to rest in. "*Ātmanā Ātmanaṁ pasyann Ātmani tusyati,*" says the *Bhagavad Gītā*. "Beholding the Self by the Self, one is satisfied in the Self." This is the highest *samādhi*.

We should all know what these things are, because one day we will certainly all reach that state. As they happen, we will see the signs. Sometimes people are frightened by the unexpected. If they suddenly lose physical consciousness in meditation, they feel, "Something is happening to me. Am I going to die?" They disturb their meditation. Instead, if we know the signs we will welcome these things.

The aforementioned are the different stages along the Yogic path. Once the first stage is achieved and we learn to go within without expecting anything from externals, we have caught hold of the first link. Then it's only a matter of pulling in order to get the entire chain. But the first one must be present.

Saint Thirūmular said, "A person was running and running in search of the Light. He spent his whole life doing that. Ultimately he collapsed and died because he couldn't reach it." Millions and millions of people collapse this way because they don't know that the Light is within.

Another saying of his is, "Even if you practice Yoga for eight thousand years, you are not going to reach the Light." By this he means external Yoga: reading books, learning all the scriptures by heart, going on pilgrimages to all the temples, *āśrams* and churches in the world. That is all *bāhya*, or external practice. Some people waste thousands of years in such effort. If we only look within, we will see the Light as if we were seeing our own image in a mirror.

All the different religions say this: We are not going to get it from outside. Turn in. Look within. Know thyself. The teachings can help you slightly, but too much learning may just muddle your mind. We should learn a little and work with that. Turning inside means turning the senses within; trying to hear something within, see something within, smell something within. All the scents are within us. All the beautiful music is within us. All art is inside. Why should we search, running after museums and gardens when every museum and garden is inside us?

We should spend a little time in the morning and evening to go within. Gradually we can extend this to our entire daily life. Whatever our limbs do outside, we can keep our minds pulled inside. As I quoted before, a Hindu saying goes, "*Man me Rām, hath me kām.*" "There is work in the hand, but

Ram (God) in the mind." Things like books are only aids which we should not hesitate to let go of when they are no longer useful. With the help of a ladder we can get to the rooftop, but once on top we let go of the ladder. We needn't continue to put garlands around the ladder and prostrate to it. Many times people adore and worship symbols. For example, there are those who bind and place their scriptures in velvet cases which they keep on their altars and carry in procession but never even read one line of.

Symbols should be used to help you transcend them. With the help of the mind, we transcend the mind. Once we reach our destination, we can throw it out and go away. There should be no sentimentality here. Make the proper use of spiritual aids, but do not hesitate to leave them and go further. When we get nice accommodations on a plane, are we going to remain seated even after reaching our destination? Many times I find a nice parking place and am tempted to say, "Such a great parking spot. If I take the car out, I won't get it again. I'll just walk to the lecture hall." But a car is no good to me kept in a parking place. Instead, I have to use it. Some students think, "If I open this book, the binding will become damaged. I better not open it. Swamiji gave it to me. I must keep it as a memento."

Instead, we should make use of these things. Study the book page by page. Digest it. You can even give it to someone else when you're through with it. That should be our attitude. Once we reach the first step, we are on an escalator that takes us to the seventh stage.

योगाङ्गानुष्ठानादशुद्धिक्षये ज्ञानदीप्तिरा
विवेकख्यातेः ॥२८॥

28. Yogāṅgānuṣṭhānād aśuddhi kṣaye jñānadīptir ā vivekakhyāteḥ.

Yoga = union; **aṅga** =limbs; **anuṣṭhānāt** = from the practice;
aśuddhi = impurities; **kṣaye** = destruction, dwindling;
jñāna = of wisdom, of knowledge; **dīptiḥ** = light, brilliance;
ā = all the way up to; **viveka** = discriminative discernment;
khyāteḥ = perception, clarity.

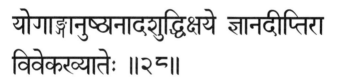

By the practice of the limbs of Yoga, the impurities dwindle away and there dawns the light of wisdom, leading to discriminative discernment.

From here onward, Patañjali gives us different ideas about Yoga practice. He divides it into eight stages or limbs. That is why these *sūtras* are also called Aṣṭāṅga Yoga, or the eight-limbed Yoga. He goes over the same ideas he has given up to now but in a more practical way.

यमनियमासनप्राणायामप्रत्याहार
धारणाध्यानसमाधयोऽष्टावङ्गानि ॥२९॥

29. Yama niyamāsana prāṇāyāma pratyāhāra dhāraṇā dhyāna samādhayo' ṣṭāvaṅgāni.

Yama = abstinence, regulation;
niyama = observances, training;
āsana = meditative posture;
prāṇāyāma = breath control, regulation or expansion of breath;
pratyāhāra = withdrawal of senses, inward flow of senses;
dhāraṇa = concentration; **dhyāna** = meditation;
samādhayaḥ = contemplation, absorption, superconscious state;
aṣṭāu = eight; **aṅgāni** = limbs, parts, components.

The eight limbs of Yoga are:
1. ***Yama* (abstinence)**
2. ***Niyama* (observance)**
3. ***Āsana* (posture practice)**
4. ***Prāṇāyāma* (breath control)**
5. ***Pratyāhāra* (sense withdrawal)**
6. ***Dhāraṇā* (concentration)**
7. ***Dhyāna* (meditation)**
8. ***Samādhi*(contemplation, absorption, superconscious state).**

अहिंसासत्यास्तेयब्रह्मचर्यापरिग्रहा यमाः ॥३०॥

30. Ahiṁsā satyāsteya brahmacaryāparigrahā yamāḥ.

Ahiṁsā = nonviolence;
satya = truthfulness;
asteya = non-stealing;
brahmacarya = continence, moderation of any sense drive;
aparigrahā = non-greed, non-grasping;
yamāḥ = abstinences, regulations

***Yama* consists of nonviolence, truthfulness, non-stealing, continence and non-greed.**

Now we come to *yama*, the first limb of Aṣṭāṅga Yoga. We should remember here that each of the eight limbs is equal to the others and necessary.

Ahiṁsā is not causing pain. Some authors translate it as non-killing, but it is not that. *Hiṁsā* means to cause pain; *ahiṁsā*, not to cause pain. Killing is different from causing pain. Causing pain can be even more harmful than killing. Even by your words, even by your thoughts, you can cause pain.

Satya is truthfulness, not lying. *Asteya* means non-stealing. These things seem so elementary but are, at the same time, "elephantary." They shouldn't be discarded as being mild. They are not easy to perfect. *Brahmacarya* is continence or celibacy. And the last part of *yama* is *aparigrahā* which can be translated in two ways. One is non-hoarding of things, not being greedy, not accumulating beyond our capacity to use things in the proper way. The other translation of *aparigrahā* is not accepting gifts. These five principles make up *yama*, the abstentions. We will discuss them in detail under *sūtras* 35 through 39.

जातिदेशकालसमयानवच्छिन्नाः सार्वभौमा
महाव्रतम् ॥३१॥

31. Jāti deśa kāla samayānavacchinnāḥ sārvabhaumā mahāvratam.

Jāti = class, species, type of birth; **deśa** = place, space;
kāla = time; **samaya** = circumstance, condition;
anavacchinnāḥ = not limited by, not cut by;
sārva = relating to all, universal, fit for all; **bhaumāḥ** = spheres;
sārvabhaumāḥ = universal; **mahā** = great; **vratam** = vow.

These great vows are universal, not limited by class, place, time or circumstance.

Patañjali calls these the *mahāvratam*, or great vows, because they can never be broken by any excuse: not time, place, purpose, social or caste rule, not by winter, summer, morning or evening, or by this country or that nationality. These points are for whole-time, dedicated Yogis; and so, for them, Patañjali allows no excuses. For people who aren't that one-pointed toward the Yogic goal, these vows can be modified according to their position in life.

शौचसंतोषतपःस्वाध्यायेश्वरप्रणिधानानि
नियमाः ॥३२॥

32. Śauca saṁtoṣa tapaḥ svādhyāyeśvarapraṇidhānāni niyamāḥ.

Śauca = purity; **saṁtoṣa** = contentment;
tapaḥ = accepting pain (heat) and not causing pain, to be purified by austerities, heat;
svādhyāya = study of spiritual book for Self understanding;
Īśvara = God; **praṇidhānā** = worship, self-surrender;
ani = all above as a group; **niyamāḥ** = observances. .

***Niyama* consists of purity, contentment, accepting but not causing pain, study of spiritual books and worship of God [self-surrender].**

The next limb, *niyama*, concerns observances. The five points of *yama*, together with the five points of *niyama*, remind us of the Ten Commandments of the Christian and Jewish faiths, as well as of the ten virtues of Buddhism. In fact, there is no religion without these moral or ethical codes. All spiritual life should be based on these things. They are the foundation stones without which we can never build anything lasting.

वितर्कबाधने प्रतिपक्षभावनम् ॥३३॥

33. Vitarka bādhane pratipakṣa bhāvanam.

Vitarka = negative thought, argument;
bādhane = upon disturbance, afflicted in;
pratipakṣa = opposite side;
bhāvanam = manifested, meditated, thought, realized.

When disturbed by negative thoughts, opposite [positive] ones should be thought of. This is *pratipakṣa bhāvana*.

Here, Patañjali gives us a very nice clue on how to control the mind and obstruct those thoughts we don't want. The best way, he says, is to invite opposite thoughts. If the thought of hatred is in the mind, we can try to bring in the thought of love. If we can't do that, we can at least go to the people we love and, in their presence, forget the hatred. So, although the hatred comes to the surface, we can keep it from coming out or staying long by changing the environment.

Sometimes we see this work between married partners. When sparks fly between them, if their little one crawls up to them, what will happen? Those of us who have had this experience will immediately know. The sparks instantly cool down. Either the mother or father picks up and hugs the child. That's because they both love the baby. In the form of the child, love comes in, and the anger or hatred is immediately banished.

We can create a positive atmosphere by looking at a holy picture, by reading an inspiring book, by meeting with a special person or simply by leaving the disturbing environment. This is a very practical point. It is very difficult to control negative thoughts while staying in a negative environment unless we have extraordinary strength. The easiest way is to change the environment. For example: if you begin to fight with your mate, even before your anger comes out, run to your baby's room and look at your sleeping child. You will forget all the anger and avoid many a divorce. At least for that reason, have a youngster at home! Or go into your shrine room, sit in front of the altar and read a nice book. Or travel to the country, look at the open sea—anything, as long as you change the environment. In that way, we create the opposite thought.

Another way to control a negative thought even before the thought overpowers us is to think of its after-effect. Stop and consider. "What will happen if I allow this thought to continue? I'll lose my friends. If that other person is strong, she may not even be affected at all. She might just laugh at me and go away. But even before the other person is affected by my anger, I will be affected. I'll shake up my nerves. My blood will boil."

वितर्का हिंसादयः कृतकारितानुमोदिता
लोभक्रोधमोहपूर्वका मृदुमध्याधिमात्रा
दुःखाज्ञानानन्तफला इति प्रतिपक्षभावनम् ॥३४॥

34. Vitarkā hiṁsādayaḥ kṛta kāritānumoditā lobha krodha moha pūrvakā mṛdu madhyādhimātrā duḥkhājñānānanta phalā iti pratipakṣa bhāvanam.

Vitarkāḥ = negative thoughts, arguments; **hiṁsā** = violence; **adayaḥ** = et cetera; **kṛta** = done; **kārita** = caused to be done; **anumoditāḥ** = approved; **lobha** = greed; **krodha** = anger;

moha = infatuation, confusion, bewilderment, loss of consciousness; **pūrvakāḥ** = preceded by; **mṛdu** = mild; **madhya** = medium; **adhimātrāḥ** = intense; **duḥkha** = pain; **ajñāna** = ignorance; **ananta** = infinite, endless; **phalāḥ** = fruit; **iti** = thus; **pratipakṣa** = opposite side; **bhāvanam** = manifested, meditated, thought, realized.

When negative thoughts or acts such as violence, etc. are done, caused to be done or even approved of—whether incited by greed, anger or infatuation—whether indulged in with mild, medium or extreme intensity, they are based on ignorance and bring certain pain. Reflecting upon this is also *pratipakṣa bhāvana.*

Here, Patañjali gives a further explanation of *pratipakṣa bhāvana.* Suppose we bring pain to someone or cause harm to be brought to another. The reactions will come and ultimately result in ignorance and misery. We need not even cause the pain directly for the reaction to occur. We can effect this just by approving of another's pain-bearing actions due to our own avariciousness, anger or ignorance.

अहिंसाप्रतिष्ठायां तत्संनिधौ वैरत्यागः ॥३५॥

35. Ahiṁsā pratiṣṭhāyām tat saṁnidhau vaira tyāgaḥ.

Ahiṁsā = nonviolence; **pratiṣṭhāyām** = upon having established; **tat** = that; **saṁnidhau** = in the presence; **vaira** = hostility; **tyāgaḥ** = given up.

In the presence of one firmly established in nonviolence, all hostilities cease.

Starting with this thirty-fifth *sūtra,* Patañjali covers the ten virtues one by one. When the vow of *ahiṁsā* is established in someone, all enmity ceases in his or her presence because that person emits harmonious vibrations. If two people who have enmity between them come to such a person, they will temporarily forget it. That is the benefit of *ahiṁsā*. When it is practiced continuously in thought, word and deed for some time, the entire personality brings out those vibrations.

Even wild animals forget their nature of causing pain in the presence of one established in *ahiṁsā*. In ancient Hindu mythology, it states that in the forests where the saints and sages lived practicing *ahiṁsā*, the animals would only kill when they were hungry. At other times, a cow and a tiger could drink water side by side. The Buddha cultivated this practice. Wherever he went he brought peace, harmony and friendliness. St. Francis is another great example of this. Mahatma Gandhi tried his best to practice and propagate *ahiṁsā*, bringing many people together. Of course, there were failures in his efforts, but he would admit, "I am still trying. I am still not that perfect." His entire life was based on the vows of *ahiṁsā* and *satya*. Even without obtaining one hundred percent perfection in them, he earned a great name throughout the world as an apostle of peace. Perhaps if Gandhi's practice had been perfected, his assassin might have forgotten the idea of shooting Gandhi when he came into Gandhi's presence. So, even with a little perfection, Gandhi was admired and revered by the entire world. Even a bit of *ahiṁsā* is enough to elevate us to a higher state.

सत्यप्रतिष्ठायां क्रियाफलाश्रयत्वम् ॥३६॥

36. Satya pratiṣṭhāyām kriyāphalāśrayatvam.

Satya = truthfulness; **pratiṣṭhāyām** = upon having established;
kriyā = actions; **phala** = fruit, result;
āśrayatvam = on which anything depends or rests.

To one established in truthfulness, actions and their results become subservient.

By the establishment of truthfulness, Yogis get the power to attain for themselves and others the fruits of work without doing the work.

In other words, things come to them automatically. All nature loves an honest person. Then you need not run after things, for they will run after you. And if you are always truthful, if no lie comes from your mouth, a time will come when all you say will come true. Even if you say something by mistake, it will happen, because by the practice of *satya* the words become so powerful and clean that honesty observes you. It wants to be with you always. If a curse is spoken, it will happen. If a blessing is said, it will happen. The more we lead a life of honesty, the more we will see the results, and that will encourage us to be more honest.

With establishment in honesty, the state of fearlessness comes. One need not be afraid of anybody and can always lead an open life. When there are no lies, the entire life becomes an open book. But this comes only with an absolutely honest mind. When the mind becomes clear and serene, the true Self reflects without disfigurement, and we realize the Truth in its own original nature.

A vow of absolute honesty means we can no longer tell white lies either. If by being honest we will cause trouble, difficulty or harm to anyone, we should keep quiet. Instead of lying and saying things like, "I don't know," we can be frank: "I know, but I don't want to tell." This does not mean you should protect a criminal, because not only should we not lie, but we should not *cause* someone else to lie either. If we do it consciously, we are a part of that lie. In fact, under law, punishment is usually greater for the person *behind* a crime than for the one who actually commits it.

So, first follow truth, and then truth will follow you. In the same way, first you learn to smoke and then the smoke teaches you. I am quite certain nobody enjoys his or her first few cigarettes. They are taken in with great difficulty, nausea and vomiting. Gradually, we can take in a whole puff without letting it out. Then, eventually, the cigarettes begin to "smoke" us. First we burn the cigarette; later it burns us, working on our tissues little by little.

Yoga is not a philosophy to be followed with blind faith. In the beginning, it is true that confidence and trust are necessary, but as you continue to practice, every step will bring more and more hope, greater and greater confidence. If we are true Yogis for just one day, we will be transformed and want more of it. It's contagious, just like any other habit. But first we must make some effort until we get a taste of the benefit. Similarly, certain candies might appear a little strange, and a child might say, "No, no. I don't want it," when the mother offers it. But if by chance the mother exerts some force and makes the child taste it, the child will want more and more. Once we get the taste, even if the whole world stands in our way, it won't keep us from our goal.

अस्तेयप्रतिष्ठायां सर्वरत्नोपस्थानम् ॥३७॥

37. Asteyapratiṣṭhāyām sarvaratnopasthānam.

Asteya = non-stealing; **pratiṣṭhāyām** = upon having established;
sarva = all; **ratna** = gems, wealth;
upasthānam = approaches, comes, permits access.

To one established in non-stealing, all wealth comes.

If we want to become the world's richest people, this is a very simple way. There's no need to get into the stock market or even to go to work. Just practice non-stealing. All of us are thieves. Knowingly and unknowingly, we steal things from nature. With every minute, with each breath, we pick nature's pocket. Whose air do we breathe? It is nature's. But that doesn't mean we should stop breathing and die. Instead, we should receive each breath with reverence and use it to serve others; then we are not stealing. If we accept it and don't give anything in return, we are thieves. We steal because of greed. We want to do little and get a lot. Many people go to the office and just sit around, use the phone to make their own appointments all day, take free supplies from the supply room and accept their paycheck at the end of the week. Aren't they stealing that money? Do we not also steal other people's ideas?

If we are completely free from stealing and greed, contented with what we have, and if we keep our minds serene, all wealth comes to us.

If we do not run after it, before long it runs after us. If nature knows we aren't greedy, she gains confidence in us, knowing we will never hold her for ourselves.

But, normally, when we get something, we tend to lock it away and put the keys in a safe place. We tend to imprison our possessions, whether money, property or even people. The moment we try to imprison money, for example, it feels, "What is this? I want free movement. They have made me round so I could roll. But here I am locked up. Oh, I've come to the wrong person. The moment I get the chance I'll roll away." Some stingy people never open their vaults. The money just sits inside and prays, "Please, somebody release me." Inevitably the prayer is heard by a robber who comes to the rescue.

Instead, if we have the attitude: "If you want to come, come; when you want to go, go," everything will say, "Why do you push me away? Let me stay with you. Don't send me away." I experience this myself. I never lock up anything. Things just come and stay. Even if I tell them to go, they beg to be with me. We can all see this situation with babies. They may come to us, play, sit in our laps, but the moment they want to go, if we try to hold them they become bored. "What is this? I made a mistake coming here." And they run away. The next time we call them, they'll think, "I don't want to come. Those people just keep me with them." Instead, if we just allow the babies to leave when they want, they'll certainly come to us again.

Another way of stealing things is by not letting others use them. Suppose we own a thousand acres of land, most of which we don't use. If there are people who want to buy a hundred acres and we don't let them, we are stealing its usage. If you have fifty garments in your closet and your neighbor doesn't have even one, you are stealing your neighbor's usage. Because certain people have the buying power to make a lot of purchases, they raise prices for poor people who don't have much money. If everyone merely bought for their own necessity, goods would be left over in stores and prices would come down. The whole world's economy is based on this. In the United States, I have heard that thousands of tons of wheat and potatoes are dumped into the ocean to keep the market in a "proper condition" and maintain prices. Instead of this practice, these goods should be given away. Because this lowers prices, though, nobody thinks much about hunger. Is this not a sin, a theft?

The land belongs to everybody. A person in a corner of Australia is just as much an equal owner of the land as anyone else. What is grown in the United States can be first given to its citizens with the surplus divided among everyone else. If we know how to care and share, no poverty or hunger need exist anywhere. In the richest country in the world, it is a pity to see things like hospitals being closed for lack of funds while billions are spent on rockets, spacecrafts and bombers. Is it more necessary to go to the moon than to take care of our neighbors? I don't negate scientific inventions and developments. They are fine. We can all ride to the moon, but only after everyone has been well-fed, clothed and educated.

A South Indian proverb says, "The stomach is crying for a piece of bread; the hair is crying for a bunch of flowers." Which is more important? The hair can live without a garland, but the stomach cannot go without a loaf of bread. So, let us satisfy the stomach first; and then, if we have money left over, we can get a number of garlands.

Here people are sick and dying while a handful of others want to go to the moon. When should we go to the moon? Only after making the earth happy. People who don't know how to live here will end up taking their same hell to the moon.

The government steals the happiness and health of hundreds and thousands of people. It is a public theft, a daylight robbery. Sometimes when I read the news, I really feel funny about all this. Everything is based on fear, pride, competition. All the antiballistic missiles are created out of fear. It is like saying, "I'm mortally afraid of you so I must protect myself with bombs and missiles." But, in the next breath the government says, "Let's be friends. Let's exchange cultural matters." How can you have both? Another thing I see are many of the secret plans of the U.S. right in the magazines. I once read an article about an antiballistic system, how it worked, what the plans were. I really don't understand this principle. If I am afraid of you, I won't say, "Here is a blueprint of the pistol I have in my pocket."

In another magazine, I saw a photo of the hot line telephone which is kept under lock and key with someone watching over it always. Agony, agony, agony. Now scientists are making lists of all the broken pieces of satellites revolving around the earth so no country mistakes them for missiles. Over a slight mistake the whole world could go to the dogs. And people can always make mistakes. Just imagine how many bombers loaded with nuclear weapons are flying around. Is there any guarantee nothing will happen to them?

So with all our modern inventions, we are really living in a horrible state. Our ancestors on horseback and carts seemed much happier. They might have eaten cruder food, they might have gone without radios, television, electronics and supersonic transport, but mentally they were happier and healthier. It's high time to get rid of this anxiety. How long can we live under such great tension?

By all this we can see richness has nothing to do with monetary wealth. The richest person is the one with a cool mind, free of tension and anxiety. Changing all these world situations is not in our hands. We are not going to stop all these things. But what *is* in our hands is the ability to find joy and peace right here and now. If we live in the present, even though the whole world might blow up in a minute, it won't bother us. We can be happy in situations of tension. If we have decided to be happy, nobody can make us unhappy. Anything might happen. An earthquake might decimate the entire world, but we need not bother about the future. Nor should we worry about the past. It has already gone. To be happy this minute is in our hands.

We are not going to change the whole world, but we can change ourselves and feel free as birds. We can be serene even in the midst of calamities and, by our serenity, make others more tranquil. Serenity is contagious. If we smile at someone, he or she will smile back. And a smile costs nothing. We should plague everyone with joy. If we are to die in a minute, why not die happily, laughing?

But a carefree life is possible only with a well-controlled mind, one that is free of anxiety, one without personal desires or possessions.

ब्रह्मचर्यप्रतिष्ठायां वीर्यलाभः ॥३८॥

38. Brahmacarya pratiṣṭhāyām vīryalābhaḥ.

Brahman = Absolute, God; **carya** = move with, remain with;
brahmacarya = continence, moderation, keeping the sense strong and calm—aligned with the creative energy;
pratiṣṭhāyām = upon having established;
vīrya = vigor, strengh, vital power, energy;
lābhaḥ = gained, obtained.

By one established in continence, vigor is gained.

By getting established in continence or celibacy, we save energy. *Vīrya* means vital energy. *Lābha* means profit. When there is no loss of *vīrya* we gain energy. What we gain by this saving is worth knowing. In the name of loving and giving, many times we lose this energy and become mentally and physically depleted. If we are not strong mentally and physically, we can never gain real spiritual wealth. The main cause for the present chaotic condition among the young is ignorance about *vīrya*. Young people say, "When you love somebody, how can you stop giving?" But, out of love, they do not know what to give. Sometimes they even give venereal disease. They lose their health and spoil the health of the ones they love. Can you say you love me and completely drain my blood and poison my system? No. If you love a child, will you make the child eat a box of candy? That isn't love. It is mere thoughtlessness. If you really loved the child you would say, "Candy is not good for you. Once in a while you can have some, but I won't buy you an entire box." Even though the child is unhappy about it, you are proving yourself to be a loving friend. The case of *brahmacarya* is like that. The seminal fluid gives strength and stamina to the brain and nerves. Nervous debility is caused by a lack of stamina because it has all been drained away.

If sex is the only form of loving, then how can a brother and sister love one another? A son and mother; a daughter and father? Sex is not the only way to show love. If love is based only on physical contact, the mind will never be satisfied with just one person. Today there will be *this* honey, tomorrow, *that* honey, the third day, another honey. Where is the limit?

Seminal fluid is our life. If stored properly, it can bring a lot of energy. When absorbed into the system it gets transformed into *prāṇa.* Conserved sexual energy in women also gets transformed. It is that vital force that allows you to really help people and have good relationships. Without much *prāṇa,* we can never give anything to anybody, just as only a fully-charged battery can give power, never a weak one. In observing *brahmacarya,* we build up this energy.

A Yogi should always keep this in mind. Teaching Yoga is not like teaching history or geometry. Teachers must impart a life force— a little current—into others. How can they do this if they are weak, if they have rundown, discharged batteries? So keep your batteries full of energy.

That doesn't mean you must completely stay away from sex. Instead, be moderate. Preserve as much energy as possible. Have sex only in the proper way, in a marital relationship. Have one or two children. Until you have a regular partner for life, store the energy. After all, when can you ask a partner to go into business with you? Only after you've saved up enough capital.

The Hindu system has four stages in life: *brahmacarya, gṛhastha, vānaprastha and sannyāsa.* Until one finishes his or her education that person is a *brahmacari,* strictly celibate. With this saved energy he or she can grasp things well. The brain power is more dynamic. In high schools and colleges now, most students learn sex and nothing else. But, instead, finish your studies and then go into partnership with another person.

This is the *gṛhastha* stage. Bring your knowledge and strength together. You should not come together because of beauty; because how long will that beauty last? However much make-up you wear, physical beauty will not last long. The real beauty is inside—in your character, your noble ideas, your aim in life. With noble ideas, a noble child can be one of your contributions to the world. Expressing your love and affections without overindulgence is not wrong. It is part of nature. Even couples who don't plan to have children should have limitations. Even animals have restrictions. Once a female dog is pregnant, no male can come near her. A lioness brings forth a cub once a year. Certain animals won't even make love in front of others—elephants, for example. So, in your own way, according to your stage of life, have limitations.

In the Hindu tradition, the *gṛhastha* stage is followed by *vānaprastha*, where the husband and wife have finished their worldly responsibilities and become totally involved in spiritual pursuits. They take pilgrimages or stay in an *āśram* somewhere. Then, at a certain point, they take *sannyāsa* and drop off all worldly ties completely. They are no longer husband and wife. In certain cases, if an individual has that much discrimination, he or she may take *sannyāsa* directly after the *brahmacarya* or *gṛhastha* stage.

But these days many people are interested in pre-marital "tests." That is something like going to a shopkeeper and asking the price of a few apples.

"A dollar," the shopkeeper says.

"Are they any good?" you ask.

"Sure."

"I think I'll try one."

Shopkeepers will never let us do that. They'll let us smell an apple and check out its size and shape, but they'll never let us sample it before buying.

Are people inferior to apples? Should they allow everyone to come and take a bite before buying? So, if you want to offer yourself to someone, do it purely, chastely. You are offering something very sacred and holy. Why should you let someone pollute this offering? If people want to know one another before marriage, they can become friends. That is how our ancestors lived. But today, in the name of freedom, people go to extremes.

By observing celibacy, we preserve not just physical energy alone but mental, moral, intellectual and, ultimately, spiritual energy as well. Sexual energy that is preserved gets transformed into a subtle energy called *ojas*. This is similar to personal magnetism. It tones the entire personality, builds the nerves, improves brain power and calms the mind. There is a similar word to *ojas* in English: ozone. In the early morning, before sunrise, we can go out and breathe the ozonic wind, which has a special vibration and energy to it. But once the sun's rays fall, this effect is lost. That's why the period between four and six in the morning is called the *Brahmamuhūrta*, the Brahmic time, or divine period, and is a very sacred time to meditate.

And *ojas*, when stored, creates *tejas*. *Tejas* is the aura or the glow. A newspaper reporter once wrote an article about me called, "The Swami Makes the People Glow." How can the Swami do this? Is it some peculiar yogic make-up? No. Everyone can glow and can transmit that energy when they preserve a lot of *ojas*. Even ordinary carbon left under the earth in an airtight chamber for a considerable time gets hardened, changes its color and becomes a diamond. If you preserve honey it gets crystallized. In the same way, the semen gets transformed and diffused.

This is why continence is a very important part of Yoga. If a handful of people come forward with strong wills, nothing is impossible. One Buddha changed half the globe; one Jesus, three quarters of the world. We all have that capacity. Let us know the value of *brahmacarya*; that it certainly will make us strong, happy, healthy, wealthy and blissful.

अपरिग्रहस्थैर्ये जन्मकथंतासंबोधः ॥३९॥

39. Aparigrahā sthairye janmakathaṁtā saṁbodhaḥ.

Aparigrahā = non-greed, renouncing possession of all but necessary items;
sthairye = upon firmness, upon resoluteness, confirmed in;
janma = birth, origin; **kathaṁtā** = how and why, questioning;
saṁbodhaḥ = thoroughly illuminated understanding, complete knowledge.

When non-greed is confirmed, a thorough illumination of the how and why of one's birth comes.

Aparigrahā is abstention from greed or hoarding—which is a form of stealing—or not receiving gifts. Many times we get gifts that are merely an advance for a future obligation. One day someone comes to us with a gift, and the next day he or she telephones to say, "Remember that gift I gave you? Well, could you please do a little something for me?" We feel obliged to do that then. Even the Internal Revenue Service won't accept business gifts as being tax-deductible because they aren't a real donation. They are only given to get something in return. A donation means something given just for the sake of giving, not for name, money or publicity.

Accepting gifts binds us and makes us lose our neutrality. The mind will say, "You received a gift from him. How can you say something against him?" On the other hand, if we are strong enough to remain free of obligation, we *can* accept gifts. Feel, "I am giving her an opportunity to use her money in the right way, but I am not obligated by this gift. She shouldn't come to me tomorrow for an obligation." Then we are not bound.

When the mind becomes this calm and clear by being free of desires and obligations, we gain the capacity to see how our desires caused our present birth. We directly see the cause and effect relationship because we are detached from it; we are no longer bound up with it.

शौचात् स्वाङ्गजुगुप्सा परैरसंसर्गः ॥४०॥

40. Saucāt svāṅgajugupsā parairasaṁsargaḥ.

Saucāt = from purification; **sva** = one's own; **aṅga** = the body; **jugupsā** = disgust, aversion; **parair** = with others; **asaṁsargaḥ** = cessation of contact.

By purification arises disgust for one's own body and for contact with other bodies.

When *śauca*, or purity, is observed, it makes you feel that even your own body is impure. Every minute there are secretions. Impurities are eliminated every second. The breath pours out carbon dioxide. The skin discharges perspiration. If we really think about it, it seems to be a very dirty place in which we live*. No matter how much perfume we put on, it only hides the dirt. If our perspiration is foul, we spray on some deodorant. If our skin looks dirty, we dab on a little powder to hide it. Every time we cover the dirt, it comes back. When we realize this, we develop an indifference toward the body; not that we neglect it, but we no longer adore it. The time we once spent on our bodies can be used for other purposes like *japa*, meditation or reading spiritual books.

When we feel our bodies are the embodiment of dirt, how can we be attracted to other bodies? These attractions will also get reduced and will certainly save us a great deal of trouble. When we spend more time on deeper things than the body, and eventually go into spiritual matters—realizing we are the true Self and not the body at all—we will not be interested in bringing two bodies together any more. We will just think of this process as two cloths rubbing together, because there is no difference between the body and a cloth. One is a skin shirt; the other, a cotton shirt.

The real union is not the union of two bodies. What is it we call masculine and feminine bodies? They are different shapes of flesh. By putting two lumps of flesh together, can we obtain *nirvana*? Not at all. Spiritual union doesn't necessarily mean physical union.

People misinterpret Tantra Yoga as something to do with sexual union. The Tibetan *Tantric* system speaks of *Śiva* and *Śakti*—*Śiva* being the masculine aspect; *Śakti*, the feminine. This doesn't refer to physical forms

**[Editor's Note; This sūtra should be understood in the light of a particular stage of discrimination on the part of a spiritual aspirant, where, for the sake of the higher goal, one develops a natural disinterest in the body and in intercourse with other bodies. However, it should be remembered that this "disgust" is not the same as aversion and that, as all the sages and scriptures have said, it is only in the human birth that a soul can attain spiritual realization. With realization, comes the perception that the body is the temple of the Divine Consciousness and is, in fact, nothing but that same Divine Consciousness.]*

but to the positive and negative forces within each individual. The Hatha Yogis call it the sun and moon. *Ha* means sun; *tha* is moon. The inner sun is in your solar plexus; the moon at the base of your spine. In order to become united, they must come together. This is known as the *prāṇa-apāna* union. "*Prāṇa apāna samayuktaḥ,*" says the *Bhagavad Gītā*. The energy that flows down should be turned up and returned to its source. The heat produced by meditation goes up and affects certain psychic glands, which start to produce nectar juices. These flow from the base of the spine through the nerves, building them up, making them more alive and helping them become almost immortal. The Sanskrit term *amṛta* (nectar) itself means "immortal." Your body becomes filled with light—*ojas* and *tejas*—and it is converted into a Yogic body. That is where the term "offering your nectar to the altar" comes from. Of course, those people interested in drinking will offer a bottle of whiskey at the altar and then take it back to drink as *prasād* (consecrated food). The mind can really deceive us.

We should be sure of the esoteric meaning in the scriptures. If we take only the surface meaning we might be misled. For example, take the offering of fruits at the altar. Who wants those fruits? Do you think God is going to eat them? It means offering the fruits of our actions to God. We are trees growing in nature; and all our energy, our actions, our thoughts, our words are the fruits of our lives which we must offer for the benefit of humanity in the name of God. This is where the term "forbidden fruit" in the *Bible* comes in. Each one of us is an Adam and an Eve because we try to eat the fruits of our actions, which we are forbidden to do. The Biblical story doesn't mean that an Adam once lived who ate the forbidden fruit and we are reaping his sins. We are doing the same thing here and now.

Every scripture has its own esoteric meanings in story form. This is because in ancient times they didn't want everybody to understand the subtle techniques and follow them without proper preparation. In the ancient Indian medical science known as *Āyurveda*, for examaple, there is a method called *kaya-kalpa,* used for the rejuvenation of the entire body. If its technique were well known, many people would wish to rejuvenate their bodies just to enjoy the world, rather than to use them selflessly.

So it is explained with code words which are not easily understood by just anyone.

Another example is a powerful herb called *musu-musukkai* in the Tamil language. This is a very powerful drug which could be misused in the wrong hands. But *musu* also means "monkey" and *kkai* has the meaning of one's "hand." So the preparation is called "double monkeys' hands." A person might just go, cut off two monkeys' hands and try to make a medicine. Ignorant people are saved from hurting themselves or others.

But once we have purity of mind, no doubt someone will come to tell us what the true meaning of these things are and what is to be done. "When the disciple is ready, the *guru* comes," is a well-known Hindu saying. When the receiver is well-tuned, the music comes. We need not send out invitations. All that is necessary is for us to tune ourselves. Then, without even a second's delay, the *guru* will come in some form. If we are not ready though, even with a hundred *gurus* around, we won't be benefited. For a *guru* can't force anything into us. We must be ready to receive. Similarly, the music is within the radio, but the radio cannot force the speaker to vibrate and bring it out. That is why preparation—developing virtues like *yama* and *niyama*—is very important.

सत्त्वशुद्धिसौमनस्यैकाग्र्येन्द्रियजयात्मदर्शन
योग्यत्वानि च ॥४१॥

41. Sattvaśuddhi saumanasyaikāgryendriyajayātmadarśana yogyatvāni ca.

Sattva = the sentient aspect of the three guṇas;
śuddhi = purification; **saumanasya** = cheerfulness of mind;
ekāgrya = one-pointedness; **indriya** = senses;
jaya = mastery over, victory; **Ātma** = Self, Soul;
darśana = realization, vision;
yogyatvāni = fitness, readiness; **ca** = and.

Moreover, one gains purity of *sattva*, cheerfulness of mind, one-pointedness, mastery over the senses and fitness for Self-realization.

First, you understand the body, then the heart is purified as well. When the heart is pure, you are always happy. Concentration of the mind comes automatically without your even trying. Only an impure mind runs here and there, forcing us to bring it back again and again. All the senses are controlled too, and then comes *Ātma darśana yogyatvāni,* fitness for Self-realization or the vision of the *Ātma.* These are all benefits of following *niyama's* first observance, purity. Just be pure in thought, word and deed. See how easy it is? But we don't want to do easy things because there's no pride in it. What is the pride in jumping over a small gutter? We want to jump rivers and break our necks. The ego never allows us to accept things easily. But even if we practice purity for just one day, we will really enjoy the benefit. Just as a sample, feel, "Today I'm going to be absolutely pure, absolutely celibate, absolutely honest." You will be tempted to repeat the experiment again and again.

संतोषादनुत्तमः सुखलाभः ॥४२॥

42. Saṁtoṣādanuttamaḥ sukhalābhaḥ.

Saṁtoṣāt = from contentment;
anuttamaḥ = supreme, unsurpassed;
sukha = joy; **lābhaḥ** = gained, attained.

By contentment, supreme joy is gained.

As a result of contentment, one gains supreme joy. Here we should understand the difference between contentment and satisfaction. Contentment means just to be as we are without going to outside things for our happiness. If something comes, we let it come. If not, it doesn't matter. Contentment means neither to like nor dislike.

कायेन्द्रियसिद्धिरशुद्धिक्षयात् तपसः ॥४३॥

43. Kāyendriya siddhiraśuddhikṣayāt tapasaḥ.

kaya = body; **indriya** = senses;
siddhiḥ (siddhir) = mastery, perfection, occult power;
aśuddhi = impurities; **kṣayāt** = from destruction;
tapasaḥ = from austerities.

By austerity, impurities of body and senses are destroyed and occult powers gained.

The direct meaning of *tapas* is "to burn," as was discussed in the first *sūtra* of this portion. By the physical *tapas* of fasting, we burn our excess fat away along with the toxins our bodies have accumulated. By mental *tapas*, we burn all our old impressions. By verbal *tapas*, observing silence, we control speech. When we burn, we feel some heat and pain. We undergo suffering. So, *tapas* also means to accept suffering. If someone suffers, he or she is blessed, because by that suffering some impurities are purged out.

In order to make our minds clean and steady we must accept suffering, pain and poverty. It is even more beneficial if, at the same time that we accept pain, we bring happiness to others. So, accept the pains of others. We never lose by accepting pain. The more the pain, the more the gain—and no pain, no gain. We should never run from it.

In our lives there are hundreds of opportunities for *tapas*. Even a cloth must undergo *tapas* to become clean. What will the laundry man do with my cloth? Will he fold it, put some sandalwood paste and a flower on it and give it back to me? No. First, he'll soak it in boiling water with soap. Then he'll beat it every which way. Then he'll tumble and roll and squeeze it in the washing machine. After that, he'll dry it in a hot chamber and iron it. Only then does the cloth lose all its dirt and grime. It undergoes *tapasya* to become pure. The laundryman has no hatred for the cloth when he does all these things to it. He only wants to make it pure. It is out of his love that he inflicts pain.

The mind too must be washed, squeezed, tossed, dried and ironed. Don't think that if someone causes us pain they hate us, but rather that they are helping us to purify ourselves. If we can think like this, we are real Yogis. If anybody hurts our feelings, we should just smile at them. "Thank you. I want more and more. I know you want me to become pure soon. Bring your friends also to inflict pain." If we understand this point and accept it, we'll never find fault with anybody who abuses, scolds or insults us. If flowery words make us happy but insults upset us, we know our minds are not yet strong. A word of abuse helps us understand our weaknesses. My Master said, "Adapt, adjust, accommodate. Bear insult. Bear injury. That is the highest *sādhana* (spiritual practice)." To go into a corner and say a *mantra* is easy *sādhana*. Anyone can do it. But if we are insulted and keep a serene mind, it is higher than saying thousands of rosaries of *japa*. That is *tapasya*.

The power to control the body and senses comes by *tapasya*. If we accept everything, what can affect us? If somebody calls us a fool, accept it; a wonderful person, accept it.

Once a man wanted to anger a saint. He began insulting him. "You dirty rogue. See how many people you have ruined with your teachings?"

The saint remained quiet, smiling at his tormentor.

"Don't you understand my language?" the man asked.

"Yes, sure."

"You mean, you've understood my insults?" The man was incredulous.

"I did."

"Then how can you keep quiet?"

The saint answered, "Son, suppose you brought me some fruit and I refused it. What would you do?"

"I would have to take it back."

"Yes," continued the saint. "In the same way, I don't enjoy all these things you have brought me. So you can just take them back."

Handling things this way takes real strength and courage. A person who can only strike back physically may be physically strong but mentally weak. Mental strength comes by *tapasya*, accepting pain. Then pain is no longer pain but is joy, because we have realized the benefit of it.

A beautiful example of this is the mother who feels so much joy in bringing forth a child, although it may be very painful. She will never avoid the pain; rather she welcomes it, knowing it is the price she pays for the great benefit later on.

स्वाध्यायादिष्टदेवतासंप्रयोगः ॥४४॥

44. Svādhyāyādiṣṭadevatāsaṁprayogaḥ.

Sva = oneself; **adhyāyāt** = from study of sacred text; **svādhyāyāt** = from Self or self study—traditionally through spiritual texts; **iṣṭa** = chosen, worshiped; **devatā** = deity, divinity; **saṁprayogaḥ** = communion, union, connection.

By study of spiritual books comes communion with one's chosen deity.

Again, *svādhyāyā*, or spiritual study, means study of scriptures and also any practice that is our own personal *sādhana* into which we've been initiated. Regular practice becomes study. By it we get *iṣṭa devatā saṁprayogaḥ*—the vision, or *darśan*, of God. By constant effort, we get a vision of the deity connected with our particular *mantra*, for each *mantra* has a deity. In other words, each name has a form. If we just stick to a certain name, eventually the form will appear automatically. It may come as a human form, a light or a sound.

समाधिसिद्धिरीश्वरप्रणिधानात् ॥४५॥

45. Samādhisiddhir īśvarapraṇidhānāt.

Samādhi = contemplation; **siddhiḥ** (siddhir) = attainment; **Īśvara** = God; **praṇidhānāt** = from total surrender, from completely placing before, from profound religious meditation.

By total surrender to God, *samādhi* is attained.

Īśvara praṇidhānā is a life of dedication, of offering everything to God or to humanity. Why do I add humanity? When we want to offer something to God, is God sitting somewhere waiting for us to give something? Where and who is God? God made the world and the world itself is God. All that is outside us is God. When we dedicate our lives to the benefit of humanity, we have dedicated ourselves to God. Whatever we do can easily be transformed into worship by our attitude. We can do anything and everything as long as we do it with the idea of serving the world at large. We can serve our tables, our chairs and everything around us. If we don't pull chairs mercilessly from one corner to another, we are serving them. If we drag them, they cry. Anything handled roughly will feel pain. There should be a gentle, Yogic touch with everything—even our spoons, forks, plates.

It reminds me of an article written by my good friend Brother David Steindl-Rast, a Benedictine monk. He wrote of how he felt God talking when he was washing dishes. If you handle them gently, he said, they make a beautiful jingling sound; but if you throw them here and there, they cry. So, dish washing can be a worship. My Master Swami Sivanandaji said, "Convert every work into Yoga with the magic wand of right attitude."

Many of us are interested in instant *samādhi*. Well, we can have it right here and now, without waiting for the *kuṇḍalinī* to be aroused and move to the *sahasrāra cakra*, if we dedicate ourselves completely.

Once we give everything to God we are renunciates; we have nothing to possess. And when we have nothing to possess, we have nothing to worry about. All worry is due to attachments and clinging to possessions. The attachment I mean is a mental attachment. What we want is a mental, rather than a physical, detachment. We can even possess things physically if we are mentally detached. This is continuous *samādhi*. We shouldn't think *samādhi* means sitting in a corner, forgetting ourselves and keeping the body still like a rock. Real *samādhi* means tranquility of mind, which is possible only when we dedicate everything and are free from all attachment.

Normally, we want everything: name, fame, money—and we become surrounded by these wants. In India, a proverb says, "If you are interested in weaving, you shouldn't keep a monkey for a pet." If you do, whenever you weave some cloth and leave it for a moment, the monkey will cut off at least a hundred strands. In the same way, if you are interested in peace, why should you have wants and possessions? They can never go together. No religion, no prophet, no saint has ever said one could have both peace and wants. Only a desireless mind, a mind free from everything, completely naked, can have peace. The *Gītā* says, "*Tyāgat śāntir anantaram.*" By total dedication, unending peace." Either give everything to the world, to the community of your fellow people, or give everything to God.

Īśvara praṇidhānā is an easy path. In one of the stanzas of the *Gītā* it is said, "Do everything in My name. Then you will get peace and joy." If we understand this, there is no reason even to read any more of these *sūtras*. But some people might want something different. Tastes differ. That is why the scriptures give different paths.

Sometimes the mother feeds the child from a different plate just for variety, but the same food still comes to the baby. It doesn't matter which plate we eat from as long as we eat. To get to the point of complete dedication, many different routes are available: hundreds of paths, religions and philosophies, all with one ultimate goal. It is immaterial what we do to achieve it as long as we achieve it.

By practicing just one of these virtues, all the rest follow. If one is perfected, concentration, meditation and even *samādhi* will come. When even one virtue becomes our nature, the mind becomes clean and tranquil. Then there is no need to practice meditation; we will automatically be meditating always.

स्थिरसुखमासनम् ॥४६॥

46. Sthira sukhamāsanam.

Sthira = steady, stable;
sukham = comfortable, happy, prosperous, easiness, pleasantly;
āsanam = posture, presence, sitting without interruption.

***Āsana* is a steady, comfortable posture.**

Āsana means the posture that brings comfort and steadiness. Any pose that brings this comfort and steadiness is an *āsana*. If you can achieve one pose, that is enough. It may sound easy, but in how many poses are we really comfortable and steady? As soon as we sit in a particular position, there is a small cramp here, a tiny pain there. We have to move this way and that. Continuously we are reminded of our legs, hands, hips and spine. Unless the body is perfectly healthy and free from all toxins and tensions, a comfortable pose is not easily obtained. Physical and mental toxins create stiffness and tension. Anything that makes us stiff can also break us. Only if we are supple will we never break.

That reminds me of a conversation between a weed and a big tree. Both grew on the bank of a swiftly running jungle river. One day the tree looked down at the tiny weed and said, "Hey, you puny little creature, why do you stand near me? Aren't you ashamed to be by my side? See how great, how big, how tall I am? How sturdy and strong? Even an elephant cannot move me. But look at you. Hah! You shouldn't have come here. People will see the difference and laugh at you. Why don't you move somewhere else?"

The weed bent its head. "Tree," the weed said, "what can I do? I didn't come here purposely. I just happen to be here. I know I'm not as strong and stiff as you. But please pardon my presence."

"All right," boomed the big tree, "but just remember your place!" This conversation happened during the rainy season. The very next day a heavy rain came, inundating the jungle and causing a terrible flood. When a river floods, it erodes the banks and pulls down anything in its way. Coming in such force, the water pulled down the great tree instantly. But the weed bent down, flattened itself completely and let the water run over it. When the flood passed, the weed rose up again. Looking this way and that, it wondered, "What happened to the great tree? I don't see it."

From far away it heard the tree's reply. "I'm being pulled down by the water. I should have been humble and simple and supple like you. Now I'm being destroyed."

What we need is the strength of steel, but with steel's flexibility—not like crude iron, which is very strong and hard but breaks. The body must be so supple it can bend any way you want it to. Such a body will always be healthy and tension-free. The moment we sit down for meditation in such a body, we'll forget it.

In order to achieve such a meditative pose, we may practice many preliminary cultural poses. This is why Hatha Yoga was created. People trying to sit quietly found they couldn't it. They encountered pain, stiffness, bile, gas, etc., and thought, "What is the reason for these things and how can we get rid of them?" They realized it was due to toxins from eating the wrong foods, at the wrong times and in the wrong quantities. These people pondered, "What is good food that won't leave toxins? What should the limit be? When is the proper time to eat?" They formed the Yogic diet, free of meat, fish, eggs, stimulants and excessive use of spices.

The next problem was what to do with the toxins already inside the body. They concluded that these could be gotten rid of by squeezing the body in all different directions. For example, they found the way to cleanse the liver, spleen and intestines was by doing the forward bending pose, *paścimottānāsana,* which is bending forward and crushing the stomach a bit. If this wasn't enough, they developed *Yoga mudrā* in order to crush it more. If toxins were still present they came up with *mayūrāsana,* the peacock pose. If this still wasn't good enough, they created *uḍḍīyāna bandha,* the stomach lift, and *nauli,* the stomach churning. When the spine was stiff and didn't want to move, they employed postures that bent it forward, backward, sideward and upside down. Although Hatha Yoga is several thousands of years old, it never becomes outdated. The truths of it are always current. They are like gold. Although other things lose their value according to time, gold is always the same.

प्रयत्नशैथिल्यानन्तसमापत्तिभ्याम् ॥४७॥

47. Prayatna śaithilyānanta samāpattibhyām.

Prayatna = persevering effort, continued effort, natural tendency for restlessness;
śaithilya = by lessening, relaxation;
ananta = infinite, unending, eternal;
samāpatti = meditation on, coalescence; **bhyām** = from both.

By lessening the natural tendency for restlessness and by meditating on the infinite, posture is mastered.

Because the senses want to taste many things, we load the system with toxins. Instead, we should control these things. Also, we can achieve steadiness through meditation on the infinite—anything great, huge, well-settled and well-established. Tiny things always shake. So, we can think of the earth or of how steady a huge mountain is.

In the Hindu tradition, the devotee thinks of *Adiśeṣa*, the thousand-hooded serpent which is said to carry the world on its head. If you take this image literally, it seems like foolishness, but this cobra stands for the gravitational force, the *prāṇa śakti*, or vital force. The force is represented by a cobra since it is believed that the cobra can live mainly on air.

But we can think of anything according to our traditions and beliefs. New Yorkers can think of the Empire State Building—of its great foundations—and how steady and firm it must be to carry over a hundred stories. A European might say, "I will be as steady as the Rock of Gibraltar." Or we can imagine we are statues or dead bodies.

If the body is still, it is easy to make the mind still. One of my masters, a great *tantric* yogi, used to say, "You need not repeat any prayers or even do *japa*. Just sit quietly for three hours in a row with no movement whatsoever, without even winking, then everything will be accomplished easily." If we sit that long, the mind comes under our control automatically.

Through the body we can put a brake on the mind. The mind will always think, "It's time for the movies. I should get up and go." Or, "I'm hungry; I must get something to eat." But if we decide, "I'm not moving for three hours," the mind ultimately has to obey us, because it needs the body's cooperation in order to get anything. That is the benefit of *āsana siddhi*, or accomplishment of *āsana*.

There are some other kinds of *siddhis* also to control the mind. *Bhojana*, or eating, *siddhi* is one. You restrict yourself to eating just a certain amount of food at a certain time each day. *Sthala siddhi* is limiting your movement by taking a vow such as, "I won't move out of this apartment for one year," or "I will not leave Manhattan for half a year." Probably the very next day, someone will offer you a free ticket to California. Tests tend to come immediately.

We all might have experienced this. The moment we decide to fast, a friend will bring us something delicious to eat. It makes us feel very sad. "Just today I decided to fast. She could have brought this cake over yesterday. Hmm. I think I'll just postpone my fast until tomorrow." In this way, we fail our exam. When we take a vow we should stick to it. There will be ample tests to tempt us to break it.

In Hindu philosophy, specifically in South Indian *Śaivism*, there are sixty-three *Śaiva Siddhānta* saints, called the *Nāyanārs*, who realized the truth by taking just one vow and sticking to it, even at the cost of their lives.

One of them, a king, vowed, "If I see holy ash on any forehead, I'll treat the bearer as Lord Śiva himself and give him all he asks for." After a while, a test came. His enemy, another king, came to know of his vow. He dressed himself as a philosophy teacher, smeared ash on his forehead, took a sharp dagger covered with a nice cloth and went to the palace. When he arrived, he asked the gatekeeper if he could see the king.

As he was ushered in, the king's minister, Tata, asked for his credentials. "I have come to teach a special scripture to the king. I am a teacher of philosophy." But the minister had some doubt. He thought he recognized the man, but he had been ordered by his king to bring in anyone with holy ash on his forehead. As he did so, he told the king, "I have my doubts about this man. I think he is your sworn enemy."

"I see the holy ash on his forehead," replied the king. "He is Lord Śiva come to teach me some scripture. Let me learn from him." Turning to his disguised enemy, he said, "Please take your seat."

The other king said, "This is a very holy scripture—very sacred and secret. It should only be taught to the proper student. You are that person. Your minister is not qualified to hear it. He should leave."

As the king was dismissing him, Tata asked, "Do you really want me to go?"

"Yes, you must." And so he was forced to leave. The king bowed before his supposed teacher; and, as he did so, was stabbed with his enemy's dagger. When the king yelled in pain, Tata rushed back in with his sword drawn. The king said, "Tata, he is my Lord. Don't do anything to him. Let no one in the country harm him. Take him safely away." With the holy name of Lord Śiva on his lips, the king fell dead. With his last breath, he had the vision of God.

The rest of the sixty-three *Nāyanār* saints invariably had this realization at the cost of their lives also. The idea behind taking one vow and sticking to it is that we become the masters of our minds. We don't give them any leniency. Once we make a vow we should stick to it unwaveringly.

Traditional Hindu marriages are made on this same principle. Once a life partner is taken by somebody, the wife becomes a goddess to the husband and he a god to her. If one partner dies, the other lives in the memory of that person—as a renunciate, never to marry again. Although the husband may be a drunkard, a devil, the wife will say, "He is my Lord. God gave him to me. Whatever he is, I will accept it."

This is a great austerity. A proverb concerning it goes, "He may be a rock, he may be grass, but still he is my husband." The wife says, "Let me adapt, adjust, accommodate. Let me live with him." By their own faith in the Lord, many women have converted their unregenerate husbands into true saints.

ततो द्वन्द्वानभिघातः ॥४८॥

48. Tato dvandvānabhighātaḥ.

Tataḥ (tato) = thereafter, in consequence;
dvandva = dualities, two by two;
anabhighātaḥ = undisturbed, not approaching.

Thereafter, one is not disturbed by the dualities.

If you make the posture firm and comfortable, then you are not affected by the dualities. Neither heat nor cold, praise nor censure, profit nor loss will affect you. You are neutral. Whether someone blesses or curses you, praises or pulls you down, whether you gain or lose a million dollars—you will be neutral. Just by posture alone you can rise above the dualities, because the mind is under your control. Even if it wants to cry, it will ask your permission first. "There is something to cry over. Can I cry?" "Yes. Otherwise, people will think you are crazy. Come on, cry a little." Just to be with the world, sometimes we must cry when other people are crying, but still we can be in control. Sometimes we must show anger. But these emotions should only come out for our use, with our permission.

तस्मिन् सति श्वासप्रश्वासयोर्गतिविच्छेदः

प्राणायामः ॥४९॥

49. Tasmin sati śvāsapraśvāsayorgativicchedaḥ prānāyāmaḥ.

Tasmin = upon that; **sati** = being acquired;
śvāsa = inhalation, hard breathing;
praśvāsa (praśvāsayor) = hard exhalation; (**yoḥ** = of these two);
gati = movement; **vicchedaḥ** = cleaving, stopping, cessation;
prāṇa = breath, vitality;
āyāmaḥ = to be stretched, to be restrained, regulation.

That [firm posture] being acquired, the movements of inhalation and exhalation should be controlled. This is *prāṇāyāma*.

After mastering the posture, we must practice control of *prāṇa* by controlling the motions of inhalation and exhalation. Some people think *prāṇāyāma* means holding the breath in as long as we can until the nerves are strained. No; our breathing should be gentle, slow and fully controlled, without any agitation. For example, in the practice of *nāḍī śuddhi,* the alternate nostril breathing, do it slowly and gently without any retention of breath to begin with. Later, you can go on to retention.

Prāṇa is the cosmic force without which nothing moves or functions. As gasoline, it moves the motorcar. As electricity, it radiates light through a bulb. Even our thoughts are moved by *prāṇa*. By *prāṇāyāma* we deal with it directly and must be very careful. It's not easy to control *prāṇa*. It takes time. In all of us there is a reserve of *prāṇa*. An automobile has a reserve tank which we can open if we run out of gas.

God is even more sensible and has given us a reserve tank that is hundreds of times greater than what we use normally. This is called *kuṇḍalinī*, or the "coiled force." People talk a lot about rousing the *kuṇḍalinī* but, when they can't control even their little day-to-day force, what is the purpose of getting into that? One should only do it after qualifying and preparing himself or herself. It is for our own safety that I say this. At the proper time, this reserve is released automatically. One shouldn't awaken it prematurely by practicing difficult or violent breathing exercises.

बाह्याभ्यन्तरस्तम्भवृत्तिर्देशकालसंख्याभिः
परिधृष्टो दीर्घसूक्ष्मः ॥५०॥

50. Bāhyābhyantara staṁbhavṛttirdeśakāla saṁkhyābhiḥ paridṛṣṭo dīrghasūkṣmaḥ.

Bāhya = external; **abhyantara** = internal;
staṁbha = stationary, suspended; **vṛitti** (vṛittir) = modification;
deśa = place, space; **kāla** = time; **saṁkhyābhiḥ** = by number;
paridṛṣṭahḥ (paridṛṣṭo) = regulated, observed; **dīrgha** = long;
sūkṣmaḥ = short, subtle.

The modifications of the life-breath are either external, internal or stationary. They are to be regulated by space, time and number and are either long or short.

Here, Patañjali talks about the retention of breath either on the exhalation or inhalation. One should be very careful about retention, however. It should be practiced properly under personal guidance, without going beyond what a teacher tells us. The *prāṇa* is very powerful energy. We shouldn't play with cobras without a proper cobra trainer nearby.

According to Patañjali, there are three types of *prāṇāyāma*: the *bāhya vṛtti, ābhyantara vṛtti* and *staṁbha vṛtti*—-or inhaling, exhaling and retention. Normally, in *prāṇāyāma* we teach only inward retention of the breath; this is easy and safe. After we have experienced the benefit of that, we can practice outward retention also.

Patañjali also includes variations on these *prāṇāyāmas* according to *deśa, kāla* and *saṁkhyā*, or place, time and count. Place means where we place our attention while breathing: the base of the spine, its middle or higher regions, etc. Time means how long we retain the breath. Count refers to the amount of counts with which we take the breath in and with which we send it out and the number with which we hold it. In the normal practice of *nāḍī śuddhi* we keep a ratio of one to two. If we take the breath in for a count of five, we send it out for a count of ten. Of course, we do not send out double the amount of breath, but we send the breath out twice as slowly as it entered. Thus, we can gain control over our exhalation. Usually we exhale more quickly than we inhale. In this practice, we try to reverse that procedure and gain mastery over the involuntary muscles.

By regulating the *prāṇa*, we regulate our minds, because the two always go together. If one is controlled, the other is automatically controlled as well. That is why *prāṇāyāma* is given by Patañjali and is so very important.

Control and discipline are very necessary in our lives. Without discipline nothing can be achieved. The whole world functions in a regulated, orderly way. If everything were merely haphazard, no great scientific inventions could be possible, nor would they be necessary. If the sun, moon and earth didn't rotate in a disciplined way, how could calculations be made to send up a rocket? If all of a sudden the earth decided, "I'm tired of rotating at this speed. Why don't I move a little faster?" where would the Apollo Mission have been? Scientists can split atoms because atoms function in an orderly way at a particular velocity.

Throughout nature we can observe discipline. It is only human beings who, in the name of freedom, say, "I can just do anything I want.

I don't want discipline. Nothing should bind me." Nobody need bind us or tell us the way if we already know how to follow a particular discipline. But when we do not know, we should listen to those who do know what to do. "I have a car that can go one hundred and twenty miles an hour, and I know how to drive it. Why should I stick to a fifty-five mile per hour speed limit? Why should I pay attention to traffic lights?" Do all these disciplines exist to enslave us? No; they are for our own safety. If I am not controlled by radar or helicopter patrol, I will be itching to press down the gas pedal a bit more. Personally, I have that weakness; and so I thank the people who have set up controls. Otherwise, I might not know my limitations. If we take these disciplines in the right sense we will welcome them.

Sukha pūrvaka is the easy, comfortable breathing with an inhalation/exhalation ratio of one to two—starting with five counts in, ten counts out and gradually increasing the count to ten/twenty. After practicing this for a while, we can add some retention: inhale for ten counts, retain for five, exhale for twenty. Then keeping the ten/twenty ratio, we can increase the retention gradually from five to fifteen, then to twenty-five, to forty and stop there. From that point on, the number of *prāṇāyāmas* we do should be increased.

Sometimes people read about a one/four/two ratio in a Yoga book and immediately begin their practice there. This can be unhealthy and dangerous. It's not the ratio with which you practice this *prāṇāyāma* that will help you, but the amount of *prāṇāyāmas* you do at a stretch. So, even without retention, if we can do thirty or forty *nāḍī śuddhis* at a stretch, it will be very beneficial.

बाह्याभ्यन्तरविषयाक्षेपी चतुर्थः ॥५१॥

51. Bāhyābhyantara viṣayākṣepī caturthaḥ.

Bāhya = external; **abhyantara** = internal; **viṣaya** = object;
ākṣepī = transcend, abandonment, throw way out;
caturthaḥ = the fourth.

There is a fourth kind of *prāṇāyāma* that occurs during concentration on an internal or external object.

The fourth type of *prāṇāyāma* happens automatically. We do not have to concentrate on retention of breath here, because it will stop automatically just by concentrating the mind on a chosen object or idea. This is also called *kevala kuṁbhaka*, the easy, unintentional retention which occurs automatically in deep meditation. When the mind comes to a standstill, the *prāṇa* automatically does the same. When we are deeply interested in something we are reading, the breath stops. If at that time we look at the breath, we will hardly be breathing. If something disturbs our concentration, we will sigh deeply to make up for that retention. Similarly, if all of a sudden some terrible news comes to us, the breath will stop completely. Afterward, we will take in a deep breath. That is because the sudden news stops the mind and, along with it, the breathing.

When breath retention happens during our *japa* or meditation, it is good. It won't happen unless the system is ready. If we are deep enough, the breath might even stop for a few minutes. In *samādhi* it stops for several hours. People don't die, because there is no wastage of energy. It is being preserved.

Normally, we are expending a lot of energy, so more must be constantly put into our systems. It is like when we drive a car, our ignition, horn, indicator lights, etc., all take current from the battery, which is thus being drained. At the same time, the dynamo within the engine compartment puts in more current, and so the battery retains its life. If the dynamo puts in too much current, the battery overheats and dies. But there is a cut-out that takes care of this, disconnecting the dynamo from the battery before it can overheat. Even though the dynamo continues to produce current, it won't go to the battery. Unfortunately, we don't have a cut-out. There is nothing to limit us but ourselves.

When we switch off the engine and park the car, there is no wastage of energy from the battery and, therefore, no need to put more energy in. In the same way, while we talk to one another we use up our human electricity—the *prāṇa*—and have to put more in. Our breathing system is the dynamo. We inhale in order to take in more *prāṇa* to maintain the battery at a certain level. If we don't talk, there is no need to breathe in so much. Also, if we move our limbs we must put in more energy. If we keep the body still, we conserve energy; but still the mind moves and consumes a little energy, so we still have to breathe in. If we do not even think, there is no wastage at all and breathing is unnecessary. *Kuṁbhaka* is automatically achieved.

Saint Thirūmular said, "Wherever the mind goes, the *prāṇa* follows." They are inseparable. If the mind is controlled first, the breath is controlled. But which is subtler, mind or breath? Which is easier to handle, a subtle thing or a gross one? Always the gross thing. Which is easier to control: steam, water or ice ? To keep ice in its place, we just have to put it down. For water, we need some sort of vessel. But for steam, even that is not enough; a covered cylinder is needed. Even though ice, water and steam are one and the same compound, they are in different stages. Similarly, it is easier to control *prāṇa* in a grosser manifestation than in a subtle one. So, first we learn to control the physical body, then the movement of the breath, then the senses and finally the mind. It is very scientific, gradual and easy.

ततः क्षीयते प्रकाशावरणम् ॥५२॥

52. Tataḥ kṣīyate prakāśāvaraṇam.

Tataḥ = therefore, as a result, from that;
kṣīyate = is destroyed;
prakāśa = inner light; **āvaraṇam** = veil.

As its result, the veil over the inner Light is destroyed.

Patañjali now comes to the benefit of *prāṇāyāma*. We destroy the veil that covers the inner light. *Prakāśa*, the light within, is covered by a veil of mental darkness. What is the best way to remove a veil? By pulling the threads out, one by one, until it exists no more.

The mind is a veil woven of thoughts. It has no substance by itself. If we pull the thoughts out one after the other, when they have all been removed, there is no mind left. It is like a heap of sugar. If we remove each grain of sugar, one after the other, the heap no longer exists. In fact, the name "heap" is absurd; because, in reality, no heap exists, only sugar. Wood, arranged in various ways, gets called different things: chair, table, bench or firewood. Different appearances get different names. But it is only the appearance that changes; the basis can never be destroyed. Our basis is the Self. As long as we identify with the body or mind, we feel we are mortal. *Prāṇāyāma* indirectly helps us to understand the Oneness, the never-changing One, because it removes the veil. And it is an easy practice. Not many people come to meditation class, but hundreds and thousands come for *āsanas* and *prāṇāyāma.*

धारणासु च योग्यता मनसः ॥५३॥

53. Dhāraṇāsu ca yogyatā manasaḥ.

Dhāraṇāsu = for concentration; **ca** = and;
yogyatā = fitness, readiness;
manasaḥ = of the mind.

And the mind becomes fit for concentration.

If the *prakāśa āvaraṇam* is removed, although the mind is not completely annihilated, its density is reduced and it becomes more capable of practicing *dhāraṇā.*

स्वविषयासंप्रयोगे चित्तस्वरूपानुकार इवेन्द्रियाणां प्रत्याहारः ॥५४॥

54. Svaviṣayāsaṁprayoge cittasvarūpānukāra ivendriyāṇām pratyāhāraḥ.

Sva = their own, its own; **viṣaya** = objects;
asaṁprayoge = in non-contact, upon disconnecting, upon withdrawal;
citta = mind-stuff; **svarūpa** = its own nature;
anukāra = imitate; **iva** = as it were, as if;
indriyāṇām = of the senses;
pratyāhāraḥ = to turn away, avert completely.

When the senses withdraw themselves from the objects and imitate, as it were, the nature of the mind-stuff, this is *pratyāhārah.*

With *prāṇāyāma*, the mind is still not completely fit, because there are other things that will try to pull the mind here and there—namely, the senses. They will always tell the mind, "Ah, there is a wonderful thing in this showcase. Come on, why not buy it?" Or, "Do you smell that wonderful odor? Get ready. Wash your hands. Some nice things are being cooked." The mind might even be quiet, but the nose won't allow it to remain so. And the moment the nose says that something is being prepared, the tongue says, "The saliva is ready," and the eyes say, "Can I have a look at it?" We must have a good rein over these turbulent senses.

In the *Bhagavad Gītā* the battle with the senses is explained, in an esoteric way, as a battlefield. The battlefield is the world, the turbulent life which distracts us. Arjuna, the individual self, is confused by it and goes to the Lord, Sri Kṛṣṇa, for help.

"Sir," he says, "I have a limited capacity. I doubt if I can win the war by myself. You take the reins and drive my war chariot for me. Let me sit quietly behind You and do what You want me to do."

When Kṛṣṇa becomes his charioteer, Arjuna becomes more steadfast and calm. The chariot's white horses—the eyes, nose, tongue, ears and sense of feeling—are called the *pāñcha indriyas*, or five sensory organs. These organs should be offered to God's service. When they are engaged in that manner they are controlled. Unless they are properly engaged, they will always drag the mind outside.

When the mind is withdrawn from the sense objects, the sense organs also withdraw themselves from their respective objects and, thus, are said to imitate the mind. If the senses are allowed to see outside, they try to grasp pictures of the outside world. If they are turned inward, they will see the purity of the mind and won't take the color of the world outside.

The senses are like a mirror. Turned outward, they reflect the outside; turned inward, they reflect the pure light. By themselves, the senses are innocent, but when allowed to turn outside they attract everything and transfer those messages to the mind, making it restless. Turned inward, they find peace by taking the form of the mind itself.

The senses are, in effect, a gateway that allows externals to come into the mind. For example, if we look at a cabinet, we can only understand it as a cabinet if our mind takes that form. This is the law of perception. That's why when we concentrate on something holy, the mind takes that form. When the mind retains it, we get those pictures even in our dreams. When we have sense control we only allow the mind to take the forms we want.

In the Hindu system, the senses are made to engage in spiritual pursuits. Each temple contains colorful things everywhere—beautiful ornaments, lovely flowers, fine dresses adorning the deities, shiny golden chariots—a feast to the eye. By burning incense, the nose is catered to. By *prasād*, the tongue is satisfied. But you are seeing and eating in the name of the Divine and are grateful to God for all these things. In India, if you want to hear beautiful music free of charge, go to a religious festival. At other times, people must pay thousands of *rupees* to hear the same artists who play for free in a temple. And the musicians play facing God, not the people. And the food is prepared first for God; then everyone else can eat it.

Pratyāhāra is another way of controlling the mind. To gain mastery in it is not easy. You shouldn't delude yourself into thinking you've gained mastery after even a few years of practice. Any minute, there can be a slip. For example, if a man is interested in observing strict celibacy, he should stay away from women. He need not dislike women, but he shouldn't casually associate with them, even to hug and kiss them as sisters. Although his mouth will call them "sister," his senses will take the action in a different way.

To achieve the full value of Yoga we must stick to all these precautions and qualify ourselves. The *Gītā* says, "Yoga is not for the person who eats a lot or for one who starves. Yoga is not for the person who sleeps too much or for one who is always keeping vigil." We shouldn't go to extremes but should have limitations.

Now we come to the last *sūtra* of the second book.

ततः परमा वश्यतेन्द्रियाणाम् ॥५५॥

55. Tataḥ paramā vaśyatendriyāṇām.

Tataḥ = thence, from that; **paramā** = supreme;
vaśyatā = mastery; **indriyāṇām** = of the senses.

Then follows supreme mastery over the senses.

By the proper practice of *pratyāhāra*, your senses come fully under your control. They become obedient horses, taking you wherever you want. You become a complete master over them. We shouldn't think we lose anything by avoiding sensual pleasures. If our senses try to pull us somewhere we should feel, "No; I'm not going to satisfy you." Although we might feel a little tension at first, it is just momentary. After that we'll really feel proud: "Ah, I have gained some mastery." If we satisfy the senses, we might feel momentary pleasure followed by a greater dejection afterward. The happiness we can receive by mastery lasts longer than temporary joys. We should all become masters. That is true freedom and real victory. If you are free from your own mind and senses, nothing can bind you; then you are really free. Even imperial power, even dictatorship, can never bind you. You are not afraid of anything.

This isn't the birthright of just a few people. It is everyone's. But we should build up our mastery, never allowing the mind to fall back. If we have that control, we can do whatever we want, find peace and joy within and share the same with all humanity.

Book Three

Vibhūti Pāda

Portion on Accomplishments

This third book is called the *Vibhūti Pāda.* The *vibhūti* are all the accomplishments which come as by-products of your Yoga practice. They are also sometimes called the *siddhis,* or supernatural powers. These powers begin to come with the practice of the final three limbs of Rāja Yoga: *dhāraṇā* (concentration), *dhyāna* (meditation) and *samādhi* (contemplation).

Note on Books Three and Four:
I have translated all the sūtras *of Books Three and Four; however, I have chosen not to comment on them all. I have taken the ones I have found most useful for the understanding of Yoga aspirants and have left out the others. Those readers who wish to study more about the* sūtras *that have no commentaries here, can consult one of the books on the* Yoga Sūtras *listed in the Selected Reading.*

देशबन्धश्चित्तस्य धारणा ॥१॥

1. **Deśabandhaścittasya dhāraṇā.**

Deśa = place, location; **bandhaḥ** = binding; **cittasya** = of the mind; **dhāraṇā** = concentration.

***Dhāraṇā* is the binding of the mind to one place, object or idea.**

When the *cittam*, or sum-total of the mind, is being bound by one thing or bound in one place, it is in *dhāraṇā*. In other words, in *dhāraṇā* you are training the mind. It is the beginning of meditation. Concentration is the beginning of meditation; meditation is the culmination of concentration. They are more or less inseparable.

Normally, we see our mind running here and there. When we try to fix it on one thing, within a fraction of a second we see it somewhere else.

Imagine you just want to fix the mind on a beautiful rose. The best practice would be to keep a physical rose in front of you as you begin, because it's easier for the mind. Concrete objects, symbols or images are very helpful for our beginning practice. It's not that easy for the mind to grasp something abstract or even to visualize something. So, keep a rose or a flame or a picture in front of you.

If it is an idea on which you wish to concentrate, at least have something physical to remind you of that. While you look at this object, think of the idea connected with it. This is where the practice of *trādak*, or gazing, also comes in handy.

Trādak is actually gazing at something, sometimes without even blinking. Don't strain the eyes. Just look at your object as long as you can. You'll be able to look longer if you put your mind on the idea behind the object: how beautiful it is, what a great gift has come from a thorny bush, etc. Like that, associated ideas will come in. When you get involved in those things, even the gaze will be forgotten; but you will still be gazing without blinking. Don't try to gaze just for the purpose of gazing; if you do that the eyes will get tired quickly.

After a while, you can gently close the eyes and try to bring a mental picture of your object of concentration. First it is outside; then you try to bring it within the mind. It might come for a while, and then you lose it. Again, open the eyes. Slowly learn to grasp it within the mind alone. That means you will be developing that impression in your mind. It is something like in photography: you take a picture; it's there on the film. How do you know whether it's there or not? You develop it. If nothing comes, you have to make another picture. It is the same with the practice of *trādak*.

As you think, so you become. If you think of the rose, the mind will take the form of the rose. After a while, you will easily be able to see it within, without the aid of any physical object outside. At that stage you no longer need altars and this and that.

Even in your *pūjā* (worship service) this is what is supposed to be done. You do the *pūjā* physically and then sit back and try to bring the whole picture in your mind. How did you begin the *pūjā*? What did you do next, next, next? Bring the whole procedure to mind in the proper sequence. Once it becomes easy, you don't even need the physical objects or *pūjā* anymore.

All this is part of *dhāraṇā*. As you look at the rose, the mind will try to go somewhere. The minute you begin, the mind will say, "Ah, yes, I remember, she sent me a rose like that for my last birthday." See? Then the rose is gone from your mind; *she* is there. And then, "After that we had dinner. Ah, it was the best dinner. Then we went to the movies. What was that movie? *King Kong*?" It will all happen within two minutes. From the rose to *King Kong* in two minutes. Even less than two minutes. So, on what are you meditating now? Not on a rose, but on *King Kong*.

The mind is like that. But it doesn't matter. That's the nature of the mind. There's no point in getting frustrated. At least at that point, say, "God, where am I? How far have I come from the rose to *King Kong*? Shame on you, my little fellow; come on, let's go back to the rose."

Never give up. And never think, "Oh, I am unfit for meditation." That is the biggest mistake many people make. They think that the minute they sit and close their eyes everything should be beautiful. If the mind runs here and there they say, "Meditation is not my thing." But it's like practicing piano or playing guitar or cooking. How many times have you cooked your fingers instead of the vegetables? Nothing is learned that easily. While learning to bicycle, how many times did you fall down? So, keep trying. Persevere. Remember what Patañjali says in Book 1, *sūtra* 14: "Practice becomes firmly grounded when well attended to for a long time, without break and in all earnestness."

This very practice itself is called concentration: the mind running, your bringing it back; its running, your bringing it back. You are taming a monkey. Once it's tamed, it will just listen to you. You will be able to say, "Okay, sit there quietly." And it will. At that point you are meditating. Until then you are training yourself to meditate. Training your mind to meditate is what is called *dhāraṇā.*

तत्र प्रत्ययैकतानता ध्यानम् ॥२॥

2. Tatra pratyayaikatānatā dhyānam.

Tatra = therein; **pratyaya** = cognition; **eka** = one, single; **tānatā** = continued flow; **dhyānam** = meditation.

***Dhyāna* is the continuous flow of cognition toward that object.**

The Hindu scriptures give a beautiful example of this "continuous flow." They say it is like pouring oil from one pot into another. It is a continuous string; it doesn't break. The mind is fixed. Communication between meditator and object of meditation is steady. That's what is called *dhyāna.* Normally, what we are doing when we say we are meditating is *dhāraṇā.* After long practice of *dhāraṇā,* gradually the "flow of cognition" gets a little longer and it becomes *dhyāna.*

When would you know that you have really meditated? There are some signs for that. Say you come and sit for meditation at 4:30. Meditation is assigned for an hour. The bell rings at 5:30. If you feel, "What, who rang the bell this soon? I just sat down five minutes ago," then you may have been meditating. But when you feel five minutes as one hour, you are not meditating; you are still concentrating.

Time has no meaning in meditation and space also is lost. You don't know where you are. If you break that meditation all of a sudden, you may wonder, "What happened to my body?" Even the body is forgotten in real meditation. You are above time and space; you are out of the body. When I say "out of the body," don't think I mean that you are traveling in space or anything like that. I mean, the mind transcends body consciousness.

In this sense, meditation is similar to sleep. You don't know you have a body. Even though you still have it, you don't know it. If your sleep is really deep and someone comes and takes your body somewhere else, you don't even know. When you wake up, you will say, "I was sleeping on the couch; who brought me to the bed?"

There are other signs of meditation also. In the beginning you feel so light when you transcend the body. Sometimes you get beautiful visions connected with the object of your meditation—or sometimes not connected, but still something beautiful and elevating. Sometimes you won't see visions. You will simply see beautiful light; you will seem to be bathed in beautiful moonlight. Or sometimes you may just hear beautiful sounds like the roaring of the ocean, the sound of a gong or the beautiful notes of a flute. These are all various signs you may come across. Normally, I don't say these things much because once you hear that, you may *imagine* it is happening to you. Instead, it should just happen.

तदेवार्थमात्रनिर्भासं स्वरूपशून्यमिव समाधिः ॥३॥

3. Tad evārthamātra nirbhāsam svarūpa śūnyam iva samādhiḥ.

Tad = that [meditation]; **eva** = indeed; **artha** = object, objective; **mātra** = alone, only; **nirbhāsam** = shining forth, illuminating; **svarūpa** = its own form; **śūnyam** = devoid, empty; **iva** = as if; **samādhiḥ** = contemplation, profound absorption, bringing into harmony.

***Samādhi* is the same meditation when there is the shining of the object alone, as if devoid of form.**

There is not much I can say about this one. You will easily understand when you have a little experience. Meditation culminates in the state of *samādhi.* It's not that you practice *samādhi.* Nobody can consciously practice *samādhi.* Our effort is there only up to meditation. You put all your effort in *dhāraṇā.* It becomes effortless in *dhyāna,* and you are just there, knowing that you are in meditation.

But in *samādhi,* you don't even know that. You are not there to know it because you are that. You think first with a lot of interruptions; that is *dhāranā.* Then when you become what you think, that is *samādhi.* In meditation you have three things: meditator, the meditation and the object meditated upon. In *samādhi* there is neither the object or the meditator. There is no feeling of "I am meditating on that."

To give a scientific analogy, if you keep on adding drops of an alkaline solution to an acid, at one point the solution becomes alkaline. At that point you are simply adding alkali to alkali; there's no more acid there. The giver and receiver become one. Earlier, the receiver was an "acid-head," and the giver was alkali. As you add the alkali, drop by drop, and, keep testing it with your litmus paper, at one point, all of a sudden you notice you are no longer an acid-head! Who are you? The same alkali as God. You and God become one. That's *samādhi.*

It's rather difficult to put it in words. If you just keep working, you will know what *samādhi* is. Of course, there are different lower *samādhis,* as we talked about in the first book, where you attain that level and then come back. These are *samādhis* connected with form, with idea, with bliss and with pure ego (*savitarka, savicāra, sa-ānanda* and *sa-asmita samādhi*). All these four still leave some parts of the mind with hidden desires. You are not completely free. The ideas in the mind are not completely roasted. They could still germinate again. That's why all these four are called *sabīja samādhi. Bīja* means seed. They are with seed. Don't think you are all clean and everything is okay. As long as the seed is in the bag it seems to be innocent. But the minute you take one seed out, dig a little hole, put it in and pour a little water, then up it comes again. The sprouting tendency is still there.

As long as you have that tendency, you are still in the *sabīja* or *savikalpa samādhi.* But once you get completely roasted, even that germinating capacity goes away. The seeds are still there. In all external appearance they are the same. But, even if they are put into holes and watered they won't germinate.

What does this mean? All the thoughts, all the desires, become selfless. Selfishness is the germ that sprouts, saying, "*I* want it!" When the selfishness is completely taken out, you become germless. That is called *nirbīja samādhi* or *nirvikalpa samādhi.*

One who has achieved this may look similar to anyone else. But the burnt nature of his or her mental seeds is the difference between ordinary people and the *jīvanmuktas* (liberated beings). They also eat, sleep and do everything like everybody else. They may be doing anything, but they are not affected by what they do. There is no moisture of attachment to cause sprouting. They are living liberated people. Liberation is not something you experience when you die. While living, you should be liberated. *Jīvanmukta: mukta* means liberated, *jīvan*, while living.

That is the final state of *samādhi.* It is not sitting stiffly with eyes closed, as some people think. If sitting like a statue is what you call *samādhi*, all the rocks in the garden must be in deep *samādhi.* No. You will be useful; you will be active—more active than other people. Your actions are more perfect than other people's. You are dynamic, but you look static.

Opposites meet; extremes look alike. A top that is not rotating is motionless. The same top at its highest velocity also looks motionless. Lack of light is darkness. Keep on increasing the light, you get blinded by the light and feel you are in darkness again. A totally *sattvic* person appears to be very quiet; a totally *tamasic* one is also quiet.

त्रयमेकत्र संयमः ॥४॥

4. Trayam ekatra saṁyamaḥ.

Trayam = consisting of three; **ekatra** = upon one;
saṁyamaḥ = quintessential concentration of mind.

The practice of these three [*dhāraṇā, dhyāna* and *samādhi*] upon one object is called *saṁyamaḥ.*

From this practice, come the *siddhis.* You dive deeply into an object or idea, and it releases its secrets. In a way, scientists have done *saṁyama* on the atomic particles. The particles released their energy, and the scientists got the knowledge of them. They accomplished the truth behind the particles. *Saṁyama* is usually done on objects or ideas connected with some results. When the results come, you call them *siddhis* or *vibhūti.*

तज्जयात् प्रज्ञालोकः ॥५॥

5. Tajjayāt prajñālokaḥ.

Tat = that; **jayāt** = from its mastery;
prajñā = true or transcendental knowledge;
ālokaḥ = glimmer, lustre, light, beholding.

By the mastery of *saṁyama* comes the light of knowledge.

This means that the truth behind the object on which we do *saṁyama* becomes known to us. That is what we call discovery. The truth was "covered" before; now we "discover" it. It's not that anyone creates anything new. Some truth was hidden. By *saṁyama,* we understood what it was. That's the true meaning of discovery.

तस्य भूमिषु विनियोगः ॥६॥

6. Tasya bhūmiṣu viniyogaḥ.

Tasya = its; **bhūmiṣu** = in stages;
viniyogaḥ = employment, application (practice).

Its practice is to be accomplished in stages.

त्रयमन्तरङ्गं पूर्वेभ्यः ॥७॥

7. Trayam antaraṅgam pūrvebhyaḥ.

Trayam = triad, the three together; **antar** = internal, interior; **aṅgam** = limb, part; **pūrvebhyaḥ** = from those preceding.

These three [*dhāraṇā, dhyāna* and *samādhi*] are more internal than the preceding five limbs.

In Aṣṭāṅga Yoga, *dhāraṇā, dhyāna* and *samādhi* are the more *antaraṅga*, or inner practices. Even to practice *yama* and *niyama*, you need the outside world. How will you practice non-injury if there is nothing outside to injure? How to deal with the outside world is taught through *yama* and *niyama*. Even your body is an outside world for you, so in *āsana* you do something with your body; in *prāṇāyāma* you do something with your *prāṇa*; in *pratyāhāra* you do something with your senses. But *dhāraṇā, dhyāna* and *samādhi* are totally inward. They are on the mental level. That is what Patañjali means by saying these three are more inner than the preceding five.

तदपि बहिरङ्गं निर्बीजस्य ॥८॥

8. Tad api bahiraṅgam nirbījasya.

Tad = these; **api** = even; **bahir** = external, exterior; **aṅgam** = limb, part; **nirbījasya** = of the seedless.

Even these three are external to the seedless *samādhi*.

When these three are compared with the preceding five steps, they are more internal. But when they are compared with *nirbīja samādhi*, they become external and gross.

व्युत्थाननिरोधसंस्कारयोरभिभवप्रादुर्भावौ निरोधक्षणचित्तान्वयो निरोधपरिणामः ॥९॥

9. Vyutthāna nirodha saṁskārayor abhibhava prādurbhāvau nirodha kṣaṇa cittānvayo nirodha pariṇāmaḥ.

Vyutthāna = rising up, awakening; **nirodha** = suppressive, checked;
saṁskārayoḥ = of the two impressions;
abhibhava = disappear; **prāduḥ** = arising;
bhāvau = appear; **nirodha** = suppression, checked;
kṣaṇa = moment; **citta** = mind; **anvayaḥ** = conjunction;
nirodha = suppression, checked;
pariṇāmaḥ = transformation, development.

The impressions which normally arise are made to disappear by the appearance of suppressive efforts, which in turn create new mental modifications. The moment of conjunction of mind and new modifications is *nirodha pariṇāmaḥ*.

तस्य प्रशान्तवाहिता संस्कारात् ॥१०॥

10. Tasya praśānta vāhitā saṁskārāt.

Tasya = of that; **praśānta** = pacified, calm, composed;
vāhitā = flow; **saṁskārāt** = through habit, from training.

The flow of *nirodha pariṇāmaḥ* becomes steady through habit.

सर्वार्थतैकाग्रतयोः क्षयोदयौ चित्तस्य समाधिपरिणामः ॥११॥

11. Sarvārthataikāgratayoḥ kṣayodayau cittasya samādhipariṇāmaḥ.

Sarva = all, everything; **arthatā** = object, wordliness; (sarvārthatā = distractedness, attending to everything); **ekāgratayoḥ** = undisturbed attention, attending to one thing (of both of these); **kṣaya** = declining, destruction [of the former]; **udayau** = appearance [of the latter]; **cittasya** = of the mind; **samādhi** = absorption, harmony; **pariṇāmaḥ** = development, maturity.

When there is a decline in distractedness and appearance of one-pointedness, then comes *samādhiḥ pariṇāmaḥ* (development in *samādhi*).

शान्तोदितौ तुल्यप्रत्ययौ चित्तस्यैकाग्रता परिणामः ॥१२॥

12. Śāntoditau tulyapratyayau cittasyaikāgratā pariṇāmaḥ.

Śānta = quieted, subsiding, past [śānti, pacified]; **uditau** = rising, present (these both); **tulya** = equal, identical; **pratyayau** = both adjacent concepts, both adjacent ideas; **cittasya** = of the mind; **ekāgratā** = one pointed undisturbed attention; **pariṇāmaḥ** = transformation, development, maturity.

Then again when the subsiding past and rising present images are identical, there is *ekāgratā pariṇāmaḥ* (one pointedness).

एतेन भूतेन्द्रियेषु धर्मलक्षणावस्थापरिणामा व्याख्याताः ॥१३॥

13. Etena bhūtendriyeṣu dharma lakṣaṇāvasthā pariṇāmā vyākhyātāḥ.

Etena = by this; **bhūta** = in the elements;
indriyeṣu = and in the senses (all elements and senses);
dharma = established visible characteristics;
lakṣanaḥ = mark, indicated invisible characteristic indirectly expressed due to time differences;
avasthā = condition, state;
pariṇāmāḥ = transformations, developments;
vyākhyātāḥ = described, explained.

By this [what has been said in the preceding three *sūtras*], the transformations of the visible characteristics, time factors and conditions of elements and senses are also described.

शान्तोदिताव्यपदेश्यधर्मानुपाती धर्मी ॥१४॥

14. Śāntoditāvyapadeśya dharmānupātī dharmī.

Śānta = latent past, quieted; **udita** = uprisen present;
avyapadeśya = unmanifested, indescribable;
dharma = nature, essential quality; **anupātī** = following through;
dharmī = substratum.

It is the substratum (*Prakṛti*) that by nature goes through latent, uprising and unmanifested phases.

क्रमान्यत्वं परिणामान्यत्वे हेतुः ॥१५॥

15. Kramānyatvam pariṇāmānyatve hetuḥ.

Krama = step, succession; **anyatvam** = different phases, otherness; **pariṇāma** = evolution, transformation, development; **anyatve** = in the differences, in the otherness; **hetuḥ** = cause.

The succession of these different phases is the cause of the differences in stages of evolution.

परिणामत्रयसंयमादतीतानागतज्ञानम् ॥१६॥

16. Pariṇāma traya saṁyamād atītānāgata jñānam.

Pariṇāma = change, transformation, moving from one stage of evolution to another; **traya** = threefold, triad; **samyamāt** = from saṁyama on; **atīta** = past; **anāgata** = future; **jñānam** = knowledge.

By practicing *saṁyama* on the three stages of evolution comes knowledge of past and future.

In this and in the following *sūtras*, Patañjali describes various *saṁyamas* and the *siddhis* which will result.

शब्दार्थप्रत्ययानामितरेतराध्यासात् संकरस्तत्प्र
विभाग संयमात् सर्वभूतरुतज्ञानम् ॥१७॥

17. **Śabdārtha pratyayānām itaretarādhyāsāt saṁkarastatpravibhāga saṁyamāt sarva bhūta ruta jñānaṁ.**

Śabda = sound, word; **artha** = meaning, purpose;
pratyayānām = presented ideas, thought;
itaretara = one with another [itara-itara = the other-another];
adhyāsāt = from superimposition;
saṁkaraḥ = mixed up [with each other], confused together;
tat = their; **pravibhāga** = distinction;
saṁyamāt = from saṁyama on; **sarva** = all;
bhūta = any living being (divine, human, animal, vegetal);
ruta = any cry or noise; **jñānam** = knowledge.

A word, its meaning and the idea behing it are normally confused because of superimposition upon one another. By *saṁyama* on the word [or sound] produced by any being, knowledge of its meaning is obtained.

संस्कारसाक्षात्करणात् पूर्वजातिज्ञानम् ॥१८॥

18. **Saṁskārasākṣātkaraṇāt pūrvajātijñānaṁ.**

Saṁskāra = activator impression [the mind];
sākṣat = from direct perception;
karaṇāt = from intuitive [perception], from [saṁyama on], immediate cause;
pūrva = previous; **jāti** = birth; **jñānam** = knowledge.

By direct perception, through *saṁyama*, of one's mental impressions, knowledge of past birth is obtained.

प्रत्ययस्य परचित्तज्ञानम् ॥१९॥

19. Pratyayasya paracitta jñānam.

Pratyayasya = of the thought, of belief, of the notion, of the idea, of the conviction;
para = other's, of another; **citta** = field of mental images;
jñānam = knowledge.

By *saṁyama* on the distinguishing signs of other's bodies, knowledge of their mental images is obtained.

न च तत् सालम्बनं तस्याविषयीभूतत्वात् ॥२०॥

20. Na ca tat sālaṁbanam tasyāviṣayī bhūtatvāt.

Na = not; **ca** = and; **tat** = that;
sālaṁbanam = together with support; **tasya** = its, of that;
aviṣayī = not proper object, being out of reach, without object;
bhūtatvāt = from existing nature, from beingness.

But this does not include the support in the person's mind [such as the motive behind the thought, etc.], as that is not the object of the *saṁyama*.

कायरूपसंयमात् तद्ग्राह्य शक्तिस्तम्भे
चक्षुःप्रकाशासंप्रयोगेऽन्तर्धानम् ॥२१॥

21. **Kāyarūpa saṁyamāt tadgrāhya śakti staṁbhe cakṣuḥ prakāśāsaṁprayoge'ntardhānam.**

Kāya = body; **rūpa** = form; **saṁyamat** = from saṁyama on; **tad** = that; **grāhya** = perception, grasped; **śakti** = power, ability; **staṁbhe** = to be checked, suspended; **cakṣuḥ** = eye; **prakāśa** = light; **asaṁprayoge** = upon being disconnected; **antardhānam** = disappearance.

By *saṁyama* on the form of one's body and by checking the power of perception by intercepting light from the eyes of the observer, the body becomes invisible.

Oh boy! Do you want to become invisible? When you want to see something, the form comes onto the retina, gets recorded and then you see the image. Until that is done, you cannot see. So, if by *saṁyama* on my own body, I disconnect the light that would affect your retina, no image will be formed on your retina, and you won't see any form.

एतेन शब्दाद्यन्तर्धानमुक्तम् ॥२२॥

22. **Etena śabdādyantardhānam uktam.**

Etena = in this way; **śabda** = sound; **adi** = et cetera; **antardhānam** = disappearance; **uktam** = has also been spoken about [is explained].

In the same way, the disappearance of sound [and touch, taste smell, etc.] is explained.

सोपक्रमं निरुपक्रमं च कर्म तत्संयमाद
परान्तज्ञानमरिष्टेभ्यो वा ॥२३॥

23. Sopakramam nirupakramam ca karma tat saṁyamād aparānta jñānam ariṣṭebhyo vā.

Sopakramam = active manifestation;
nirupakramam = inactive manifestation; ***ca*** = and;
karma = latent results from past actions; **tat** = that;
saṁyamāt = from saṁyama on; **apara** = final, distant;
anta =end; (aparānta = final/distant end, death);
jñānam = knowledge;
ariṣṭebhyaḥ = and the portents too (i.e. with the karmas); **vā** = or.

***Karmas* are of two kinds: quickly manifesting and slowly manifesting. By *saṁyama* on them, or on the portents of death, the knowledge of the time of death is obtained.**

मैत्र्यादिषु बलानि ॥२४॥

24. Maitryādiṣu balāni.

Maitri = friendliness; **adiṣu** = et cetera, et cetera;
balāni = strengths, powers.

By *saṁyama* on friendliness and other such qualities, the power to transmit them is obtained.

बलेषु हस्तिबलादीनि ॥२५॥

25. Baleṣu hasti balādīni

baleṣu = on the strengths; **hasti** = elephant;
bala = strengh; **adīni** = et cetera, et cetera.

By *saṁyama* on the strength of elephants and other such animals, their strength is obtained.

That means you do *saṁyama* on a very strong animal; for example, an elephant. It is not that the elephant will come to you, but the strength of the elephant. You acquire that strength. If you do *saṁyama* on the Rock of Gibraltar, you will become real rocky. That means you become so heavy. You just simply stand on the scale and weigh 110 pounds. Stand on it doing *saṁyama* on the Rock of Gibraltar, the scale will immediately burst. In the same way, if you do *saṁyama* on a feather, the scale will record only zero. You can lighten yourself; you can make yourself heavy. It's all achieved by *saṁyama*. Do it; try it. Nice things will happen.

प्रवृत्त्यालोकन्यासात् सूक्ष्मव्यवहित विप्रकृष्टज्ञानम् ॥२६॥

26. Pravṛttyāloka nyāsāt sūkṣma vyavahita viprakṛṣṭa jñānaṁ.

Pravṛtti = super sense faculty; **āloka** = inner light, perception;
nyāsāt = from directing, from projection, from sitting near;
sūkṣma = subtle; **vyavahita** = hidden, concealed;
viprakṛṣṭa = remote, distant; **jñānam**= knowledge.

By *saṁyama* on the Light within, the knowledge of the subtle, hidden and remote is obtained. [Note: subtle as atoms, hidden as treasure, remote as distant lands.]

भुवनज्ञानं सूर्ये संयमात् ॥२७॥

27. Bhuvanajñānam sūrye saṁyamāt.

Bhuvana = universe, world; **jñānam** = knowledge;
sūrye = on the sun; **saṁyamāt** = from saṁyama.

By *saṁyama* on the sun, knowledge of the entire solar system is obtained.

चन्द्रे ताराव्यूहज्ञानम् ॥२८॥

28. Candre tārā vyūha jñānaṁ.

Candre = upon moon; **tārā** = star;
vyūha = arrangement; **jñānam** = knowledge.

By *saṁyama* on the moon, comes knowledge of the stars' arrangement.

ध्रुवे तद्गतिज्ञानम् ॥२९॥

29. Dhruve tadgati jñānaṁ.

Dhruve = on the polestar; **tad** = their;
gati = movement, procession; **jñānam** = knowledge.

By *saṁyama* on the pole star comes knowledge of the stars' movements.

नाभिचक्रे कायव्यूहज्ञानम् ॥३०॥

30. Nābhicakre kāyavyūha jñānam.

Nābhi = navel; **cakre** = on the plexus; **kāya** = body; **vyūha** = orderly arrangement, distribution; **jñānam** = knowledge.

By *saṁyama* on the navel plexus, knowledge of the body's constitution is obtained.

You won't need an x-ray. You can understand the whole body and its constitution because the solar plexus is the center of the body. It is something like saying that if you understand the sun, you understand the whole solar system.

कण्ठकूपे क्षुत्पिपासानिवृत्तिः ॥३१॥

31. Kaṇṭha kūpe kṣut pipāsā nivṛttiḥ.

kaṇṭha = throat; **kūpe** = on the pit; **kṣut** = hunger; **pipāsā** = thirst; **nivṛttiḥ** = cessation, satisfaction.

By *saṁyama* on the pit of the throat, cessation of hunger and thirst is achieved.

Some of these *siddhis* are simple enough to attain if anybody wants to try. Patañjali gives this nice, simple one that will make the one who cooks very happy! Put your entire attention on the pit of the throat and you don't need to visit the kitchen. All these examples are given mainly to test yourself. They don't take that long to achieve.

कूर्मनाड्यां स्थैर्यम् ॥३२॥

32. Kūrmanāḍyām sthairyaṁ.

Kūrma = tortoise; **nāḍyām** = subtle channel, tube;
sthairyam = stability, motionlessness.

By *saṁyama* on the *kurma nadī* (a subtle tortoise-shaped tube located below the throat), motionlessness in meditative posture is achieved.

मूर्धज्योतिषि सिद्धदर्शनम् ॥३३॥

33. Mūrdha jyotiṣi siddha darśanaṁ.

Mūrdha = crown of head; **jyotiṣi** = on the light;
siddha = masters and adepts; **darśanam** = vision, seeing.

By *saṁyama* on the light at the crown of the head (*sahasrara chakra*), visions of masters and adepts are obtained.

प्रातिभाद्वा सर्वम् ॥३४॥

34. Prātibhād vā sarvaṁ.

Prātibhād = spontaneous intuitive light-flash, luster, illumination, pure presence of mind;
vā = or; **sarvam** = everything, all.

Or, in the knowledge that dawns by spontaneous enlightenment [through a life of purity], all the powers come by themselves.

हृदये चित्तसंवित् ॥३५॥

35. Hṛdaye citta saṁvit.

Hṛdaye = on the heart; **citta** = mind-stuff;
saṁvit = knowledge, understanding.

By *saṁyama* on the heart, the knowledge of the mind-stuff is obtained.

सत्त्वपुरुषयोरत्यन्तासंकीर्णयोः प्रत्ययाविशेषो भोगः परार्थात् स्वार्थसंयमात् पुरुषज्ञानम् ॥३६॥

36. Sattva puruṣayor atyantāsaṁkīrṇayoḥ pratyayāviśeṣo bhogaḥ parārthāt svārthasaṁyamāt puruṣajñānaṁ.

Sattva = of the buddhi (intellect), of the mind;
puruṣayoḥ = Self (of these both);
atyanta = completely different, all the way to the end different;
asaṁkīrṇayoḥ = (and) not mixed together (sattva & puruṣayoḥ);
pratyaya = cognition, thought;
aviśeṣaḥ = without distinction (of these both);
bhogaḥ = experience; **para** = another;
arthāt = from the interest, from the purpose;
sva = Self; **artha** = interest, purpose; **saṁyamāt** = from saṁyama;
Puruṣa = Self; **jñānam** = knowledge.

The intellect and the *Puruṣa* (*Ātman*, Self) are totally different, the intellect existing for the sake of the *Puruṣa*, while the *Puruṣa* exists for its own sake. Not distinguishing this is the cause of all experiences; and by *saṁyama* on the distinction, knowledge of the *Puruṣa* is gained.

ततः प्रातिभश्रावणवेदनादर्शास्वादवार्ता
जायन्ते ॥३७॥

37. **Tataḥ prātibha śrāvaṇa vedanādarśāsvāda vārtā jāyante.**

Tataḥ = thence; **prātibha** = spontaneous, illuminated, divine, intuitive and extraordinary; **śrāvaṇa** = hearing (clairaudience); **vedana** = touch; **adarśa** = seeing (clairvoyance); **āsvāda** = taste; **vārtā** = smell; **jāyante** = are born, arises.

From this knowledge arises superphysical hearing, touching, seeing, tasting and smelling through spontaneous intuition.

ते समाधावुपसर्गा व्युत्थाने सिद्धयः ॥३८॥

38. **Te samādhāvupasargā vyutthāne siddhayaḥ.**

Te = these; **samādhau** = in samādhi; **upasargāḥ** = obstacles; **vyutthāne** = in outward going, in worldly pursuits; **siddhayaḥ** = accomplishments, powers.

These [superphysical senses] are obstacles to [*nirbija*] *samādhi* but are *siddhis* (powers or accomplishments) in the worldly pursuits.

बन्धकारणशैथिल्यात् प्रचारसंवेदनाच्च चित्तस्य परशरीरावेशः ॥३९॥

39. Bandhakāraṇa śaithilyāt pracāra saṁvedanāc ca cittasya paraśarīrāveśaḥ.

Bandha = bundle, bind, bound; **kāraṇa** = cause;
śaithilyāt = from loosening; **pracāra** = procedure, propagation;
saṁvedanāt = known from sensation, perception, and feeling;
ca = and; **cittasya** = of the mind-stuff; **para** = another, other;
śarīra = body; **āveśaḥ** = enter.

By the loosening of the cause [of the bondage of mind to body] and by knowledge of the procedure of the mind-stuff's functioning, entering another's body is accomplished.

उदानजयाज्जलपङ्ककण्टकादिष्वसङ्ग उत्क्रान्तिश्च ॥४०॥

40. Udāna jayāj jala paṅka kaṇṭakādiṣvasaṅga utkrāntiś ca.

Udāna = the nadī current of upward moving prāṇa;
jayāt = from mastery; **jala** = water; **paṅka** = mud, swamp;
kaṇṭaka = thorn; **adiṣu** = et cetera et cetera;
asaṅga = without contact;
utkrāntiḥ = passing over, levitate, passing away (leaving the body):
ca = and.

By mastery over the *udāna* nerve current (the upward vital air), one accomplishes levitation over water, swamps, thorns, etc. and can leave the body at will.

समानजयाज्ज्वलनम् ॥४१॥

41. Samānajayāj jvalanaṁ.

Samāna = the nadī current of prāṇa flowing in the navel region; **jayāt** = from mastery; **jvalanam** = radiance, fire.

By mastery over the *samāna* nerve current (the equalizing vital air) comes radiance to surround the body.

श्रोत्राकाशयोः संबन्धसंयमाद्दिव्यं श्रोत्रम् ॥४२॥

42. Śrotrākāśayoḥ saṁbandhasaṁyamād divyam śrotraṁ.

Śrotra = ear; **ākāśayoḥ** = and either (both); **saṁbandha** = relationship, link, connection; **saṁyamāt** = from saṁyama on; **divyam** = divine, celestial, heavenly; **śrotram** = hearing.

By *saṁyama* on the relationship between ear and ether, supernormal hearing becomes possible.

कायाकाशयोः संबन्धसंयमाल्लघु
तूलसमापत्तेश्चाकाशगमनम् ॥४३॥

43. Kāyākāśayoḥ saṁbandha saṁyamāllaghu tūla samāpatteścākāśagamanaṁ.

Kāya = body; **akāśayoḥ** = and either (both); **saṁbandha** = relationship, link, connection; **saṁyamāt** = from saṁyama on; **laghu** = light; **tūla** = cotton fiber; **samāpatteḥ** = profound meditation; **ca** = and; **ākāśa** = ether, sky; **gamanam** = travel.

By *saṁyama* on the relationship between the body and ether, lightness of cotton fiber is attained, and thus traveling through the ether becomes possible.

बहिरकल्पिता वृत्तिर्महाविदेहा ततः प्रकाशावरणक्षयः ॥४४॥

44. Bahirakalpitā vṛttirmahāvidehā tataḥ prakāśāvaraṇakṣayaḥ.

Bahiḥ = external, projected outside; **akalpitā** = unidentified, formless; **vṛttiḥ** = thought wave, activity; **mahā** = great; **videhā** = bodiless, disincarnate; **tataḥ** = from that; **prakāśa** = inner light of the Self; **āvaraṇa** = veil, covering; **kṣayaḥ** = destroy, remove.

By *saṁyama* on the thought waves unidentified by and external to the body [*maha-videha*, or the great bodilessness], the veil over the light of the Self is destroyed.

स्थूलस्वरूपसूक्ष्मान्वयार्थवत्त्वसंयमाद् भूतजयः ॥४५॥

45. Sthūla svarūpa sūkṣmānvayārthavattva saṁyamād bhūta jayaḥ.

Sthūla = gross; **svarūpa** = essential nature (sva = self; rūpa = form, color, nature); **sūkṣma** = subtle; **anvaya** = correlative, connectedness; **arthavatva** = purposefulness; **saṁyamāt** = from saṁyama; **bhūta** = elements (earth, etc.); **jayaḥ** = mastery.

By *saṁyama* on the gross and subtle elements and on their essential nature, correlations and purpose, mastery over them is gained.

ततोऽणिमादिप्रादुर्भावः कायसंपत् तद्धर्मानभिघातश्च ॥४६॥

46. Tato'ṇimādi prādurbhāvaḥ kāyasaṁpat taddharmānabhighātaśca.

Tataḥ = from that;
aṇimā = the power of becoming miniature, atomic size;
adi = et cetera (and other related powers);
prādur = appear, manifest;
bhāvaḥ = occurring, state of (prādur);
kāya = body; **saṁpat** = perfection; **tad** = their;
dharma = characteristics, functions;
anabhighātaḥ = without obstruction, non-resistance;
ca = and.

From that comes attainment of *anima* and other *siddhis*, bodily perfection and the non-obstruction of bodily functions by the influence of the elements.

[The eight major *siddhis* alluded to here are:
1. *Aṇimā* (to become very small)
2. *Mahima* (to become very big)
3. *Laghima* (to become very light)
4. *Garima* (to become very heavy)
5. *Prāpti* (to reach anywhere)
6. *Prākāmya* (to achieve all one's desires)
7. *Iṣṭva* (ability to create anything)
8. *Vaśitva* (ability to command and control everything)]

रूप लावण्यबलवज्रसंहननत्वानि
कायसंपत् ॥४७॥

47. Rūpa lāvaṇyabalavajrasaṁhananatvāni kāyasaṁpat.

Rūpa = beauty, appearance; **lāvaṇya** = gracefulness, attractive;
bala = strength; **vajra** = adamantine hardness;
saṁhananatva = robustness, solidness, compactness;
ani = plural for this group of five; **kāya** = body;
saṁpat = perfection.

Beauty, grace, strength, adamantine hardness and robustness constitute bodily perfection.

ग्रहणस्वरूपास्मितान्वयार्थवत्त्व
संयमादिन्द्रियजयः ॥४८॥

48. Grahaṇa svarūpāsmitānvayārthavattva saṁyamād indriya jayaḥ.

Grahaṇa = power of perception, apprehension, grasping nature;
svarūpa = essential nature (sva = self; rūpa = form, color, nature);
asmitā = ego sense, I-ness; **anvaya** = correlation, connectedness;
arthavattva = purposefulness; **saṁyamāt** = from saṁyama on;
indriya = senses; **jayaḥ** = mastery.

By *saṁyama* on the power of perception and on the essential nature, correlation with the ego sense and purpose of the sense organs, mastery over them is gained.

ततो मनोजवित्वं विकरणभावः
प्रधानजयश्च ॥४९॥

49. Tato manojavitvam vikaraṇabhāvaḥ pradhānajayaśca.

Tataḥ = thence, by that; **manaḥ** = mind;
javitvam = quickness, fast movement;
vikaraṇa = without organs of sense; **bhāvaḥ** = state of being;
pradhāna = fundamental primary cause behind manifestation, prakṛti; **jayaḥ** = mastery; **ca** = and.

From that, the body gains the power to move as fast as the mind, the ability to function without the aid of the sense organs and complete mastery over the primary cause (*Prakṛti*).

सत्त्वपुरुषान्यताख्यातिमात्रस्य सर्वभावाधिष्ठातृत्वं
सर्वज्ञातृत्वं च ॥५०॥

50. Sattvapuruṣānyatākhyātimātrasya sarvabhāvādhiṣṭhātṛtvam sarvajñātṛtvam ca.

Sattva = essential purity of the mind field, purest intelligence;
puruṣa = Self, pure awareness, consciousness;
anyatā = distinction between; **khyāti** = discernment, clarity;
mātrasya = of only; **sarva** = all; **bhāva** = states of existence;
adhiṣṭhātṛtvam = supremacy; **sarva** = all;
jñātṛtvam = knowingness, (omniscience, all-knowingness);
ca = and.

By recognition of the distinction between *sattva* (the pure reflective nature) and the Self, supremacy over all states and forms of existence [omnipotence] is gained, as is omniscience.

तद्वैराग्यादपि दोषबीजक्षये कैवल्यम् ॥५१॥

51. Tadvairāgyādapi doṣabījakṣaye kaivalyam.

Tad = that; **vairāgyāt** = from non-attachment;
api = even; **doṣa** = deficiency, disease, detrimental effect;
bīja = seed; **kṣaye** = upon destruction;
kaivalyam = independence, absolute unity, perfect isolation, detachment of the soul from matter.

By non-attachment even to that [*siddhis*], the seed of bondage is destroyed and thus follows *kaivalya* (independence).

This means that all these *siddhis* are beautiful, but they will bind us, because *siddhis* are the outcome of mind. The mind *wants* something. It wants to achieve this or that. What for? To be proud of itself. It develops ego. It makes your "I" and "mine" bigger. Selfish desires are still there. If you are after *siddhis* like astral traveling, clairvoyance and clairaudience, I ask you why. You may say, "Oh, I thought I could help people." I say that this is just an excuse. You want to show you can do something. You want to be proud of it.

Are the *siddhis* bad then? If so, why are they there? I say they are not bad. They are beautiful; they are good. When? When *they* come to *you.* When you run after them they are bad. That's all the difference. Let the *siddhis* come and beg, "Hey, can't I do something for you?" Then they are beautiful. If you don't run after them and you don't crave them, they are not yours. They want to have you as theirs. They want to be with you and serve you. Then they are okay. That's why, even in the *Bible,* you come across these powers. Everything will come to you. When? When you seek the Kingdom. "Seek ye first the Kingdom of Heaven; everything else will be added unto you." You don't need to run after them one by one. When you become the boss, you get everything. You don't need to run after small jobs.

Not only these *vibhūti,* these *siddhis,* are like that, but everything is like that: beauty, money, power, strength, scientific knowledge. All these things are becoming misused, and the whole world is trembling with fear. Why? Because we have not sought God first. What is God? Peace, contentment, egolessness. So, we are not really condemning *siddhis.* They are God's powers, by-products of the search for God. Let them come after you.

When your mind is that clean and calm, then you will be able to handle them well for good purposes, not for your ego. You won't be beating your own drum, "Oh, I can do this; I can do that." *Siddhis* are not for that. Patañjali clearly explains these things, because as a scientist he has to place the facts before his students. But it is not that he is encouraging you to acquire *siddhis.* That is the beauty of Patañjali. He is not hiding anything. He says, "These are all the possibilities, no doubt, but don't run after them. You may get hurt by them. Let them run after you."

स्थान्युपनिमन्त्रणे सङ्गस्मयाकरणं
पुनरनिष्टप्रसङ्गात् ॥५२॥

52. Sthānyupanimantraṇe saṇgasmayākaraṇam punaraniṣṭa prasaṅgāt.

Sthāni = celestial beings, deities, devas;
upanimantraṇe = upon the invitation, on the offer, upon admiration; **saṅga** = encounter, come into contact, attachment;
smaya = smile, smile with pride;
akaraṇam = not accepting, without cause for action;
punaḥ = again; **aniṣṭa** = undesirable;
prasaṅgāt = getting caught, attachment, indulgence.

The Yogi should neither accept nor smile with pride at the admiration of even the celestial beings, as there is the possibility of getting caught again in the undesirable.

क्षणतत्क्रमयोः संयमाद्विवेकजं ज्ञानम् ॥५३॥

53. Kṣaṇa tat kramayoḥ saṁyamād vivekajam jñānaṁ.

Kṣaṇa = a single moment, twinkling of an eye; **tat** = that;
kramayoḥ = in sequence, progressing step by step;
saṁyamāt = from saṁyama on;
viveka = discrimination, discernment;
jam = born of; **jñānam** = knowledge.

By *saṁyama* on single moments in sequence comes discriminative knowledge.

जातिलक्षणदेशैरन्यतानवच्छेदात् तुल्ययोस्ततः प्रतिपत्तिः ॥५४॥

54. Jāti lakṣaṇa deśairanyatānavacchedāt tulyayostataḥ pratipattiḥ.

Jāti = species, class; **lakṣaṇa** = characteristic mark,
invisible characteristic, time characteristic;
deśaiḥ = and position (these three); **anyatā** = distinction, difference;
anavacchedāt = from the indistinguishable, from the undefined;
tulyayoḥ = of equals, of comparables;
tataḥ = thus (refers to the above described saṁyama);
pratipattiḥ = distinguishable knowledge.

Thus, the indistinguishable differences between objects that are alike in species, characteristic marks and positions become distinguishable.

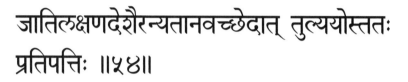

तारकं सर्वविषयं सर्वथाविषयमक्रमं
चेति विवेकजं ज्ञानम् ॥५५॥

55. Tārakam sarvaviṣayam sarvathāviṣayamakramam ceti vivekajam jñānaṁ.

Tārakam = transcendent; **sarva** = all; **viṣayam** = object, condition; **sarvathā** = in all ways; **viṣayam** = object, condition; **akramam** = non-sequential; **ca** = and; **iti** = thus; **viveka** = discrimination; **jam** = born of; **jñānam** = knowledge.

The discriminative knowledge that simultaneously comprehends all objects in all conditions is the intuitive knowledge which brings liberation.

सत्त्वपुरुषयोः शुद्धिसाम्ये कैवल्यम् ॥५६॥

56. Sattva puruṣayoḥ śuddhi sāṁye kaivalyam.

Sattva = buddhi (intellect), mind field, tranquil and pure mind; **puruṣayoḥ** = and (both) of the Self, of pure consciousness; **śuddhi** = purity; **sāmye** = upon equality, in exactly the same; **kaivalyam** = independence, absolute unity, perfect isolation, detachment of the soul from matter.

When the tranquil mind attains purity equal to that of the Self, there is Absoluteness.

We are not here to grasp a little of this and a little of that. What is the biggest fish you can catch? The "self-fish." Hook that fish. Then you can probably have a nice big aquarium. You don't need to kill the self-fish. Just keep it in your aquarium. Show it to others: "See, this is my fish." That would make the best aquarium.

We should never lose sight of this and simply settle for little things. Never. That's not a good business. Don't settle for these tiny, tiny things.

Sometimes they come and tempt you, "Hey, come on, I am here, I am here. Use me." Say, "No; my purpose is something different. I am going straight ahead. I don't even want to stand and wait and watch the sideshows here and there."

I say this because, as you progress along the spiritual path, the sideshows will tempt you. It's like a king is sitting there ready to give you everything. He has invited you to come to his party and be his friend, and you are going toward that party. On the way, you see all kinds of variety shows, magician's tricks, some music being played. But you should know that they are all on their way to the party to play according to the king's orders. When you get there, all of them will also be there; and you can see them while you sit by the side of the king. But when you forget that, you stand on the pavement and see only them and miss the king.

Never, never settle for these little things. Our goal is something very high. It is eternal peace, eternal joy. Don't settle for a little peace, for a little joy, for petty happiness.

Book Four

Kaivalya Pāda
Portion on Absoluteness

Book Four has the heading *Kaivalya Pāda*, or the portion that talks about absoluteness. The root of *kaivalya* is *kevala*, which means without qualities or conditions, that which is cosmic. The one who has the quality of *kevala* is called *kaivalya*. It's an experience of absoluteness, unlimitedness.

Note on Books Three and Four:
I have translated all the sūtras *of Books Three and Four; however, I have chosen not to comment on them all. I have taken the ones I have found most useful for the understanding of Yoga aspirants and have left out the others. Those readers who wish to study more about the* sūtras *that have no commentaries here can consult one of the books on the* Yoga Sūtras *listed in the Selected Reading.*

जन्मौषधिमन्त्रतपःसमाधिजाः सिद्धयः ॥१॥

1. **Janmauṣadhi mantra tapaḥ samādhijāḥ siddhayaḥ.**

Janma = birth; **auṣadhi** = herbs;
mantra = sacred speech, Vedic hymn, incantation;
tapaḥ = consume or destroy by heat, purification by austerity, undergo penance, acceptance of sufferings;
samādhi = concentration of thoughts, intense contemplation on a particular object, absorption; **jāḥ** = born, produced or caused by;
siddhayaḥ = psychic powers, accomplishments, attainments.

***Siddhis* are born of practices performed in previous births, or by herbs, mantra repetition, asceticism or by *samādhi*.**

Patañjali begins this book by reviewing the methods by which the *siddhis* can be obtained by the Yoga practitioner. Some people attain the *siddhis* without even doing any practices in this life. They don't know what they did to have these kinds of powers. That is the proof that they have done something in their past lives to merit such powers in this one. He also gives us some clues about the people who get some experiences through their LSD and marijuana. The so-called "grass" is an herb, is it not? Mushrooms could be considered herbs also.

Or *siddhis* come by the practice of *mantra japa* or by asceticism. Asceticism, or *tapas*, means accepting suffering willingly, thus exercising your will power and gaining control over the mind.

And finally Patañjali says that the *siddhis* can come through *samādhi* gained through the proper procedure of concentration and meditation.

So, there are various ways of accomplishing the psychic powers. But normally it is recognized that all the others except *samādhi* are not natural. For example, using herbs means inducing *siddhis* by the use of certain external stimuli. It's not an "organic" *siddhi*. It may come and then fade away. So, *siddhis* should come in the regular process of Yoga, not through external stimuli.

जात्यन्तरपरिणामः प्रकृत्यापूरात् ॥२॥

2. Jātyantarapariṇāmaḥ prakṛtyāpūrāt.

Jati = species, class by birth, category;
antara = another, different;
pariṇāmaḥ = transformation; **prakṛiti** = nature;
āpūrāt = from inflow, from overflow, from flooding.

The transformation of one species into another is brought about by the inflow of Nature.

निमित्तमप्रयोजकं प्रकृतीनां वरणभेदस्तु ततःक्षेत्रिकवत् ॥३॥

3. Nimittam aprayojakam prakṛtīnām varaṇabhedastu tataḥ kṣetrikavat.

Nimittam = incidental cause, instrumental or efficient cause;
aprayojakam = not causing, not initiating;
prakṛtīnām = natural evolution, primary material cause;
varaṇa = choosing, mound, obstacle;
bhedaḥ = piercing, separation, bursting open, blossoming, sprouting, breaking through;
tu = but; **tataḥ** = thence, from that;
kṣetrikavat = like a farmer.

Incidental events do not directly cause natural evolution; they just remove the obstacles as a farmer [removes the obstacles in the water course running to the field].

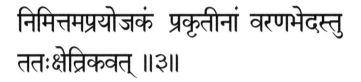

Here, Patañjali gives a nice example of how a farmer allows the water to run into the field simply by removing the obstacles in the water course. Your mind also wants to run to its original source of tranquility, but there are impediments on the way that obstruct the flow.

Your practices and your teacher do the job of an agriculturist. The *guru* is not really bringing you anything new; instead, he or she is simply removing the obstacles so the flow of consciousness will be continuous and the water can reach its source. Water is already running in the canal. The cultivator simply goes looking for some obstacles and takes them out. Once the cultivator removes them, he or she doesn't need to tell the water it can flow. It is like the sun outside; it is always there, ready to come into your house. The obstacles are the closed door and windows. If you simply open them, the light shines in.

निर्माणचित्तान्यस्मितामात्रात् ॥४॥

4. Nirmāṇacittānyasmitāmātrāt.

Nirmāṇa = created, produced, constructed; **cittāni** = minds; **asmitā** = ego sense, I-ness; **mātrāt** = due to only, from aloneness.

A Yogi's ego sense alone is the cause of [other] artificially created minds.

प्रवृत्तिभेदे प्रयोजकं चित्तमेकमनेकेषाम् ॥५॥

5. Pravṛttibhede prayojakam cittamekamanekeṣām.

Pravṛtti = functions, activities, appearance, manifestation;
bhede = on difference, in the division;
prayojakam = director, instigator;
cittam = mind, mind-stuff;
ekam = one; **anekeṣām** = of the many.

Although the functions in the many created minds may differ, the original mind-stuff of the Yogi is the director of them all.

तत्र ध्यानजमनाशयम् ॥६॥

6. Tatra dhyānajam anāśayaṁ.

Tatra = of these; **dhyāna** = meditation; **jam** = born; **anāśayam** = free of karmic impressions, without residue.

Only the minds born of meditation are free from karmic impressions.

कर्माशुक्लाकृष्णं योगिनस्त्रिविधमितरेषाम् ॥७॥

7. Karmāśuklākṛṣṇam yoginastrividhamitareṣām.

Karma = action; **aśukla** = not white (not good); **akṛṣṇam** = not black (not bad); **Yoginaḥ** = of a Yogi; **trividham** = three kinds; **itareṣām** = of others.

The actions of the Yogi are neither white [good] nor black [bad]; but the actions of others are of three kinds: good, bad and mixed.

The esoteric meaning of white and black is good and bad, or pure and impure. But in the Yogi's case there is no pure or impure *karma.* As a Yogi, your actions are performed with such equanimity that you don't bring them into either category. You are above good and bad. Others may categorize your actions; but to you they are just something that has to be done and they are happening.

It is like the case of any instrument—a knife, for example. A knife just cuts. If the knife cuts a fruit you may say it is good and if it cuts a throat it is bad. But to the knife, a cut is a cut. It doesn't matter where it cuts or what it cuts. The one who wields the knife might face the good and bad reactions. Like that, the Yogi is not an agent for his or her actions. The Yogi is above the dualities. For a normal person, however, actions are of three kinds: good, bad and a mixture of the two. Part of an act may be good, part bad. For example, you may do something beautiful but your motive may be a little selfish. The act is good but the motive is bad. It's good for others but not for you. So you can see the difference between a Yogi's *karma* and the *karma* of others. Others say, "Oh, this is good; I did it perfectly," or "Oh, I goofed," or "This is just so-so." But with a Yogi, you can't categorize it that way.

ततस्तद्विपाकानुगुणानामेवाभिव्यक्तिर्वासनानाम् ॥८॥

8. Tatastadvipākānuguṇānāmevābhivyaktirvāsanānām.

Tataḥ = of these; **tad** = their; **vipāka** = fruition;
anuguṇānām = following favorable conditions, corresponding to gunas;
eva = only, alone; **abhivyaktiḥ** = manifestation;
vāsanānām = subconscious impressions, latent potentials.

Of these [actions], only those *vasanas* (subconscious impressions) for which there are favorable conditions for producing their fruits will manifest in a particular birth.

जातिदेशकालव्यवहितानामप्यानन्तर्यं
स्मृतिसंस्कारयोरेकरूपत्वात् ॥९॥

9. Jāti deśa kāla vyavahitānām apyānantaryam smṛti saṁskārayorekarūpatvāt.

Jāti = class or species born into, incarnation;
deśa = space, place; **kāla** = time; **vyavahitānām** = separated;
api = although, even; **ānantaryam** = uninterrupted relationship;
smṛti = of memory;
saṁskāra = of impression, of subliminal activator;
(**oḥ** = dual ending, of both) **ekarūpatvāt** = identical, from oneness.

Although desires are separated from their fulfillments by class, space and time, they have an uninterrupted relationship because the impressions [of desires] and memories of them are identical.

तासामनादित्वं चाशिषो नित्यत्वात् ॥१०॥

10. Tāsāmanāditvam cāśiṣo nityatvāt.

Tāsām = of these, belonging to these [impressions];
anāditvam = beginninglessness;
ca = and; **āśiṣaḥ** (āśiṣo) = desire to live;
nityatvāt = from eternality.

Since the desire to live is eternal, impressions are also beginningless.

हेतुफलाश्रयालम्बनैः संगृहीतत्वादेषामभावे तदभावः ॥११॥

11. Hetu phalāśrayālambanaiḥ saṁgṛhītatvādeṣāmabhāve tadabhāvaḥ.

Hetu = cause; **phala** = effect, fruit;
aśraya = basis, substratum;
alambanaiḥ = by (plural for all four) support;
saṁgṛhītatvāt = from the state of being held together, from interconnectedness;
eṣām = of these; **abhāve** = upon the disappearance;
tad = they; **abhāvaḥ** = disappear.

The impressions being held together by cause, effect, basis and support, they disappear with the disappearance of these four.

अतीतानागतं स्वरूपतोऽस्त्यध्वभेदाद्धर्माणाम् ॥१२॥

12. **Atītānāgatam svarūpato'styadhvabhedāddharmāṇām.**

Atīta = past, gone by; **anāgatam** = future, not yet come;
svarūpataḥ = in its own form; **asti** = it exists;
adhva = conditions, course, orbit, path;
bhedāt = from the difference;
dharmāṇām = of characteristics.

The past and future exist in the real form of objects which manifest due to differences in the conditions of their characteristics.

ते व्यक्तसूक्ष्माः गुणात्मानः ॥१३॥

13. **Te vyaktasūkṣmāḥ guṇātmānaḥ.**

Te = they [the characteristics]; **vyakta** = manifest;
sūkṣmāḥ = subtle; **guṇa** = primal force, primary attributes: sattvas, rajas, tamas; **ātmānaḥ** = having nature (of).

Whether manifested or subtle, these characteristics belong to the nature of the *guṇas.*

परिणामैकत्वाद्वस्तुतत्त्वम् ॥१४॥

14. **Pariṇāmaikatvādvastutattvam.**

Pariṇāma = transformation, alteration;
ekatvāt = due to oneness, from uniformity;
vastu = thing, real object; **tattvam** = that-ness, reality.

The reality of things is due to the uniformity of the *guṇas'* transformations.

वस्तुसाम्ये चित्तभेदात् तयोर्विभक्तः पन्थाः ॥१५॥

15. Vastusāmye citta bhedāt tayorvibhaktaḥ panthāḥ.

Vastu = thing, real object; **sāmye** = on being the same;
citta = minds; **bhedāt** = from the differences;
tayoḥ = of these two; **vibhaktaḥ** = different, separation;
panthāḥ = way, path.

Due to differences in various minds, perception of even the same object may vary.

न चैकचित्ततन्त्रं वस्तु तदप्रमाणकं तदा किं स्यात् ॥१६॥

16. Na caika citta tantram vastu tad apramāṇakam tadā kim syāt?

Na = not; **ca** = and; **eka** = one, single; **citta** = mind;
tantram = dependent, underlying principle; **vastu** = object;
tad = that; **apramāṇakam** = not perceived; **tadā** = then;
kim = what?; **syāt** = perhaps, perchance, might be.

Nor does an object's existence depend upon a single mind, for if it did, what would become of that object when that mind did not perceive it?

तदुपरागापेक्षित्वाच्चित्तस्य वस्तु
ज्ञाताज्ञातम् ॥१७॥

17. **Taduparāgāpekṣitvāccittasya vastu jñātājñātaṁ.**

Tad = that, thereby, thus; **uparāga** = coloring, influence;
apekṣitvāt = from or due to need; **cittasya** = of the mind;
vastu = object; **jñāta** = known; **ajñātam** = unknown.

An object is known or unknown dependent on whether or not the mind gets colored by it.

सदा ज्ञाताश्चित्तवृत्तयस्तत्प्रभोः
पुरुषस्यापरिणामित्वात् ॥१८॥

18. **Sadā jñātāścittavṛttayastatprabhoḥ puruṣasyāpariṇāmitvāt.**

Sadā = always; **jñātāḥ** = known;
citta = mind, mind-stuff, mind-field;
vṛttayaḥ = modification, changes; **tat** = that;
Prabhoḥ = of the master, of the excelling, of the consistency, of the eternality; **Puruṣasya** = of the pure consciousness;
apariṇāmitvāt = from or due to changelessness.

Due to Its changelessness, changes in the mind-stuff are always known to the *Puruṣa,* who is its master.

Here, Patañjali speaks of the changes in the mind-stuff. The *citta* changes constantly because that is its natural tendency. Mind is a part of the ever-changing nature. However clever we are, we can only keep the mind quiet for a little while. Therefore, our aim is not to keep the mind peaceful but to rise above the mind and realize the ever-peaceful Self.

Puruṣa is the owner of the mind-stuff or, as Patañjali puts it, its master. The *Puruṣa* knows all the changes that happen in it. How could *Puruṣa* know them if it is also changing? A changing thing cannot recognize the changes in something else, like an insane person cannot recognize the insanity of another person. So *Puruṣa*, being changeless, can always recognize the changing nature of the mind.

न तत् स्वाभासं दृश्यत्वात् ॥१९॥

19. Na tat svābāsam dṛśyatvāt.

Na = not; **tat** = that [mind]; **svābhāsam** = self-luminous; **dṛśyatvāt** = because of its perceptibility, from its ability to see.

The mind-stuff is not self-luminous because it is an object of perception by the *Puruṣa*

Here we see more or less the same idea. The mind-stuff is not the subject. It is the object to the one subject who is the *Puruṣa.* The mental functions are what you, as *Puruṣa,* perceive. The perceived can never become the perceiver, nor vice-versa. If a perceiver is perceived by something, then he or she is no longer a perceiver but, rather, the perceived. To really have this awareness, this isolation of perceiver and perceived, is Yoga.

It seems easy. So why don't we always have it? Because the quality of the mind is not that clear. It still drags us down. It does not allow us to stay separated from the mind. *Māyā* (illusion) tricks us.

You know that yesterday you had an experience on the mental level and it didn't bring you lasting satisfaction. You may say, "I don't like it anymore and I don't want it. This is the last time I will run after that." Then, two days later you want the same thing again. What does it mean? At a certain point, the true wisdom comes up, but then again *māyā* tricks you. "Oh, yesterday it brought pain, but today it's going to be wonderful. Come on."

That is because there is still the ego, which is the mind's basis. It really doesn't allow you to know and be who you are. That's why, even though you *are* the *Puruṣa*, you don't experience that always. When you hurt somebody else you say, "Oh, *I* didn't do it; it was only my *mind*." When somebody hurts you, *you* should feel the same way. "Well, *you* didn't hurt me, your *mind* did it, so I can't be angry with you."

When we do it we put the blame on the mind. When somebody else does it, we usually say, "How dare you do that?" In *savāsana* (the Hatha Yoga Corpse Pose) you may say, "I'm not the body; the body is just lying here." But when you get up, if somebody says, "Oh, how plump you are!" you get disturbed. "How dare you?" The person didn't call *you* chubby, but called your body chubby.

The realization doesn't stay with us for long. We should try to retain that awareness always. It will slip; but bring it back again and again and again. That is spiritual practice.

एकसमये चोभयानवधारणम् ॥२०॥

20. Ekasamaye cobhayānavadhāraṇaṁ.

Eka = one; **samaye** = in time [in one time—simultaneous];
ca = and; **ubhaya** = both;
anavadhāraṇam = not perceived, not cognized.

The mind-stuff cannot perceive both subject and object simultaneously [which proves it is not self-luminous].

The mind-stuff perceives objects outside. At other times, if it is clean enough, it can turn within and reflect the *Puruṣa* also. So, it can be either subject or object. As subject, it sees other things. As an object, it is seen by the *Puruṣa*. But the *Puruṣa* can never be both. It is always the subject.

चित्तान्तरदृश्ये बुद्धिबुद्धेरतिप्रसङ्गः
स्मृतिसंकरश्च ॥२१॥

21. **Cittāntara dṛśye buddhibuddheratiprasaṅgaḥ smṛtisaṁkaraśca.**

Citta = mind; **antara** = another; **dṛśye** = on the seeable;
buddhi = perceiver; **buddheḥ** = from perception;
atiprasaṅgaḥ = endless, ad infinitum; **smṛti** = memory;
saṁkaraḥ = confusion; **ca** = and.

If the perception of one mind by another mind be postulated, we would have to assume an endless number of them and the result would be confusion of memory.

चितेरप्रतिसंक्रमायास्तदाकारापत्तौ
स्वबुद्धिसंवेदनम् ॥२२॥

22. **Citerapratisaṁkramāyāstadākārāpattau svabuddhisaṁvedanam.**

Citeḥ = of the consciousness;
apratisaṁkramāyāḥ = of [that which] absolutely stays put, of the strictly unmoving, of the unchangeable; **tad** = that [citta];
ākāra = appearance, outward sign, expression;
apattau = upon assuming, upon arising, in the reflection;
sva =one's own; **buddhi** = intelligence (mind);
saṁvedanam = becomes conscious, known.

The consciousness of the *Puruṣa* is unchangeable; by getting the reflection of it, the mind-stuff becomes conscious of the Self.

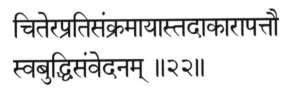

द्रष्टृदृश्योपरक्तं चित्तं सर्वार्थम् ॥२३॥

23. Draṣṭṛ dṛśyoparaktam cittam sarvārtham.

Draṣṭṛ = Seer; **dṛśya** = seen, visible;
uparaktam = colored, dyed;
cittam = mind-field, mind-stuff;
sarva = all, every; **artham** = object, thing.

The mind-stuff, when colored by both Seer and seen, understands everything.

तदसंख्येयवासनाभिश्चित्रमपि परार्थं संहत्यकारित्वात् ॥२४॥

24. Tad asaṁkhyeyavāsanābhiścittamapi parārtham saṁhatyakāritvāt.

Tad = that; **asaṁkhyeya** = countless;
vāsanābhiḥ = latent potentials, subliminal traits linked to past desires;
cittam = mind-field; **api** = even, also;
para = another [the *Puruṣa*];
artham = for the sake, purpose;
saṁhatya = in association, keeping together, combined, forming one mass or body;
kāritvāt = from (due to) activation.

Though having countless desires, the mind-stuff exists for the sake of another [the *Puruṣa*] because it can act only in association with It.

विशेषदर्शिन आत्मभावभावनाविनिवृत्तिः ॥२५॥

25. Viśeṣadarśina ātmabhāva bhāvanā vinivṛttiḥ.

Viśeṣa = distinction;
darśinaḥ = of the one who sees;
Ātma = Self;
bhāva = turning into, becoming [mind becoming Self], existing as;
bhāvanā = idea, imagining, projection;
vinivṛttiḥ = ceases forever.

To one who sees the distinction between the mind and the *Ātman*, thoughts of mind as the *Ātman* cease forever.

तदा हि विवेकनिम्नं कैवल्यप्राग्भारं चित्तम् ॥२६॥

26. Tadā hi vivekanimnam kaivalya prāgbhāram cittam.

Tadā = then; **hi** = indeed, further;
viveka = discrimination, discernment;
nimnam = inclines toward, slopes to;
kaivalya = absoluteness, independence;
prāk (prāg) = directed towards, inclined, promote;
bhāram = heavy mass, weight, gravitate;
cittam = mind-field.

Then the mind-stuff is inclined toward discrimination and gravitates toward Absoluteness.

तच्छिद्रेषु प्रत्ययान्तराणि संस्कारेभ्यः ॥२७॥

27. Tacchidreṣu pratyayāntarāṇi saṁskārebhyaḥ.

Tad (Tac) = those; **chidreṣu** = in-between, in the gaps;
pratyaya = content of the mind, notion, thought;
antarāṇi = others, other ones;
saṁskārebhyaḥ = from past impressions.

In-between, distracting thoughts may arise due to past impressions.

हानमेषां क्लेशवदुक्तम् ॥२८॥

28. Hānameṣām kleśavaduktaṁ.

Hānam = removal, relinquishing, getting rid of;
eṣām = their [the old impressions];
kleśavat = as the obstacles, just like the afflictions (kleśa);
uktam = (were) described, explained, discussed.

They can be removed, as in the case of the obstacles explained before. [See Book Two, *sūtras* 1, 2, 10, 11 and 26.]

प्रसंख्यानेऽप्यकुसीदस्य सर्वथा विवेकख्यातेर्धर्ममेघः समाधिः ॥२९॥

29. Prasaṁkhyāne'pyakusīdasya sarvathā viveka khyāterdharmameghaḥ samādhiḥ.

Prasaṁkhāne = in the attainment of the highest reward, in perfect discrimination; **api** = even;
akusīdasya = totally disinterested, without self interest, non usury, non usuriously; **sarvathā** = constant, in every way, in all ways;
viveka = discrimination, discernment; **khyāteḥ** = of clear cognition;
dharma = virtue, morality, customary observance, according to the nature;
meghaḥ = cloud; **samādhiḥ** = deep meditation, absorption

One who, due to his or her perfect discrimination, is totally disinterested even in the highest rewards, remains in the constant discriminative discernment, which is called *dharmamegha* (cloud of *dharma*) *samādhi*. [Note: The meaning of *dharma* includes virtue, justice, law, duty, morality, religion, religious merit and steadfast decree.]

Here, Patañjali talks about a *samādhi* called *dharmamegha samādhi*—the cloud of *dharma samādhi*. *Dharmamegha* means that all the beautiful qualities are there. One gets into that state when even the desire to be high is gone. Why? Because who desires to get high? Is it the one who is already high? No. As long as the desire to get high is there, you are not high; and when you really get high the desire fades away. You will have attained what is to be attained, and all the desires drop out of you. It is only then that you are totally liberated.

Saint Thirūmular says, "Even with God, please be without desire." That means that desire itself is a bondage. Ultimately, even the desire to get God should go. Then only will you have God. When will that desire go? When you get God! It's kind of a tricky thing. The fulfillment of this desire and becoming desireless happen simultaneously. It's something like saying, "I want to sleep, I want to sleep." At one point you fall asleep. Only when "I want to sleep" goes, you are asleep.

So, this *dharmamegha samādhi* cannot be attained by your effort. Although you put all your efforts up to a certain point, when you really reach that place, even that effort goes away and it becomes effortless. At that point, further effort would keep you down.

Until we reach this stage, there is no harm in having certain good wants to help us stay away from the so-called undesirable wants. Then, when you are able to eliminate the undesirable ones, it is easy to eliminate the good ones also.

It's exactly like the example of using soap to clean a cloth. Imagine you have a pure, clean, white cloth, and then somehow it becomes dirty. You want the cloth to stay away from "wanting" the dirt. What do you do? You want a piece of soap. What is soap? Another piece of dirt, is it not? Maybe it's good-looking and good-smelling and you have to pay for it, but it's still dirt. Once you get the soap, what do you do? You bring the paid-for dirt and allow it to chum up with the unpaid-for dirt. At the proper time, when you know positively that all the unwanted dirt is really playing with the newcomer dirt, you just rinse the cloth in clean water and take it out. What happens? Both kinds of dirt are washed away.

In the same way, you have to have a good want to push away the old bad ones. When the old wants are ready to go, the good want will go also. "Okay, my purpose is over; I leave you free." If, instead, you are pushing an undesirable want away with the help of another undesirable want, it may help in ridding you of the first one, but the second will remain with you. To give an example, even our government is making this mistake in its approach to curing heroin addiction. They prescribe methadone to push away the heroin. It works, but what remains? Methadone addiction. Then you will need something else to push out this addiction. It becomes a vicious cycle.

Another example has occurred many times in history when a government tries to rid itself of some unwanted group with the help of another unwanted group. At one point, the Muslims wanted to take control over a part of India. They sought the help of the British. The British came and helped the Muslims subdue the Indians, but once the Muslims were victorious, the English said, "Having made you successful, you will have to give us some royalty. Otherwise, we will push you out." Who is the real ruler then? The Muslims thought that by getting the help of the English they could put down the Indians and get everything; instead, they were stuck under the thumb of the English.

Therefore, whether it is in the daily life or the national life, before we seek the help of something, we should know whether it is the right kind of help or not. Otherwise, it may bind us later on.

ततः क्लेशकर्मनिवृत्तिः ॥३०॥

30. Tataḥ kleśa karma nivṛttiḥ.

Tataḥ = from that; **kleśa** = root affliction;
karma = resulting action; **nivṛttiḥ** = cessation, retreat, finished, vanish.

From that *samādhi* all afflictions and *karmas* cease.

By *dharmamegha samādhi,* all that affects the mind goes away. One becomes a *jīvanmukta.* Such a person is not affected by anything. He or she is there and things happen; that person is a constant witness. The body and mind, which were trained well before liberation, just continue certain functions because of their *prārabda*, or residual *karma.*

To review the workings of *karma*, all our actions are grouped into three sections. As you know, all *karmas* that are performed leave their results. Those results are stored in a big "bag" called the *karmasaya*, literally, the bag of *karma.*

Prārabda karma is the allotment taken out of the bag to be experienced in this life. You have lived before in a number of different bodies and have performed a lot of actions. The results are now bundled up in the *karmasaya. Sañjīta karma* is the sum total of all your past *karmas. Prārabda* is the amount allotted for you to experience in this lifetime. It is according to your *prārabda* that you come into this world with different qualities of body and mind. If you are a girl and I am a boy, it means your *prārabda* gave you a feminine body and mine gave me a masculine one, because we each have to undergo certain experiences for which that type of body is needed.

That is why sometimes we see bodies with certain deformities. There's no other reason for a newborn child to be deformed. It has done some *karma* to get a body in which the soul should suffer this result.

While experiencing the *prārabda* we are doing new *karma* also. How can we distinguish between the *prārabda* and the *āgami*, or new *karma*? Anything that happens without your expectation, unforeseen, is due to *prārabda*. But anything that you consciously plan and do is your new *karma*. If you purposely go and kick a stone and hurt your toe, it is *āgami karma*. If you are just walking around and all of a sudden hit a stone and get hurt, that is due to *prārabda*. So these are the three kinds of *karmas: sañjīta, prārabda* and *āgami*.

In the case of *jīvanmuktas*, they have come into the world with human bodies because of their *prārabda*. Until they got liberated they were just like anybody else. Now, with their Self-knowledge, they decide not to do any new *karma* to bind themselves, so there is no *āgami* for them. But that doesn't mean they are not doing any actions. Some things seem to be happening. They seem to be doing many things. But they are not. And because of this isolation from the mind and body, they are not affected by the reactions of the acts you see them perform. It is the mind that performs all the *karmas*.

When you realize you are the *Puruṣa*, you know that any *karma* belongs to the mind. When that isolation, or *kaivalya*, comes, the *sanjita* gets burned because there is no stimulation for the body and mind to continue anything. And because the *sañjīta* cannot affect you, there is no further birth for you. But still, the *prārabda* that brought this mind and body remains. Until that is over, the body and mind will still function.

Jīvanmuktas are neither to be blamed nor praised for their actions. Just as you watch them acting, they watch themselves. All the praise and blame go to the body and mind—not to the *jīvanmuktas*.

Sometimes students ask what happens to the *jīvanmuktas* after they die. Do they come back, or do they go to another plane and continue evolving or what happens? They never worry about it. They don't even want to know. If they wanted to know, they would not be *jīvanmuktas*. They are free.

You might wonder then about the saints and prophets who appear in our midst sometimes. They may have come back because they had that desire; then they are not *jīvanmuktas*. Or, sometimes, *jīvanmuktas* are sent back into the world. It is not because they want it, but because the cosmic law wants it. "Hey, you are a good example. Go, live in the midst of people. Let them see you appear to be acting, although you are not acting." Sometimes teachers are sent like that.

Sri Ramakrishna Paramahamsa gives a beautiful parable about this. Once, a few people went to visit a garden, having been told that there were beautiful big fruit trees there. But the garden was completely surrounded by high walls, and they couldn't even see what was inside. With great effort one person managed to climb the wall and see inside. He saw such luscious fruit that the minute he saw it, he jumped in. Another person climbed up and immediately jumped in the same way. Finally, a third person climbed up, but when she saw it, she said, "My gosh, how can I jump in now? There are so many hungry people below who don't know what is here or how to climb up." So, she sat on the wall and said, "Hey, there are a lot of fruits, come on. If you try hard, you can come up like I have." She lent a hand, pulling people in.

Such people are called teachers. They know what is there, but they don't just want to go and experience it themselves. They want to wait and pull as many people over as they have the strength to do. It is the cosmic consciousness or cosmic law that takes care of that. Sometimes, even if such a person *wants* to jump over the wall, God says, "No; you stay there. It's not your business to jump. Sit there and help everybody. Until you finish, you can't jump in." They simply have to obey the cosmic law.

And how can you recognize a *jīvanmukta*? Only by becoming a *jīvanmukta*. Until then, he or she may appear to you to be like anybody else. Still, we *seem* to recognize it in some people. We just see something, and if we think the person is a *jīvanmukta*, we may follow him or her. But we should know that we are understanding that person in our own way, according to our own imagination. That's the problem with gods and religion. Each person imagines the unimaginable God in his or her own way, and each imagination varies; so, we fight. But, in the case of wanting a realized person to guide you, ultimately you have to judge by the results. What happens in your life by following the imagination that so-and-so is a *jīvanmukta*? If you become more unhappy, don't follow that person anymore. If you are becoming better and happier, continue. The proof of the pudding is in eating. Lick a little and see how it tastes. If it tastes good, eat a little more. It's an important point. Why are my students with me? What have they seen in me? Are they all seeing the same thing? Have any of them really seen me ? Do they really know who I am? No. According to their own thinking they have taken a liking to me. "Oh, this guy seems to be a good person to guide me." That's all. It's their own imagination. They imagine a *guru* should be a certain way. If he or she fits all their expectations, they say, "This is the one I am looking for." In reality, only a snake knows a snake; only a saint knows a saint.

तदा सर्वावरणमलापेतस्य
ज्ञानस्यानन्त्याज्ज्ञेयमल्पम् ॥३१॥

31. Tadā sarvāvaraṇamalāpetasya jñānasyānantyājjñeyamalpam.

Tadā = then; **sarva** = all; **avaraṇa** = coverings;
mala = impurity, imperfection, dirt;
apetasya = of that removal; **jñānasya** = of knowledge;
anantyāt = from (because of) the infinity (endlessness);
jñeyam = to be known; **alpam** = very little, nearly nothing, trifling.

Then all the coverings and impurities of knowledge are totally removed. Because of the infinity of this knowledge, what remains to be known is almost nothing.

What is impurity? It is like the sensitive coating on photographic film. The "I" and "mine" coat our mental film and then want to "catch" everything they see. If not for the sensitive film, you may see many things, but they wouldn't affect you, because nothing would get recorded. A *jīvanmukta's* mind is like an uncoated, crystal-clear mica sheet. It runs through the camera and pictures are shot, but nothing gets recorded. There's nothing to process, nothing to develop and nothing to fix. That means there are no "fixations."

ततः कृतार्थानां परिणामक्रमसमाप्तिर्गुणानाम् ॥३२॥

32. Tataḥ kṛtārthānām pariṇāmakramasamāptirguṇānām.

Tataḥ = then; **kṛta** = having fulfilled, done;
arthānām = purposes (of);
pariṇāma = transformation, transition;
krama = sequence, succession; **samāptiḥ** = terminate, end;
guṇānām = of the primal attributes
(all three—*sattvas, rajas and tamas*).

Then the *guṇas* terminate their sequence of transformations because they have fulfilled their purpose.

This is a beautiful *sūtra* to understand. The three *guṇas* (*sattva, rajas* and *tamas*) constantly intermingle; and, thus, *Prakṛti* functions. Why should they do this; or, in other words, why does nature function? The nature functions to give experience to the reflected *Puruṣa.* (In other words, the mind. The scriptures sometimes say *Puruṣa* itself, but the meaning is the *Puruṣa* reflected upon the mind-stuff.")

Unfortunately, the *Prakṛti,* of which our mental mirror is made, is itself made up of the three *guṇas,* so it is not always the same. It's a sort of psychedelic mirror. Occasionally it is straight, but most of the time it moves around. If you stand in front of it, you see yourself as constantly changing. You forget the truth, because you see it so rarely; whereas, the ugly image is almost constant. You mistake yourself to be the changing images and say, "Oh, I am terribly ugly; I am terribly unhappy; I am terribly this or that." You put yourself in the position of the image. So, the duty of *Prakṛti* is to torture the soul in every way until it really gets enough knocks and bumps.

Then, at one point, the soul says, "No; I cannot be affected by all this. I should stay away." When this understanding comes, the soul renounces the world. "I don't want you anymore, because the minute I come you simply put me into difficult situations. You never allow me to be quiet. Now and then you give me a little happiness, but you seem to be bringing me mostly unhappiness." That is what is called *sannyāsa*, or renunciation. "I don't want."

Why do people come to my talks? Because they don't want to be in the nightclubs; they don't want Miami Beach; they don't want Las Vegas. The very fact they want to be at the talks means they don't want the other things out there. Why? They've had enough. As the previous *sūtra* says, when the soul detaches itself, there's no more impurity for it.

And then what happens to *Prakṛti*? I will give an analogy to explain it. Imagine a mama with a number of children. They all go out to play and get dirty. When they return, totally covered with grime, she puts them into the bathtub and turns on the shower. Of course, she can't clean everybody at the same time, so she washes them one by one. Once a baby is clean, what will she do with it? She takes it out of the tub and says, "Go, get dry and hop into bed." Will she stop working? No. There are still more dirty children in the tub. Mother *Prakṛti* is just like that. She stops functioning with the clean child.

"Okay, you are clean. Go, and don't come to me again. My job is over with you. But I still have a lot of work to do with other children." That is what is meant in this *sūtra*. *Prakṛti*—the qualities and their continuous transformations—stop their action on the free soul because they have fulfilled their purpose. They have given enough experience to the *Puruṣa*.

क्षणप्रतियेगी परिणामापरान्तनिर्ग्राह्यः क्रमः ॥३३॥

33. Kṣaṇapratiyogī pariṇāmāparāntanirgrāhyaḥ kramaḥ.

Kṣaṇa = moments; **pratiyogī** = dependent existence, partnership, uninterrupted succession;
pariṇāma = transformation, transition;
aparānta = other end, final end;
nirgrāhyaḥ = graspable, recognizable;
kramaḥ = sequence.

The sequence [referred to above] means an uninterrupted succession of moments which can be recognized at the end of their transformations.

पुरुषार्थशुन्यानां गुणानां प्रतिप्रसवः
कैवल्यं स्वरूपप्रतिष्ठा वा चितिशक्तेरिति ॥३४॥

34. Puruṣārthaśūnyānām guṇānām pratiprasavaḥ kaivalyam svarūpa pratiṣṭhā vā citiśakter iti.

Puruṣa = Self, pure consciousness; **artha** = purpose, meaning; (**Puruṣārtha** = the four purposes of the human: artha, kāma, dharma and mokṣa);
śūnyānām = devoid of, loss of existence, of being zero;
guṇānām = of the primal attributes (sattvas, etc.);
pratiprasavaḥ = reabsorb, involution, recede, return back in reverse;
kaivalyam = absolute freedom, independence;
svarūpa = its own nature, own form;
pratiṣṭhā = settles, established; **vā** = or;
citi = pure consciousness; **śakteḥ** = of its power;
iti = thus, the end.

Thus, the supreme state of Independence manifests while the *guṇas* reabsorb themselves into *Prakṛti*, having no more purpose to serve the *Puruṣa*. Or [to look from another angle] the power of pure consciousness settles in its own pure nature.

Patañjali does not mean here that the *guṇas* and *Prakṛti* are really different. But we use the term *Prakṛti* when the *guṇas* are not manifesting separately. When the *guṇas* manifest, *Prakṛti* functions with the *Puruṣa*. Once that job is over, the *guṇas* withdraw their action from that *Puruṣa*. Or you can put it another way: "The power of pure consciousness settles in its own pure nature." That means that when the *guṇas* withdraw, finishing their job, the *Puruṣa*—having gotten completely cleaned—stops running around. It is settled. It is happy in its own true nature. It is no longer seeking happiness and peace from outside because it realizes it is happiness personified.

Now, if we go all the way back to the very beginning of the *Yoga Sūtras*, the second *sūtra* in the first Book says, "*Yogas' citta vṛtti nirodhaḥ.*" "Restraint of the modifications of the mind-stuff is Yoga." The third *sūtra* is "*Tadādraṣṭuḥ svarupe'vasthanam.*" "Then the Seer rests in its own state." The entire four books are the explanations of these two *sūtras*. *Citta vṛtti nirodhaḥ* is the practice. *Svarupevasthānam* is the experience. That's why he again talks about the experience at the end. "You just rest in your own true nature. You have played your games, you have gotten all your experiences and now you are resting." By resting, Patañjali means that the true you is resting while your body and mind function.

It's not that your body and mind necessarily rest always. They have to continue to fulfill the jobs for which they were created. According to the *prārabda*, a momentum has been created like a wheel that has been set in motion. You gave a push earlier and the body and mind are facing that now as *prārabda*. When you attain the *jīvanmukta* state, the pushing hand is taken away, but the wheel won't stop immediately. It will continue until the momentum is lost. While the momentum continues, you just rest and watch what is happening as a witness. It's like an old grandpa watching the children but not being affected by them.

In one sense, you are the witness; in another, you are the actor. It depends on where you put yourself. In reality, you are the witness, but if you miss the reality, you are the actor. When you become the actor you are responsible for your actions. When you are the witness you are not responsible for your actions because *you* are not acting. So, either act and be responsible, or allow the mind and body to act and be a witness, totally free.

If the body and mind do something wrong, they will undergo certain sufferings. If my mind wants to push my finger into the fire, I am watching. My mind is pushing *my* finger into the fire. But because I am watching and not doing anything, that doesn't mean the finger won't get burned or that the mind won't feel the agony of it. When the mind cries, "It got hurt," I must still watch that. The finger got hurt; the mind is suffering.

But, normally, Yogis do actions only for the sake of others. They are not affected by these actions they are not doing anything for their own sake. Whatever the outcome, it goes to somebody else. Karma Yoga—selfless service without personal expectation—is done by the mind. In fact, it is the mind that does all Yoga practice, not the real you. That's why we rarely even talk about the true you. You can leave the real you alone. It is the image-you or the ego-you that needs Yoga. It is to the ego that the teaching is given. "If you want to be quiet and happy, perform actions for others' sake." No scripture is necessary for the true Self. The entire practice is for the ego or lower self, the individual self.

So, let the lower self or ego or *citta* free itself from its egoistic activity. Then, it can also rest in peace, reflecting the Self. The mind need not always be functioning; and even if it is functioning, it can function peacefully and joyfully. Then it won't be a burden for the mind to function. When a Yogi performs something, he or she enjoys it. It's a play—a game—to act. Scriptures talking of the Self are just for the sake of our intellectual understanding. But the practical truth for the ego is very simple. Just learn to be selfless. Learn to lead a dedicated life. Whatever you do, do it for others. The dedicated ever enjoy peace. That's the reason I really don't speak about the scriptures very much. My students wanted to make a book about the *Yoga Sūtras*, so I have said all this. But for myself, I feel we don't really need scriptures. The entire life is an open book, a scripture. Read it. Learn while digging a pit or chopping some wood or cooking some food. If you can't learn from your daily activities, how are you going to understand the scriptures?

In conclusion, it is my sincere wish and prayer that each one of you experience the peace and joy of Yoga through the help and grace of the great Yoga adept Patañjali Mahāṛṣi and that you all attain the supreme achievement to which his *Yoga Sūtras* point. May you go beyond mere book knowledge and attain realization through purity of heart in your very lives.

OM Śāntiḥ, Śāntiḥ, Śāntiḥ. OM Tat Sat.

Glossary of Sanskrit Terms

A

abhiniveśa — clinging to bodily life
ābhyantara vṛtti — internal retention of breath
abhyāsa — spiritual practice
Adiśeṣa — the thousand-headed cobra upon which the world rests according to Hindu mythology
āgami karma — *karma* being performed in the present
Agni — fire; the *deva* (god) or ruling power of fire
aham — I
ahaṁkāra — ego feeling
ahiṁsā — non-injury (one of the *yamas*)
ajapa — unrepeated
akartā — non-doer
ākāśa — the ether
amṛta — nectar; immortality
ānapānasati — (Pali) Buddhist meditation technique involving watching the incoming and outgoing breath
anāgata — not yet come (refers to the silence beyond the *OM* vibration, the unpronounced *praṇava*); the heart *cakra*
ānanda — bliss
antaraṅga — internal part
aṇu — atom
anuśāsanam — exposition, instruction
apāna — energy descending from the navel pit within the human body
aparigrahā — non-greed, non-hoarding, non-acceptance of gifts (one of the *yamas*)
apuṇya — non-virtuous; wicked
artha — meaning; wealth
asaṁprajñata — undistinguished *samādhi* (see Book One, *sūtra* 18)
āsana — pose (the 3rd of the eight limbs of Aṣṭāṅga Yoga); seat
āsana siddhi — accomplishment of an *asāna*
asmita — egoity, ego sense, egoism, I-ness

āśrama — a spiritual community where seekers practice and study under the guidance of a spiritual master; every stage of life, such as *brahmacarya, gṛhastha, vānaprastha,* and *sannyāsa*

aṣṭāṅga — eight-limbed

Aṣṭāṅga Yoga — the Yoga of eight limbs; another name for Rāja Yoga (see Book Two, *sūtra* 29)

asteya — non-stealing (one of the *yamas*)

Ātma, Ātman — the Self

avyakta — unmanifested

āyu — life

Āyurveda — (lit. scripture of life) one of the Indian systems of medicine

B

bāhya — external

bāhya vṛtti — external retention of breath

bandha — bondage; lock

Bhagavad Gītā — Hindu scripture in which Lord Kṛṣṇa instructs his disciple Arjuna in the various aspects of Yoga

bhāvana — thought, feeling; attitude

bhoga — enjoyment

bhuvana — universe

bījam — seed

brahmacarya — (lit. relating to *Brahman*) continence, sense control, celibacy (one of the *yamas*); the stage in life of the celibate student

brahmamuhūrta — two-hour period before sunrise (between four and six a.m.), especially conducive to meditation

Brahman — the unmanifest supreme consciousness or God;

buddhi — intellect; discriminative faculty of the mind

C

cakra — (lit. wheel) one of the subtle nerve centers along the spine which, when concentrated upon, yields experiences of various levels of consciousness

cit — the principle of universal intelligence or consciousness
citta-nāśa — (lit. death of the mind) dissolution of mind in meditation
cittam — mind-stuff

D, E

Dakṣiṇāmūrti — (lit. south-faced deity) an aspect of Lord Śiva in which he instructs through silence
darśana — vision or experience of a divine form or being
deśa — space; place of concentration during Yoga practice
deva — celestial being; controller of an aspect of nature
deva loka — the plane where the gods abide
dhāraṇā — concentration (the sixth of the eight limbs of Aṣṭāṅga Yoga)
dharma — duty, righteousness, moral
dharmamegha samādhi — cloud of virtue" *samādhi* (see Book Four, *sūtra* 29)
dhyāna — meditation (the 7th of the eight limbs of Aṣṭāṅga Yoga)
divya — divine
duḥkha — suffering
dveṣa — dislike
ekāgrata pariṇāma — mental modification of one-pointedness

G, H

gṛhastha — householder stage of life
guṇa — one of the qualities of nature (*sattva, rajas* and *tamas* or balance, activity and inertia)
guru — (lit. remover of darkness) spiritual guide, teacher
hāna — removal
hāno-pāya — method for the removal of sorrow
hatha — (lit. *ha* — sun; *tha* — moon)
Hatha Yoga — the physical aspect of Yoga practice, including postures (*āsanas*), breathing techniques (*prāṇāyāma*), seals (*mudras*), locks (*bandhas*) and cleansing practices (*kriyas*)
hiṁsā — injury or pain; violence

I, J

Indra — the king of the gods or ruling powers of nature

indriya — sense organ

Iṣta devatā — one's chosen deity

Īśvara — the supreme cosmic soul; God

Īśvara praṇidhāna — worship of God or self-surrender (one of the *yamas*)

japa — repetition of a *mantra*

Japa Yoga — science of *mantra* repetition

jaya — victory, mastery

jīva(tman) — individual soul

jīvanmukta — liberated living soul

jñāna — wisdom of the Self; knowledge, idea

Jñāna Yoga — Yoga of Self-inquiry

jyotiḥ — illumination, effulgence, light

K

kaivalya — experience of absoluteness; non-qualified experience

kāla — time

karma — action and reaction

Karma Yoga — performing actions as selfless service without attachment to the results

karmāśaya — womb, or bag, of *karmas*

karunā — mercy, compassion

kāya-kalpa — a tonic for physical rejuvenation

kevala — without qualities or conditions

kevala kuṁbhaka — natural, automatic breath retention during deep meditation

kleśa — obstruction or obstacle

kriyā — action, practice; (Hatha Yoga) cleansing practice

Kriyā Yoga — according to Patañjali: the three preliminary steps in Yoga (*tapas, svadhyaya* and *Īśvara praṇidhāna* or austerity, study and self-surrender)

kuṁbhaka — breath retention

kuṇḍalinī — (lit. coiled energy) the energy stored at the base of every individual's spine

L, M

loka — a world of names and forms

mahat — great

maharṣi — great sage

mahāvrata — (lit. great vows) refers to the *yamas*

maitrī — friendliness

manas — the desiring faculty of the mind-stuff

Māṇḍukya Upaniṣad — the *Upanishadic* treatise of *OM*, considered the crest jewel of all the *Upaniṣads*

mano-nāśa — death or dissolution of the mind

mantra — (lit. that makes the mind steady) a sound formula for meditation

mara — (Tamil) tree

māyā — illusion

mayūrāsana — (Hatha Yoga) the peacock pose

mokṣa — liberation

mudrā — sign, seal or symbol

mukta — set free, released, liberated

mukti — liberation, freedom

musu-musu-kkai — (Tamil) herb used for *Ayurvedic* healing; it also means "hand of monkey" and "monkey"

N, O

nāḍī suddhi — (Hatha Yoga) nerve-cleansing *prāṇāyāma* in which one breathes alternately through left and right nostrils

Nārada — a sage and celestial singer of divine names

nauli — (Hatha Yoga) stomach *kriyā* where one isolates and then churns the abdominal recti muscles

Nāyanārs — the sixty-three Saivite saints of South India

nirbīja — without seed, seedless
nirodha — cessation, restraint
nirodha parināma — the moment of conjunction of a thought and one's effort to restrain it
nirvāna — (lit. nakedness) in the Buddhist teachings, the state of liberation
nirvicāra — without reflection (see Book One, *sūtra* 44)
nirvikalpa — without thought or imagination
nirvitarka — without reasoning (see Book One, *sūtra* 43)
nitya — eternal, permanent
niyama — observance (the second of the eight limbs of Aṣṭāṅga Yoga; see Book Two, *sūtra* 32)
OM — the cosmic sound vibration which includes all other sounds and vibrations, the basic *mantra*, the absolute *Brahman* as sound
ojas — the subtle energy resulting from the preservation of sexual energy

P

pāda — portion
pādārtha — a thing; the substance and its meaning
pāñca indriya — the five senses
Pāñca Tantra — (lit.) five attitudes or approaches
Parabrahman — the supreme unmanifest consciousness or God
parama — highest, supreme
paścimotanāsana — (Hatha Yoga) the full-forward bending pose
Patāñjali Mahārṣi — Yogi and sage who compiled the *Yoga Sūtras;* considered to be the "Father of Yoga"
phalam — fruit; effect
prakāśa — illumination; *sattva*
Prakṛti — the Nature
prāṇa — the vital energy
prāṇa-apāna — the ascending and descending energy within the human body
praṇava — *OM*, the basic hum of the universe

prāṇāyāma — the practice of controlling the vital force, usually through control of the breath (the fourth of the eight limbs of Aṣṭāṅga Yoga)

praṇidhāna — total dedication

prārabdha karma — the *karma* which has caused one's present birth

prasādam — consecrated food offering; grace

pratipakṣa bhāvana — practice of substituting opposite thought forms in the mind

pratyāhāra — sense control; withdrawal of the senses from their objects (the 5th of the eight limbs of AṣṭāṅgaYoga)

pūjā — worship service

puṇya — virtuous

Puruṣa — the divine Self which abides in all beings

R, Ṛ

rāga — liking, desire; tune

rājā — king

Rāja Yoga — the "Royal Yoga;" the system of concentration and meditation based on ethical discipline

rajas — activity; restlessness (one of the three *guṇas*)

Rām(a) — a name of God; a powerful seed *mantra*

Ramakrishna Paramahamsa (1836-1886) — saint of India; Guru of Swami Vivekananda

Rāmana Maharṣi — (1879-1950) sage of Thiruvannamalai; *jñāni* of India

Rāmāyana — epic telling the story of Lord Rāma as a dutiful son, brother, husband, warrior and king

ṛtaṁbharā prajñā — absolute true consciousness

rūpa — appearance; form

S

sa-ānanda — *samādhi* on the *sattvic* mind (see Book One, *sūtra* 17)

sa-asmita — *samādhi* on the egoity alone (see Book One, *sūtra* 17)

śabda — sound, word or name
sabīja — with seed
sādhana — spiritual practice
sadhu — a spiritual person, often a wandering mendicant
sahasrāra (cakra) — thousand-petaled lotus; the subtle center at the crown of the head, where the consciousness and energy go in the higher *samādhis*
Śaiva Siddhānta — a philosophy which leads to the worship of the Absolute as Lord Śiva
Śaivism — sect of Hinduism which worships the Absolute as Lord Śiva
sākṣī — witness
śakti, Śakti — energy; the Divine Mother
samādhi — contemplation, superconscious state, absorption (the eighth and final limb or culmination of the eight limbs of Aṣṭāṅga Yoga)
samādhi pariṇāma — development in *samādhi*
saṁkyā — count in *prāṇāyāma*
saṁprajñāta — distinguished *samādhi* (see Book One, *sūtra* 17)
saṁsāra — round of births and deaths; family
saṁskāra — mental impression
saṁtoṣa — contentment
saṁyama — practice of *dhārāṇa, dhyāna* and *samādhi* upon one object, usually for the attainment of a particular power
saṁyoga — perfect union
sanjita karma — *karma* awaiting another lifetime to bear fruit
śānti — peace
sannyāsa — renunciation
sannyāsi — a renunciate; member of the Holy Order of *Sannyās*, having taken formal initiation from another *sannyāsi*
saptadhā bhūmi — the seven planes of understanding
Sat — existence or Truth
Sat-cid-ānanda — existence-knowledge-bliss absolute
sattva — purity; balanced state (one of the three *guṇas*)
satya — truth; truthfulness (one of the *yamas*)
śauca — purity (one of the *niyamas*)

savāsana — (Hatha Yoga) the corpse pose
savicāra — *samādhi* with reflection (see Book One, *sūtra* 17)
savikalpa — *samādhi* with thought or imagination
savitarka — *samādhi* with reasoning (see Book One, *sūtras* 17 & 42)
siddha — an accomplished one, often with supernatural powers
siddhi — accomplishment
Śiva — God as auspiciousness
Śivananda, Swami (1887-1963) — sage of the Himalayas, founder of the Divine Life Society; Guru of Swami Satchidananda
smṛti — memory; code of law
śraddhā — faith
Śri — Goddess of Divine Wealth; eminent or illustrious; used in names to show respect or reverence
staṁbha vṛtti — breath retention
sthala siddhi — mastery over staying in one place (usually for at least twelve years)
sthiti — inertia; *tamas*
sukha — happiness
sukha pūrvaka — (lit. easy, comfortable breathing) alternate nostril breathing with retention
sūtra — (lit. thread) aphorism
svādhyāya — spiritual study (one of the *niyamas*)
svarūpa — essential nature
swāmī — renunciate; member of the Holy Order of *Sannyās*

T, U

tamas — inertia, dullness (one of the three *guṇas*)
tanmātram — subtle element
Tantra Yoga — a practice using *yantra* and *mantra* to experience the union of Śiva and Śakti (or the masculine and feminine, positive and negative forces) within the individual
tapas(yā) — (lit. to burn) spiritual austerity; accepting but not causing pain (one of the *niyamas*)

Tat — That; the unlimited, unmanifested Absolute
tattva — principle
tejas — illumination; the aura of a *brahmacari*
Thirumūlar — Tamil saint of South India
trādaka — gazing, concentration practice
tyāga — dedication
uḍḍyana bandha — (Hatha Yoga) stomach lift
Upaniṣads — the final portion of each of the *Vedas* which gives the non-dualistic *Vedānta* philosophy

V

vairāgyam — dispassion, detachment or non-attachment
Vālmīki — legendary Indian sage and poet who wrote the *Rāmāyana*, the epic story of the life of Śri Rāma
vānaprastha — recluse or pilgrim who has finished family responsibilities and taken to the spiritual life; the stage prior to *sannyāsa* or formal renunciation
Varuṇa — the *deva* (god) or ruling power of water
vāsanā — (lit. smell) the impression of actions that remains unconsciously in the mind and induces a person to repeat the action (example: the smell of perfume is the *vāsanā* of perfume)
Vedānta — final experience of the study of the *Vedas*
Vedas — the wisdom scriptures of Hinduism (*Rig, Sama, Yajur and Atharva*)
vibhūti — blessing or power
videha — bodiless
vidyā — knowledge, learning
vikalpa — thought or imagination; verbal delusion
viparyaya — misconception
vīrya — vital energy, strength; semen
viveka — discrimination of the real from the unreal

Vivekānanda, Swami (1862-1902) — a disciple of Sri Ramakrishna and one of the founders of the Ramakrishna Order

vṛtti — modification

Y

yama — abstinence (the 1st of the eight limbs of Aṣṭāṅga Yoga; see Book Two, *sūtra* 30)

yantra — a sacred geometrical figure representing a particular aspect of the Divine

Yoga — (lit. union) union of the individual with the Absolute; any course that makes for such union; unruffled state of mind under all conditions

Yoga mudrā — (Hatha Yoga) the symbol of Yoga; a posture which awakens the spiritual force within the individual

Index

Please note: references given denote Book and sūtra numbers

manas (desiring faculty of mind) I-2
mantra I-28, I-32; *mantra* repetition I-14, I-28, I-29
marriage II-38, II-47
mastery (self-) I-15; II-22, II-55
māyā II-22; IV-19
meditation I-5, I-15, I-17, I-41 through I-51; II-11, II-29, II-45, II-51; III-1 through III-4, III-7, III-8; and *OM* I-27; practice of (see concentration)
memory I-6, I-11
merit II-14
mind I-2, I-4, I-7, I-15, I-17, I-33, I-46, I-49; II-6, II-13, II-18, II-20, II-27, II-54; III-1, III-2, III-9, III-10, III-56; IV-15 through IV-28, IV-32, IV-34; (see also body and mind) and *prāṇa* I-34; II-51
minds IV-4 through IV-6
mirror (analogy) I-3
misconception I-7, I-8
monkey and sparrow (story) I-33
name and form I-27; II-26, II-44
Nārada story about patience I-14; story about Valmiki I-41
nature I-17 through I-19; I-45; II-17 through II-19, II-21 through II-26, II-50; IV-32 through IV-34; nature three qualities of balance, activity and inertia (see *guṇas*)
nature (one's own true) I-3; II-25, II-27; IV-34
Nayanar saints II-47
niyamas (observances) II-29, II-32; listed individually II-40 through II-45
nirodha parināma III-9, III-10
non-attachment I-4, I-12, I-15, I-16; II-15, II-18, II-45
non-greed II-30, II-31, II-39
non-injury II-1, II-30, II-31, II-35
non-stealing II-30, II-31, II-37
non-violence (see non-injury)
observances II-29, II-32; *niyamas*, outlined individually II-40 through II-45

II-18, II-20, II-21, II-23 through II-27; III-56; IV-18 through IV-25, IV-32 through IV-34
realization I-49, I-51; II-24, II-41
religion I-15, I-26; II-27, II-32, II-45; IV-29, IV-30
renunciation I-15; II-45; IV-32
ṛtaṁbharā prajñā (absolute true consciousness) I-48, I-49
ritual I-7; III-1
saint(s) I-7, I-15, I-50; II-25, II-27; IV-30; Nayanar saints II-47
sacrifice (see giving)
samādhi I-41 through I-51; II-2, II-27, II-29, II-45; III-3, III-4, III-7, III-8; IV-1, IV-29 through IV-32; development in III-11; distinguished I-17; kinds of I-17, I-42 through I-51; non-distinguished I-18, I-20 through I-23
saṁskāra I-16; III-9, III-10; IV-9 through IV-11, IV-27, IV-28
saṁyama (practice of) III-4 through III-6, III-9 through III-56
saṁtoṣa (contentment) II-32, II-42
saṁyoga (perfect union) II-23 through II-27
sannyāsa (renunciation) IV-32
saptadhā bhūmi (seven planes of understanding) II-26, II-27
satya (truthfulness) II-30, II-31, II-36
śauca (purity) II-32, II-40, II-41
science I-4, I-27, I-46; II-50
scorpion sting (example) II-25
scripture(s) I-7; II-1, II-40; IV-34
Self I-3, I-4, I-15, I-16, I-18, I-23 through I-27, I-29, I-47; II-1, II-5, II-6, II-17, II-18, II-20 through II-27, II-52; III-56; IV-18 through IV-25, IV-32 through IV-34; realization of (see realization)
selfishness I-5, I-15; III-3
senses I-2, I-15; battle of (analogy of *Bhagavad Gītā*) II-54, II-55; withdrawal of II-29, II-54, II-55
seven planes of understanding II-26, II-27
siddhis (psychic powers) II-43, II-47; III-4 through III-6, III-9 through III-56; IV-1
silence I-49
silk worms (story) II-18

Stories, Examples and Analogies

Please note: references denote Book and sūtra numbers.

Book One

How the Mind Works

Example of smell coming from kitchen: I-2

Example of how a stranger becomes your daddy: I-2

Prison

Analogy of difference in attitude of prisoner and prison guard though both are locked in; prison and life both as places for reformation: I-2

Reflection

Analogy of mind as lake: I-3

Analogy of mind as mirror: I-3, I-16

Wardrobe

Analogy of Truth inside all scriptures as same man inside different clothes: I-7

Feeding a Child

Analogy of tricking the mind by removing the thoughts in small portions: I-7

Snake in the Rope

Analogy of unreality imposed on reality: I-8 (see also II-15)

Nārada

Story of patience: I-14

Classes

Example of how people respond to a vibration: I-15

Obstacle Race

Analogy of life's lesson: I-30

Four Keys to Four Locks

Happiness toward the happy, compassion toward the unhappy, delight in the virtuous and disregard for the wicked: I-33

Monkey and Sparrow

Story: I-33

H.G. Wells Story

Analogy of other parts weakening as one is developed: I-41

Nārada

Story of Valmiki: I-41

Dakṣiṇāmūrti

Story: I-49

Book Two

Self as Charioteer

Analogy from *Bhagavad Gītā:* II-1 (see also II-54)

Snake in the Rope

Analogy of unreality imposed on reality: II-5 (see also I-8)

Musk Deer

Analogy: II-8

Reflection

Example of how others reflect our happiness: II-8

Asafoetida

Example of lingering impressions: II-11

Karma

Analogy of kinds as arrows in air, in bow or in quiver: II-12

Indra

Story of pigs: II-18

Silk Worms

Analogy of desire and its results: II-18

Factory

Analogy of world as: II-22

Scorpion Sting

Story of "cure": II-25

Change of Name and Form

Analogy of how wood becomes plank, chair, firewood, ash: II-26

Fruits

Explanation of offerings of fruit to God as fruits of our actions: II-40

Explanation of "forbidden fruit" (story of Adam and Eve): II-40

Laundryman

Analogy of *tapas*: II-43 (see also IV-29)

Saint

Story of returning insults: II-43

Weed and Tree

Story of humility: II-46

Battery

Analogy of recharging with *prana*: II-51

Bhagavad Gītā

analogy of the battle with the senses II-54 (see also II-1)

Book Three

Goal

Analogy of sideshow distractions on way to palace: III-56

Book Four

Laundry

Analogy of soap IV-29: (see also II-43)

Garden

Sri Ramakrishna's story of helping others over the wall: IV-30

Mother Bathing Babies

Analogy of how nature functions: IV-32

Sanskrit Quotes

Please note: references denote Book and sūtra numbers.

Book One

Mana eva manuṣyanam karaṇam bandha mokṣayoho.

As the mind, so the person; bondage or liberation is in your own mind. (Sanskrit saying) I-2; see also II-25

Mokṣabhekṣo bandhaḥ.

Even the desire for liberation is a bondage. (*Vedantic* scriptures) I-15

Man me Rām, hath me kām.

In mind, Ram (God); in the hand, work.
(Hindi saying) I-16; see also II-27

Ekam sat, viprahā bahudha vadanti.

Truth is one; seers express it in many ways. (*Upaniṣads)* I-27

Nantaḥ-prajñām, na bahis prajñām, nobhayatah-prajñām, na prajñām-ghanam, na prajñām, nāprajñām.

Not the outside knowledge, nor inside knowledge, not knowledge itself, not ignorance (*Māṇḍūkya Upaniṣad)* I-49

Mauna vākya Prākṛtita Parabrahma tattvam.

The *Parabrahma tattvam,* or unmanifested supreme principle, can only be explained by silence, not by words.
(*Dakṣiṇāmūrti Stothram)* I-49

Book Two

Satyam bruyat priyam bruyat.

Speak what is truth, speak what is pleasant. (*Vedas)* II-1

Aham sakṣiḥ.

I am the eternal witness. (*Vedantic* scriptures*)* II-25

Mana eva manuṣyanam.

As the mind, so the person. (Sanskrit expression) II-25; see also I-2

Ko vidhi ko niṣedaḥ?

What is a must and what is not? (Vedic teaching) II-27

Ātmana Ātmanam pasyann Ātmani tuṣyati.

Beholding the Self, by the Self, one is satisfied in the Self. (*Bhagavad Gītā)* II-27

Man me Rām, hath me kām.

In mind, Ram (God); in the hand, work. (Hindu saying) II-27; see also I-16

Prāṇa apāna samayuktah.

By the unity of *prāna* and *apāna*... (*Bhagavad Gītā)* II-40

Tyāgat śāntir anantaram.

Unending peace by total dedication. (*Bhagavad Gītā)* II-45

Selected Reading

Carrera, Reverend Jaganath
Inside the Yoga Sutras
Yogaville, Virginia: Integral Yoga® Publications, 2006
(commentary for each *sūtra*, extensive cross-referencing, a *sūtras*-by-subject index)

Prabhavananda, Swami and Christopher Isherwood
How to Know God, the Yoga Aphorisms of Patanjali
New York: New American Library 1969 (translation and commentary)

Sivananda, Swami
Rāja Yoga
Rishikesh: The Divine Life Society, 1937
(translation, commentary, plus Sanskrit Devanagari)

Taimni, I. K.
The Science of Yoga
Wheaton, Illinois: The Theosophical Publishing House, 1967
(translation and commentary, plus Sanskrit Devanagari
and transliteration)

Venkatesananda, Swami
Enlightened Living: The Yoga Sutras of Patanjali
Cape Province, South Africa: The Chiltern Yoga Trust, 1975
(interpretive translation with transliteration)

Vivekananda, Swami
Rāja Yoga
New York: Ramakrishna-Vivekananda Center, 1970
(translation, commentary and supplementary talks)